THE WINTER'S TALE

BROADVIEW / INTERNET SHAKESPEARE EDITIONS

Broadview Editions Series Editor
L.W. Conolly
Internet Shakespeare Editions Coordinating Editor
Michael Best
Internet Shakespeare Editions Textual Editor
Eric Rasmussen

THE WINTER'S TALE

William Shakespeare

EDITED BY

Hardin L. Aasand

BROADVIEW / INTERNET SHAKESPEARE EDITIONS

Library and Archives Canada Cataloguing in Publication

Shakespeare, William, 1564–1616, author
The winter's tale / William Shakespeare ; edited by Hardin L. Aasand.

(Broadview / Internet Shakespeare Editions)
Includes bibliographical references.
ISBN 978-1-55481-090-1 (pbk.)

1. Fathers and daughters—Drama. 2. Kings and rulers—Drama. 3. Married people—Drama. 4. Castaways—Drama. 5. Sicily (Italy)—Kings and rulers—Drama. I. Aasand, Hardin L., 1958–, editor II. Title. III. Series: Broadview / Internet Shakespeare Editions

PR2839.A2A28 2014 822.3'3 C2014-906255-9

Broadview Press is an independent, international publishing house, incorporated in 1985.

We welcome comments and suggestions regarding any aspect of our publications—please feel free to contact us at the addresses below or at broadview@broadviewpress.com.

North America
PO Box 1243
Peterborough, Ontario
K9J 7H5, Canada
555 Riverwalk Parkway
Tonawanda, NY 14150
USA
Tel: (705) 743-8990
Fax: (705) 743-8353
email: customerservice@broadviewpress.com
www.broadviewpress.com

UK, Europe, Central Asia, Middle East, Africa, India, and Southeast Asia
Eurospan Group
3 Henrietta St.
London WC2E 8LU
United Kingdom
Tel: 44 (0) 1767 604972
Fax: 44 (0) 1767 601640
email: eurospan@turpin-distribution.com

Australia and New Zealand
NewSouth Books
c/o TL Distribution
15-23 Helles Ave.
Moorebank, NSW 2170
Australia
Tel: (02) 8778 9999
Fax: (02) 8778 9944
email: orders@tldistribution.com.au

Copy-edited by Denis Johnston
Book design by Michel Vrana
Typeset in MVB Verdigris Pro

Broadview Press acknowledges the financial support of the Government of Canada through the Canada Book Fund for our publishing activities.

PRINTED IN CANADA

CONTENTS

FOREWORD

The Internet Shakespeare Editions (http://internetshakespeare.uvic.ca) and Broadview Press are pleased to collaborate on a series of Shakespeare editions in book form, creating for each volume an "integrated text" designed to meet the needs of today's students.

The texts, introductions, and other materials for these editions are drawn from those prepared by leading scholars for the Internet Shakespeare Editions, modified to suit the demands of publication in book form. The print editions are integrated with the fuller resources and research materials that are available electronically on the site of the Internet Shakespeare Editions. Consistent with other volumes in the Broadview Editions series, each of these Shakespeare editions includes a wide range of background materials, providing information on the the play's historical and intellectual context, in addition to the text itself, introduction, chronology, essays on Shakespeare's life and theater, and bibliography; all these will be found in more extensive form on the website.

The Internet Shakespeare Editions, a non-profit organization founded in 1996, creates and publishes works for the student, scholar, actor, and general reader in a form native to the medium of the Internet: scholarly, fully annotated texts of Shakespeare's plays, multimedia explorations of the context of Shakespeare's life and works, and records of his plays in performance. The Internet Shakespeare Editions is affiliated with the University of Victoria.

The Broadview Editions series was founded in 1992 under the title "Broadview Literary Texts." Under the guidance of executive editors Julia Gaunce and Marjorie Mather, of series editors Eugene Benson and Leonard Conolly, and of managing editors Barbara Conolly and Tara Lowes, it has grown to include several hundred volumes—lesser-known works of cultural significance as well as canonical texts. Designed with the needs of undergraduate students in mind, the series has also appealed widely to scholars—and to readers in general.

Michael Best, Coordinating Editor, University of Victoria
Eric Rasmussen, General Textual Editor, University of Nevada, Reno
Don LePan, Broadview Press

ACKNOWLEDGEMENTS

Following in the footsteps of David Bevington, whose Broadview/ISE edition of *As You Like It* set a standard for all who follow, I too must express my deepest gratitude to Michael Best, Coordinating Editor, and Eric Rasmussen, General Textual Editor, of the Internet Shakespeare Editions. Their collegiality and professionalism are profoundly appreciated. Marjorie Mather of Broadview Press coordinated the production of this edition from its earliest stages, and Denis Johnston's prompt and thoughtful copy-editing saw it through to its final published state. The library staff at Helmke Library at Indiana-Purdue University Fort Wayne assisted me with the acquisition of material to give life to this edition. Finally, I need no oracle to be reminded of the invaluable and loving contributions of my wife, Amy, whose patience and graciousness make this dedication especially resonant.

The brief essays on Shakespeare's life and Shakespeare's theater are reprinted from the Broadview edition of *As You Like It*, courtesy of David Bevington. Quotations from Shakespeare's plays other than *The Winter's Tale* are from David Bevington's *Complete Works*, 5th edition (New York: Pearson Longman, 2004).

The ISE website has many pages designed to enrich readers' understanding of the plays' context in Shakespeare's life and times. To access these, visit internetshakespeare.uvic.ca/, click on the tab Life & Times, and search for the desired topic. Ones that apply especially to *The Winter's Tale* include:

- "Autolycus"
- "Children"
- "Coney-catching"
- "The country: pastoral"
- "Country fairs"
- "A cutpurse"
- "Exit pursued by a bear"
- "Forman sees *The Winter's Tale*"
- "The Late Renaissance: Mannerism"
- "The marriage ceremony"
- "The Masque"
- "Music of the streets and fairs"
- "The Private Theater"
- "Romantic comedy"
- "Village celebrations"

All were written by Michael Best, Coordinating Editor of the Internet Shakespeare Editions.

INTRODUCTION

The Winter's Tale is a play that defies simple classification. Neither comedy nor tragedy—despite appearing in the "Comedy" section of the First Folio of 1623 (see A Note on the Text, p. 63)—the play incorporates themes and conventions from several genres. The geographic shifts of the play—the wintry oppression of Sicilia, the pastoral warmth of Bohemia, and the redemptive return to a Sicilia desperate for rebirth—allow Shakespeare to crisscross generic boundaries as dramatically as they traverse the Mediterranean setting of Sicilia and the Northern climes of Bohemia. The wide "vast" (1.1.25, TLN 32) of the play's geographical reach and generic filiation also provide Shakespeare with the opportunity to revisit themes played out in some earlier plays: the abrupt, senseless jealousy of Othello finding its parallel in Leontes's motiveless distrust of Hermione's fidelity in 1.2; the remorseful contriteness of Lear following his own delusional follies surfacing in Leontes's 16-year period of penitential withdrawal (3.2.218–29, TLN 1424–35); Camillo's loyal service to Leontes hearkening back to Kent's long-suffering devotion to Lear (4.2.3–7, TLN 1617–22); the green world of burgeoning love and fertile beginnings in *As You Like It*'s Arden forest informing the pastoral festivity of Bohemia's sheep-shearing celebration (4.4, TLN 1797 ff.); Puck's impishness in *A Midsummer's Night Dream* or Feste's pranks in *Twelfth Night* reborn in Autolycus's cozening of peasant clowns and willing maidens (4.4.210 ff., TLN 2044 ff.). All these elements and more converge in this "late play" and reflect the masterful hand of Shakespeare returning to and transforming earlier characters and situations. In characterizing it as "late," modern critics avoid the nebulous issue of the play's genre: pastoral, tragicomedy, romance, tragicomic romance—all categories proposed as labels for this most bedeviling of plays. The thorny question remains, however: what "kind" of play is *The Winter's Tale*?[1]

That the play is "late" in Shakespeare's career is evident from its performance history, which includes productions at the Globe playhouse in 1611 and the court of King James in both 1611 and 1613. Whether the royal family beheld the same play in private performance in 1611 and in 1613 at Princess Elizabeth's nuptial celebrations as the public

1 See also ISE website, internetshakespeare.uvic.ca, "Romantic comedy."

viewed at the Globe in 1611 remains a vexing, unanswerable question. Critics have proposed that the marriage of the youthful Elizabeth to Frederick V, Elector Palatine, who later became King of Bohemia, may account for the shifting polarities in Shakespeare's manipulation of his source—*Pandosto* by Robert Greene, which invests the king of Bohemia with a jealousy borne from his suspicion that his wife has slept with his friend, the king of Sicilia (see Appendix A1, p. 204). However, Shakespeare's play makes Bohemia the more festive, more appropriate setting for the young lovers, Florizel and Perdita, relegating the themes of jealousy and infidelity to Sicilia.

Simon Forman, court astrologer and amateur occultist, provides accounts of four of Shakespeare's plays in his 1611 "Booke of Plaies," *The Winter's Tale* one of them. His well-known account is as striking for what it omits as for what it includes in its three paragraphs: "Observe there how Leontes, the king of Sicilia, was overcome with jealousy of his wife with the king of Bohemia, his friend that came to see him; and how he contrived his death and would have had his cupbearer to have poisoned, who gave the king of Bohemia warning thereof and fled with him to Bohemia."[1] Forman gives a cursory listing of the plot that follows: the oracle's pronouncement of Leontes's isolation unless his banished daughter is restored and the subsequent return of the daughter 16 years later with her betrothed (3.2.129–32 ff., TLN 1313–16 ff.). No mention is made, however, of the bear that devours Antigonus (3.3.55, TLN 1500), nor of Hermione's death and magical restoration as a kinetic statue (5.3.18 ff., TLN 3208 ff.)—a puzzling exclusion given Forman's own occult proclivities. Forman concludes his account with a paragraph devoted to Autolycus, "the Rogue that came in all tattered like coll pixci [a will-o'-the-wisp]...." Forman's concluding admonition is that one should "beware of trusting feigned beggars or fawning fellows."[2]

For the modern audience, Forman's skeletal account of the play jars with the magical, fantastical elements that dramatically redeem the play's tragic beginning. The promise of domestic bliss that opens the

1 See Simon Forman's *Booke of Plaies and Notes thereof per formans for Common Pollicie*, reprinted in *William Shakespeare*, ed. E.K. Chambers, 2 vols. (Oxford: Clarendon P, 1930), 2: 340–41. For an online version, see ISE website, internetshakespeare.uvic.ca, "Forman sees *The Winter's Tale*."

2 See also ISE website, internetshakespeare.uvic.ca, "Autolycus," "Coney-catching," and "A cutpurse."

play is abrupt and fleeting. Two old friends, Leontes and Polixenes, share their nostalgic memories of a childhood free from worry and anxiety, an innocence that is shattered by Leontes's sudden onset of jealousy over his pregnant wife Hermione's persuasiveness in extending his friend's stay in Sicilia, and his unsubstantiated doubt over the paternity of his yet unborn child. Perhaps Shakespeare hints at the tragic turn of the play in the brief opening scene in which the competitive nature of reciprocating hospitality is implied in the dialogue between Camillo and Archidamus:

ARCHIDAMUS. If you shall chance, Camillo, to visit Bohemia on the like occasion whereon my services are now on-foot, you shall see (as I have said) great difference betwixt our Bohemia and your Sicilia.
CAMILLO. I think this coming summer the King of Sicilia means to pay Bohemia the visitation which he justly owes him.
ARCHIDAMUS. Wherein our entertainment shall shame us, we will be justified in our loves. For indeed—
CAMILLO. Beseech you—
ARCHIDAMUS. Verily, I speak it in the freedom of my knowledge. We cannot with such ma gnificence—in so rare—I know not what to say. We will give you sleepy drinks, that your senses (unintelligent of our insufficiency) may, though they cannot praise us, as little accuse us.
CAMILLO. You pay a great deal too dear for what's given freely.
(1.1.1–15, TLN 4–21)

Implicit in the courteous modesty of competing hosts is the more lacerating emotion that surfaces in Leontes's psychotic outburst against his spouse and his best friend:

There have been,
Or I am much deceived, cuckolds ere now,
And many a man there is, even at this present,
Now, while I speak this, holds his wife by th' arm,
That little thinks she has been sluiced in's absence,
And his pond fished by his next neighbor, by
Sir Smile, his neighbor. (1.2.189–94, TLN 273–78)

Leontes's fear that Polixenes has bested him and stolen his wife is abrupt and unexpected, but the insecurity behind the sentiment may permeate the subsequent Sicilian atmosphere of mistrust, jealousy, and irrational fear.

In the opening scene of Act 2, the doomed Mamillius unwittingly points to the bleakness unfolding in Sicilia when he asks his mother to tell him a sad tale: "A sad tale's best for winter" (2.1.24, TLN 618). He of course will become part of the collateral damage of Leontes's actions. Indeed, were the play to end at the conclusion of 3.2, the audience would be entitled to leave the theater hopeless and despairing of any redemptive intervention: friendships can be torn asunder by mere suspicion; children can be drained of life by unraveling family order; wives can be indicted by a husband's capricious jealousy and imprisoned on a whim; and innocent babies can be banished to the wild because of an irrational hint of bastardy. Yet Shakespeare pivots the play away from tragedy by relocating the action to Bohemia, a pastoral realm of shepherds, a charming conman, and disguised lovers blocked from consummation by obstinate fathers—all features of romantic comedies. Bohemia promises the green world of rebirth and regeneration common in Shakespeare's greatest comedies such as *A Midsummer Night's Dream*, *As You Lke It*, and *Love's Labor's Lost*. To reach Bohemia, however, Shakespeare entrusts the play's transformation to an allegorical figure of Time and the inexplicable bear whose maw swallows up the fleeing Antigonus and the tragic remains of Sicilia. This brings us back to the question of the play's genre.

THE QUESTION OF GENRE

Some Shakespearean scholars consider these late plays as "outriders" (Mowat, "Name" 4:132), a group of plays that have a suppleness of plotting, a flirting with tragic outcomes, and the miraculous appearance of gods or god-like devices that hint at the spectacular. Often this experimentation has been associated with the rise of the tragicomic works of Francis Beaumont and John Fletcher. The "tragicomedies" that Beaumont and Fletcher conceived were based on Giovanni Battista Guarini's Italian model that, while taking its characters to the precipice of death, pulled them back from its culmination. In his play *The Faithful Shepherdess* (c. 1608), John Fletcher provides us in his address to the reader with the operative definition that suggests how distinct are Shakespeare's "romances" from typical tragicomic structure: "A tragic-comedy is not so called in respect of mirth and killing, but in respect it wants deaths, which is enough to make it no tragedy, yet brings some near it, which is enough to make it no comedy."[1] Despite certain features (dramatic revelations, unconventional plots, and exotic settings) discernible in Shakespeare's "romances," the presence of death and of emotional states that have tragic, highly affective potential for its characters make the "tragicomic" label unsatisfying.

Turning elsewhere, perhaps nostalgically to Shakespeare's past, others trace *The Winter's Tale* elements to Shakespeare's invocation of native romances such as *Mucedorus* (c. 1590)— revived in the public playhouses as recently as 1610—and miracle plays such as the Digby *Mary Magdelene*, which were popular in the late fifteenth and early sixteenth centuries.[2] From *Mucedorus*, Shakespeare could have teased out the story of a prince disguised as a lowly shepherd who saves a princess from a ravenous bear. Moreover, suggestively, the allegorical appearance of Comedy and Envy as characters to wrestle with the play's theme provides Shakespeare with a blueprint for the generic tension he establishes more subtly in *The Winter's Tale*. From the Digby miracle play of Mary Magdelene, Shakespeare could have excavated the themes of tested faith, the maritime separation of families, and the miraculous return of those once thought dead. The spiritual implications of Mary's faithful service and her ascent into heaven are perhaps echoed in Hermione's providential return to "life" in Paulina's chapel. Given the iconoclastic nature of the Protestant church, the appearance of a venerated statue of a "deceased" queen evokes the outlawed Catholic belief in the intercession of saints. If this element of the play—missing in Shakespeare's source—hints at Shakespeare's own Catholic sentiments (a view suggested most recently by Stephen Greenblatt), Hermione's re-animation points to the role of grace in enabling forgiveness and reunion. This appearance of conventions attributable to prose romances and miracle plays provides us with a glimpse into Shakespeare's dramatic method.

---

1 *The Faithful Shepherdess* <https://archive.org/details/faithfulshepher00fletgoog>.

2 For a thorough consideration of Shakespeare's romantic precursors in Tudor miracle or saint's plays, see Felperin, *Shakespearean Romance* chapter 1, and Snyder (ed.) 3–9.

Other factors can be extracted from the dramatic skein presented by *The Winter's Tale*. Shakespeare was writing for three different venues: the public outdoor Globe, the private indoor Blackfriars, and the court of James I and his family.[1] Certainly the dance of the satyrs in the sheep-shearing festival of Act 4 reflects the power of the court masque to influence Shakespeare's dramatic choices, and the acquisition of the Blackfriars venue gave Shakespeare and his company a theater that appealed to an elite audience with particular sensibilities of genre and spectacle. With the play's performance for Princess Elizabeth's nuptials to Frederick, the play's ability to address contemporary politics enlarges its generic girth.

In conclusion, the issue of genre requires us to expand our definition to encompass a broad range of sources and influences. For *The Winter's Tale*, genre invites an expansion of the geography, content, and temporal influences to such an extent that the artifice draws attention to itself, to become a tale that "should be hooted at" in Paulina's terms (5.3.116, TLN 3327). The "sad tale" that Mamillius requests from Hermione in 2.1 takes on different forms and pursues different ends. The first three acts in Sicily promise a tragic conclusion. Were the play to end with the ursine removal of Antigonus, the abandonment of Perdita to the fortunes of nature, and the announced deaths of Mamillius and Hermione, Leontes would be an isolated tragic figure, devoid of any possibility for a restoration of family. He would confront a lonely death looming in the distance, the pathetic end Lear submits to without his Cordelia, or the suicidal stroke that Leontes's prototype, Pandosto, inflicts on himself: a sad tale indeed. Shakespeare's decision, however, to revert to "mouldy tales"—Ben Jonson's contemptuous jeer in his *Ode to Himself*—provides him with a means of generating hope and recovery. It is an admission that there are indeed costs to one's actions but that "providential forces" provide hope: "the benevolent coincidences that provide the occasion for final resolution ... all seem part and parcel of a providence that has operated throughout" (Bliss 156).

1 See also ISE website, internetshakespeare.uvic.ca, "Private Theater."

CORRESPONDING CHARACTERS IN *PANDOSTO* AND *THE WINTER'S TALE*

In *Pandosto*	In *The Winter's Tale*
Pandosto	Leontes
Bellaria	Hermione
Garinter	Mamillius
Fawnia	Perdita
Franion	Camillo
Egistus	Polixenes
Dorastus	Florizel
Capnio	Autolycus
none	Antigonus, Paulina, Emilia, Clown, Dorcas, Mopsa

While Robert Greene's *Pandosto*: *The Triumph of Time* (1588) provides us with the narrative structure, basic characters (see chart above), and essential pastoral and romance elements for *The Winter's Tale*, Shakespeare's adoption and manipulation of the narrative elements display his ingenuity in choosing sources and synthesizing those sources with the vast storehouse of personal readings and dramatic influences that were available to him.[1] The story (see Appendix A1, p. 201 ff.) outlines King Pandosto's emerging jealousy over his wife Bellaria's presumed trysts with his lifelong friend, Egistus. Though it provides the essential ingredients for *The Winter's Tale*, Greene's novel constructs a narrative that is straightforward and predicated on a reader's engagement with a story that is lurid and devoid of the enigmatic motivation and spiritual aura found in Shakespeare's play. As in *The Winter's Tale*, Pandosto's jealousy leads to both the death of Bellaria (Hermione)—in this case an actual death—and their son, Garinter (Mamillius). Like *The Winter's Tale*'s Camillo, Pandosto's cupbearer Franion spirits away Egisthus to his home in Sicilia—not Bohemia, which Pandosto rules in Greene's prose narrative. Pandosto's wrath,

1 Stanley Wells, ed., *Perymedes the Blacksmith and Pandosto* by Robert Greene (New York: Garland, 1988).

once the king learns of the departure of Egisthus and Franion, is now trained on Bellaria, whom Pandosto conjectures committed her adultery with Franion's assistance. Pandosto's jealousy is prompted by an extended narrative in which Bellaria's involvement with Egisthus becomes more intimate and more "familiar": Bellaria's desire to please her husband extends to her visiting Egisthus in his bedroom.

Bellaria's subsequent imprisonment, trial, and exoneration through the Delphic oracle are all repeated in *The Winter's Tale*. The birth of a daughter—in Greene named Fawnia—similarly elicits Pandosto's enraged jealousy and suspicion that the child is not his; and after pledging to have the girl burned to death, he retreats in his anger thanks to his advisors' intercession. Despite this reprieve, Pandosto still orders that the daughter be set adrift on the ocean and left subject to Fortune's whimsical treatment. Bellaria's and Garinter's deaths provided Shakespeare with the same tragic coda to the first half of his play. Despite the desire to commit suicide—which he fulfills by the end of the narrative—Pandosto persists, as does Leontes.

Greene, like Shakespeare, transports the narrative across the sea, where the infant Fawnia floats ashore in Sicilia and is discovered by a shepherd, Porrus, who raises her. As with Perdita, Fawnia matures in her beauty and wit with tremendous modesty, qualities that ultimately draw to her side at a chance encounter the young prince, Dorastus, son of Egisthus. Greene's attention to these star-crossed lovers is so extensive that, in its 1635 printing, *Pandosto* was retitled *The Pleasant History of Dorastus and Fawnia*. As in Shakespeare, Greene's second half focuses on the young lovers and their flight from Sicilia and arrival in Bohemia, where Pandosto imprisons Dorastus and attempts to seduce his own daughter.

While Shakespeare brings Polixenes and Leontes together in Sicilia for their emotional reunion, Egisthus sends a message to Pandosto asking that his son be released and Fawnia executed; Pandosto agrees to this request until the shepherd Porrus describes Fawnia's orphan past, a recounting which reveals her to be Pandosto's daughter. This reversal overturns the potential tragedy that has been building: Pandosto apologizes for his lust, knights the peasant Porrus, and sails with Dorastus, Fawnia, and Porrus to Sicilia to reconcile with his friend Egisthus. Overwhelmed by grief for his suspicious treatment of Egisthus, for his role in bringing on Bellaria's death, and for his incestuous feelings towards his daughter, Pandosto commits suicide and is returned home posthumously by Dorastus and Fawnia. Greene characterizes this suicide as a "tragical stratagem" to "close up the comedy."

Besides the obvious reversal of kingdoms—Pandosto's Bohemia becomes Leontes's Siclia while Egistus's Sicilia becomes Polixenes's Bohemia—Shakespeare invests the play with two dramatic alterations to Greene's novel, both of which give the lie to Greene's subtitle ("the Triumph of Time") and the presence of "Fortune" as a blind impetus for the novel's tragedies. As the critic Inga-Stina Ewbank has astutely observed, Shakespeare's "triumph" of time is a regenerative force that restores Hermione after 16 years and provides Leontes with a penitential opportunity to atone for violent acts that sent his wife into isolation, his son to an early grave, and his daughter abandoned to the wilds. Greene's novel, which concludes with Pandosto's suicide, following his wife's and son's earlier deaths, ends with no opportunity for providential intervention, and thus provides only the aftertaste of satisfaction. Shakespeare's choice to resurrect Hermione as a statue affords the play a redemptive turn:

> LEONTES. Her natural posture.
> Chide me, dear stone, that I may say indeed
> Thou art Hermione—or rather, thou art she
> In thy not chiding, for she was as tender
> As infancy and grace. But yet, Paulina,
> Hermione was not so much wrinkled, nothing
> So aged as this seems.
> (5.3.23–29, TLN 3212–18)

For Phebe Jensen, this moment "makes [Hermione] miraculously present, in a ceremony performed under the direction of a Pauline practioner [*sic*], during which stone is transformed into flesh, just as bread and wine become body and blood in the Catholic Mass" (304). The theater that makes this moment possible is aligned with the performance of ritual that transforms lives and provides for rebirth. Such a conclusion would have been irrelevant for Greene's novel, which celebrates melodramatic situations that prompt emotional excesses and Pandosto's anticlimactic, seemingly appropriate suicide. The logical, linear movement provided by Greene, in which narrative heaps situation upon situation, outcome upon outcome, is given a cyclical, sacramental dimension by Shakespeare, in which Leontes's precipitous jealousy and Mamillius's premature demise are bound up by a gracious Hermione and a banished daughter restored. This would have been beyond Greene's story and outside of his authorial capacity.

CLASSICAL INFLUENCE

Ovid was an important storehouse of mythic influences for Shakespeare throughout his career. He drew on Ovid's *Metamorphoses* for his earliest narrative poems and sonnets, and wove Ovidian allusions into plays as diverse as *Titus Andronicus*, *A Midsummer Night's Dream*, and *The Tempest*. *The Winter's Tale* afforded Shakespeare the opportunity to incorporate a number of Ovidian myths to amplify the play's narrative structure (see Appendix A2, pp. 250–64 ff.). In Perdita, Shakespeare created echoes of Flora, the goddess of fertility and spring, an allusion also noted by Robert Greene in *Pandosto* (see Appendix A1, p. 222; and extended note, p. 138). Shakespeare's dramatic adaptation of the Flora myth is also present in subtle hints such as allusive names, as Jonathan Bate suggests: "... is the goddess really Flora? We also know that Time has taken it upon himself to name Bohemia's son *Florizel*, so for the latter to call Perdita Flora is to stake a claim for her by grafting his own name to her" (229).

Ovid's presence is palpable in Florizel's unwittingly ironic allusions to Apollo's penchant for transforming himself to achieve sexual congress (4.4.24 ff., TLN 1825 ff.). The greater tapestry of Ovidian influence, however, is found in Shakespeare's overarching dramatic structure. The cyclical return of Proserpina governs the two-part—diptych—structure of the play: the first three acts take place in a Sicily made tragically wintry by Mamillius's death, Hermione's apparent death, and the mortuary climate that surrounds the court; the last two acts introduced by Time are initially relocated to the pastoral climes of Bohemia, where life is restored—despite Antigonus's violent end—and obstinacy replaced by youthful vigor. Shakespeare's choice of the Proserpina myth is especially poignant for this play. Daughter of Ceres, Proserpina was abducted by Dis, god of the underworld, and cloistered there for six months in his death-like clutches, followed by six months of fertile growth with her annual restoration to her mother. As Jonathan Bate proposes, *The*

Winter's Tale can aptly be named for this dormancy of hope: "Waiting for Proserpina" (220).

Ovid's presence is given more resonance in the statue scene, in which Shakespeare unobtrusively interweaves two separate myths to capture the profound reach of this final reunion of husband and wife. By alluding to the myths of Orpheus's descent to regain his Eurydice and the power of Pygmalion's imagination to turn an ivory statue into a warm, vital woman, Shakespeare invests Hermione's own resurrection before the rapt Leontes with a profound magic. Paulina's warning to Leontes resonates with Orphic power: "do not shun her / Until you see her die again, for then / You kill her double" (5.3.106–08, TLN 3313–15).

Leontes's faith in Paulina's vision recasts Pygmalion's miracle as a metaphorical restoration: Hermione's cloistered statuary is exchanged for a domestic life she had forsaken 16 years earlier. Leontes's language betrays its Ovidian origins: "... methinks / There is an air comes from her. What fine chisel / Could ever yet cut breath?" (5.3.77–79, TLN 3278–80). Though Giuliano Romano[1] is credited with carving this figure, the sculpture is Hermione's own aging visage that beholds her daughter and penitent husband, a charitable gesture that Leontes little deserves but one which is provided for by Paulina's intercession. Shakespeare found in these Ovidian transformations the power of faith to restore life from stone and to transform living beings into ossified figures entranced by magic. The implications of the moment are given special weight by Leonard Barkan: "Hermione's life as a sixteen-year statue is her own winter's tale, but the whole world of Sicilia has in fact been similarly hardened. Only with the discovery of Perdita does the softening begin to take place" (661).

Shakespeare's provocative grafting of Ovid's *Metamorphoses* onto his drama mitigates the melodrama he gleaned from Greene's *Pandosto* and humanizes the obdurate figures of Leontes and Polixenes. Both stifle love by repudiating, respectively, Hermione's potent love and the emerging youthful love of Perdita and Florizel,[2] and both are metamorphosed into passionate, responsive figures who promote love over suspicion, trust over mistrust, and faith over the lunacy of prejudice.

---

1 See extended note, p. 188; and ISE website, internetshakespeare.uvic.ca, "The Late Renaissance: Mannerism."

2 See ISE website, internetshakespeare.uvic.ca, "The marriage ceremony."

In the midst of the sheep-shearing festival in Act 4, a group of artisans performs a "gallimaufry of gambols" (4.4.308, TLN 2150), a dance of satyrs that resounds for the court audience who witnessed Ben Jonson's earlier *Masque of Oberon* (1611).[1] The masque entertainment—a spectacle of dance, song, and elaborate scenic devices by Inigo Jones—was a trademark of King James's court and James's own penchant for spectacles of state. Though the dance of satyrs is often seen as a detachable interlude inserted into the play by Shakespeare to take advantage of his company's role in Jonson's entertainment, the presence of the dance and the spectacle clearly reflects both a Jacobean aesthetic influence and the courtly venue of the Banqueting House, site of the November 1611 performance and the February 1613 performances arranged for the festivities surrounding the wedding of Princess Elizabeth.

Masques were allegorical extensions of the royal court in which panegyric praise of the monarch performed an embellishment of courtly power. As Stephen Orgel puts it (*Illusion* 39):

> Masques were essential to the life of the Renaissance court; their allegories gave a higher meaning to the realities of power and politics, their fictions created heroic roles for the leaders of society.... In form they were infinitely variable, but certain characteristics were constant: the monarch was at the center, and they provided roles for members of the court within an idealized fiction.

The ascension of James I to the throne of England in 1603 provided not only patronage for court masques but also, more importantly, a domestic and political break from Elizabethan rule, during which dynastic succession had remained a public concern. As David Bergeron (*Royal Family* 27 ff.) has noted, James I brought with him a family of potential successors who provided a stability desirable to a country ruled previously by the childless Elizabeth I. James's reign provided, thus, a domestic model that made him not only *pater patriae* at the national level but also *paterfamilias* domestically. Despite the promise of orderly succession, the relationship between James and his queen, Anne of Denmark, and more specifically between the monarch and

1 See ISE website, internetshakespeare.uvic.ca, "Country fairs" and "The Masque."

his children, Prince Henry and Prince Charles, engendered a public display of familial rivalries and domestic discord, a theme that is prevalent in *The Winter's Tale*. The promise of succession and the potential ruptures between father and son are profoundly relevant in the relationships between Leontes and Mamillius and between Polixenes and Florizel.[1]

While the Jacobean royal family may not be responsible for the dynamics reverberating within *The Winter's Tale*, their presence reminds us of the power of theater to reflect its cultural milieu. As Jonathan Goldberg has observed (*James I* 85–112), James I frequently applied domestic metaphors to the promulgation of regal doctrine. In his 1597 *Trew Law of Free Monarchies*, he wrote: "as the Father of his fatherly duty is bound to care for the nourishing, education, and virtuous government of his children even so is the king bound to care for all of his subjects" (*Political Works* 55).[2] In the more intimate *Basilikon Doron* addressed to Prince Henry and intended as a royal handbook for a future monarch (see Appendix B1, p. 265 ff.), James reminds his son of his "fatherly authority" and the need to regard his future subjects in patriarchal terms. More dramatically, Leontes's discussion with Mamillius over their physical resemblance is itself a representation of the very real need for monarchs to guarantee their legitimacy through dynastic succession and a visual, emblematic imprinting of the royal patriarch upon his children. This dialogue is worth citing in full, for its content is nothing less than the patriarchal need to guarantee a succession that duplicates the legitimacy of its ancestry:

LEONTES. ... How now, you wanton calf,
Art thou my calf?
MAMILLIUS. Yes, if you will, my Lord.
LEONTES. Thou want'st a rough pash and the shoots that I have
To be full like me, yet they say we are
Almost as like as egg—women say so
That will say anything. But were they false
As o'er-dyed blacks, as wind, as waters? False
As dice are to be wished by one that fixes
No bourne 'twixt his and mine, yet were it true

1 See ISE website, internetshakespeare.uvic.ca, "Children."

2 *The Political Works of James I*, ed. Charles H. McIlwain (Cambridge: Harvard UP, 1918), 55.

> To say this boy were like me? Come, Sir Page,
> Look on me with your welkin eye, sweet villain,
> Most dearest, my collop. (1.2.125–36, TLN 201–213)

In a famous double portrait of 1583,[1] James and his mother, Mary Queen of Scots, are captured on canvas in a pose that asserts their visual resemblance: face, gestures, and posture are exactly duplicated, and mother and son mirror each other. James's authority is affirmed by his physical resemblance to his mother, a fact not lost on Leontes as he looks on his own progeny.[2]

CRITICAL HISTORY

Simon Forman's May 1611 account (see above, p. 12) may be considered the first critical reception of the play. Forman treats the play as a cautionary tale against roving peddlers like Autolycus; the transformative restoration of Leontes's family fails to provoke any comment. Taking into account classical principles of play production, Ben Jonson and eighteenth-century neoclassicists after him dismissed *The Winter's Tale* as rife with "mouldy tales" and plot absurdities. For John Dryden (1672), *The Winter's Tale* reflects a poetry that lacked "vigor and maturity" and displayed a "lameness of ... [Plot]": "Besides many of the rest as *The Winter's Tale*, *Love's Labour Lost*, *Measure for Measure*, which were either grounded on impossibilities, or at least, so meanly written, that the Comedy neither caus'd your mirth, nor the serious part your concernment."[3] Alexander Pope chose to deny Shakespeare's hand in the creation of *The Winter's Tale* in order to dissociate Shakespeare's genius from a "meanly" written play. The sensibility underlying these sentiments can be found in eighteenth-century productions such as Macnamara Morgan's *The Sheep-Shearing; Or, Florizel and Perdita*, produced in 1754, or David Garrick's *Florizel and Perdita, a Dramatic Pastoral* in 1756. While Garrick retains in abbreviated form both Leontes and Hermione—including Hermione's

---

1 See <http://www.tudorplace.com.ar/images/Stuart,Mary09.jpg>, accessed [1 August 2012].

2 See ISE website, internetshakespeare.uvic.ca, "Children."

3 "Defence of the Epilogue," *Second Part of the Conquest of Granada*, qtd. in Hunt, *Critical Essays* 4–5.

truncated resurrection as a statue—both plays excise the problems highlighted by Samuel Johnson, Pope, and Dryden:

> Both Morgan and Garrick solved the eighteenth-century problem of the play's purportedly inchoate form by excising the first half of *The Winter's Tale*, the Sicilian scenes of Leontes' jealous rapture, Camillo's and Polixenes' flight, Hermione's trial, Paulina's intercession, the casting out of the babe, Antigonus's death on the seacoast of Bohemia, and Time the Chorus narration of the passage of sixteen years. (Hunt, *Critical Essays* 6)

The discordant halves of the story, Antigonus's dispatching by a mischievous bear, and the restoration of family through the Pygmalion-like animation of Hermione—all elements that captivate a modern audience—are subjugated to the pastoral romance of two lovers from apparently disparate social classes and the denouement that provides for the comic nuptials. Until John Philip Kemble's 1802 production at Drury Lane, which restored the tragic jealousy and brooding ambience that resonates in the play's first three acts, *The Winter's Tale* remained a truncated pastoral shell of Shakespeare's original play.

Nineteenth-century Romantic critics found their inspiration in productions that restored the tragic dimensions of Leontes and Hermione's story. Kemble's 1802 production influenced criticism of the early Romantic period. Moved by both Kemble's portrayal of Leontes and Sarah Siddons's riveting realization of Hermione, William Hazlitt rehabilitated Shakespeare's play as a drama worthy of consideration: "These slips or blemishes [i.e., the choric role of Time, the leaping forward over 16 years, and the mythical seacoast of Bohemia] however do not prove it not to be Shakespear's; for he was as likely to fall into them as any body; but do not know any body but himself who could produce the beauties" (qtd. in Hunt, *Critical Essays* 65). Hazlitt singles out the "stuff" of the tragic dimensions contained within the play: the "romantic sweetness, the comic humour" are demonstrably Shakespeare's work, and Leontes's "crabbed and tortuous style" betrays the "thorny" labyrinthine depths of an unreasonable tragedy. Leontes's psychopathology and Hermione's saintly patience persuaded Hazlitt that this play is indubitably Shakespeare's work.

Similarly, Samuel Taylor Coleridge's regard for the play derived from Leontes's impassioned conviction of Hermione's infidelity, a trait that for Coleridge is given its tragic force in *Othello*: "an excitability by the most inadequate causes, and an eagerness to snatch at proofs; secondly, a grossness of conception, and a disposition to degrade the object of the passion by sensual fancies and images; thirdly, a sense of shame of his own feelings exhibited in a solitary moodiness of humor, and yet from the violence of the passion forced to utter itself ..." (qtd. in Hunt, *Critical Essays* 72). Despite the Romantic attention to Leontes and his incipient jealousy, the play in the nineteenth century failed to generate more than passing theatrical criticism prompted by performance.

The emergence of structural, mythic, and new critical approaches to literature in the twentieth century provided the play with some of its more memorable and powerful commentary. New Criticism, which treated literature as logical artifacts with poetic and symbolic wholeness, opened up *The Winter's Tale* to a wide array of critics who found the work unified around either a cluster of symbolic features or verbal structures that were either archetypal (Frye) and primal in scope or more narrowly Christian in intent (Tillyard, Bethell, Wilson Knight, Traversi). E.M.W. Tillyard (1938) made an early examination of Shakespeare's "last plays" as plays of contemplation in which Shakespeare constructed a plot that accentuated the tragic suffering of an evil King (Leontes), the repentance that leads to regeneration (the return of Perdita), and the forgiveness that allows for reunion and restoration (the animated statue of Hermione). Tillyard asserted (60) that *The Winter's Tale* provides for distinct planes of reality that represent the everyday world of courtly life, the paranoid delusional world of Leontes, the frozen world of Hermione that occurs offstage, and the heightened pastoral world that promotes regeneration and restoration. Tillyard and Traversi anticipated the archetypal criticism of Northrop Frye, who systematized these "planes" of reality around seasonal myths of spring, summer, fall, and winter. Though the schematics of Tillyard's criticism would never entirely encapsulate the play's dramatic structure—Wilson Knight would later supplement him by creating a Christian framework for the play's movement—Tillyard's perceptive treatment of Shakespeare's heightened tragic and pastoral worlds remain far-reaching: Shakespeare created "something that can vaguely be called metaphysical, some sense of the complexity of existence, of the different planes on which human life can be lived" (60).

Northrop Frye returned dramatic structure to critical studies of the play, though, like Traversi, he saw *The Winter's Tale* as a series of movements that are cyclical and mythic in nature. Following from his *Anatomy of Criticism*, Frye connects the play's plot structure to the movements from winter to spring, with the promise of summer romance in the marriage of Perdita and Florizel; Leontes's delusional winter of isolation and deprivation gives way to the emergence of spring in Perdita's haven in Bohemia, ending with the marriage of Florizel and Perdita as a comic resolution. Leontes's reunion with Hermione is not quite the typical comic resolution of festivity, however: "It is the world symbolized by nature's power of renewal; it is the world we want; it is the world we hope our gods would want for us if they were worth worshiping" (*Natural Perspective* 116). Thus, for Frye, the romances promote the civil and societal order promised in the comedies with a grim recognition that not all loss can be recompensed or death forestalled.

While mythic criticism grounds *The Winter's Tale*—indeed, all of Shakespeare's romances—within a cycle of nature that resonates in all literature and unifies it into a vast mythic narrative, later critics lament the reduction of specific works into the "same, omnivorous myth" (Ryan 10) at the expense of the play's subtleties. It is important to note the seminal work of J.I.M. Stewart, whose early treatment of Leontes's jealousy, while hearkening back to Coleridge's Romantic treatment, is an important foreshadowing of later psychologically informed treatments of the play. Stewart's profoundly influential treatment considers that the play's significance "may be like that of an iceberg, most massive below the surface" (37). His metaphor reflects the psychological trenchancy of his critical practice; for Stewart, Leontes's jealousy is not a botched theatrical display but an internalized defense of his homosexual passion for Polixenes: "Wanting to be unfaithful to Hermione but consciously unable to entertain the thought, Leontes's ego defends itself by imagining from the details of Hermione's joking hospitality that she means sexually to betray him." Leontes's protection is "I don't love him; she does" (qtd. in Hunt, *Critical Essays* 16).

Early Freudian criticism by scholars such as Stephen Reid and Murray Schwartz discuss the oedipal fears Shakespeare dramatizes. For Reid, Leontes can safely respond to his paranoid jealousy only by projecting his affection for Polixenes through the marriage of Perdita—his offspring—with Florizel—Polixenes's surrogate. Schwartz treats Leontes's jealousy as a psychic drama in which Hermione assumes the role of the dominant rival for Polixenes's affections. Her success in "wooing" Polixenes to stay in Sicilia when Leontes has failed to do so is recast as the father's successful courtship of the maternal. C.L. Barber and Richard P. Wheeler's interpretative strategy recuperates these earlier narratives by arguing that Leontes's friendship with Polixenes must be salvaged and redeemed from a "gross sexuality" through the surrogacy of their children. Only then can he be restored to Hermione and the family be reunited: "The sexual bond of Perdita and Florizel in the new generation makes possible the restoration of Leontes's friendship and the recovery of family bonds purged of sexual degradation" (331–32). Barber and Wheeler identify a progressive movement from the early festive comedies to the tragedies and later romances in terms of how Shakespeare renders older and younger generations. If early festive comedies focus on the assertion of young lovers' rights over paternal prerogative to block love, and later tragedies attend to the dissolution of family bonds just as they are being asserted as paramount for a stable society, the romances provide a redemptive restoring of familial balance after death and abandonment.

While earlier psychoanalytic critics focused on Leontes's psychic state, the unfathomable origins of his jealousy, and his homoerotic regard for Polixenes, later scholars found the three major female characters worthy of equal attention: Hermione, Paulina, and Perdita. These are "three female roles of the first significance" (Overton 46) who function to restore societal order and the female voice. While most feminist critics characterize Leontes's—and also Polixenes's—"oppressive misogyny" and "dark incestuous desires" as responsible for the "static, barren, masculine world" that deprives women of voice (Neely 170), reproductive energy, and maternal influence, the concluding restorations and resurrections of feminine voice are characterized differently: some critics (see French, Neely) view the "patriarchal" society created at the end as either a recuperative moment in which marriage makes women crucial and "freed and enfranchised" (2.2.60, TLN 891) members of the unified family, while others (see Adelman, Enterline, Erickson) conclude that the later restoration of these three women is one that limits their voices within a reconstituted masculine estate.

Lyn Enterline underscores further how Shakespeare uses his Ovidian source to capture this "contraction of power" revealed by Erickson. Enterline examines how Shakespeare uses the Ovidian context of the Proserpina myth within Pygmalion's desire for his statue to take breath and live. For Enterline, Leontes fails to exorcize his narcissistic control of Hermione and her speech such that, like Pygmalion who shapes and finds his image animated, Hermione is so "narrowly" constricted by Leontes's delusions that there is "*nothing* Hermione can say to Leontes" (43). The final scene, thus, is devoted to the three women: Paulina who reanimates Hermione, and Perdita and Hermione who share the scene as if Leontes lacks presence. Hermione and Paulina reify Ovid's tales of rape, misogyny, and female revenge for a Leontes who himself becomes more "stone" than Hermione.

New Historicism, which found its voice in the 1980s, has as its underlying premise the belief that literature is a social product. Literature provides a nexus or intersection for individuals and power structures within which to negotiate or subvert identity and discursive practices. The law, the royal court, the church, the marketplace, and the home are all implicated in this negotiation. As Joan Hall notes, "[New Historicists] uncover strategies by which texts may subvert the dominant ideology of the age but eventually reinscribe it once any socially transgressive elements are contained" (147). Within this construct, the marginalized voices of the powerless or subjected make evident the means by which power is practiced and enforced.

Crtitics such as Leonard Tennenhouse, Stuart Kurland, and William Morse read Shakespeare's romances—including *The Winter's Tale*—as strictly political plays. For them, the play interrogates the underlying foundation of Jacobean absolutism, calling into question its use of patriarchalism to construct a kingship absolute and divinely ordained. The psychological dimensions of this play—an anxious son doomed to deprivation of family and then death, a jealous husband who discards his family, and an abused wife estranged from her son and newborn baby—extend beyond the family to the state itself: the loss of familial order portends, in Tennenhouse's phrase, an "assault on the body politic" (176). This is a conservative criticism: Leontes's failure as father is redeemed by the resurrection of Hermione, the restoration of a family, and a royal genealogy that reauthorizes a royal patriarchy. For David Bergeron (*Royal Family*), the royal family was truly a "text" that infuses

Shakespeare's romances; Bergeron believes not in an allegorical one-to-one correspondence but rather an appropriation by Shakespeare of the mystique that surrounded the Jacobean family. Bergeron draws on the anthropological theories of Clifford Geertz that a mythologized world is concomitantly a political world.

Michael Bristol's New Historicist reading has a Marxist foundation based on the market economy. For him, *The Winter's Tale* betrays "spatiotemporal" gaps in time itself between a gift economy of Sicilia and the emergent market economy of Bohemia. Shakespeare manipulates time as it is experienced in both halves of the play: Leontes's jealousy—a "derangement" predicated on a culture of gift-giving and "potlatch"—occurs during the Winter Festival or Christmastide and reflects a "gift economy" in which Leontes's extravagance transforms Hermione into a form of currency to be fulfilled in the market economy of Bohemia: "Polixenes's attempt to thwart this plan is what actually prompts the otherwise incomprehensible outburst of the king. On this view the ensuing sacrifice of family members is the final, violent stage of potlatch undertaken by Leontes as a primitive affirmation of honor" (156). Just as Time, the choric figure, signals verbally the dramatic fissure of time and place, the bear is an androgynous, spatiotemporal sign that marks the boundaries between the deaths encountered in the first half of the play and the promise of life and a new organic economy of strategic calculation in the latter half.

Phebe Jensen's focus is on the religious dimension of the play, especially the festivities in Bohemia and the fulcrum established in the closing scene in Hermione's dramatic restoration through Paulina's "art, lawful as eating" (5.3.110–11, TLN 3320). Scholars such as Jensen, Julia Lupton, and Huston Diehl have read this transformation of Hermione into a living statue as a mingling of Renaissance aesthetics and Catholic, specifically Marian, iconography. While critics such as Diehl view Shakespeare's modification of Catholic ritual—Shakespeare's statue is truly a living, breathing Hermione—as a Protestant revision and repudiaton of Catholic adoration of iconic efficacy, others (Lupton, Jensen, Ruth Vanita) suggest that Shakespeare's own Romanist upbringing informs a scene with Catholic vitality: "In the context of such direct Catholic and Eucharistic overtones, the apparent transformation of marble into flesh seems to confirm both the efficacy of praying to statues and the Catholic doctrine of Real Presence" (Jensen 303).

Beyond the statue's reanimation, Shakespeare invests the play with an aura of Catholic sensibility: the festivities of Bohemia (the sheep-shearing and the pastoral dances) reflect the transformative power of theater and ritual in human existence. Leontes's earlier, tragic iconoclasm gives way to a grace of art and faith to restore community and family. Furthermore, as Vanita suggests, the play also reaffirms the feminine power of Marian ideology through the triad of Hermione, Paulina, and Perdita, whose "triangular kinship" subordinates and nullifies Leontes's earlier tyranny.

If New Historicism opened up *The Winter's Tale* to a wealth of cultural significations, the deconstructive turn taken by other critics denies the play a final, singular interpretation. Howard Felperin represents this interpretative strategy for *The Winter's Tale*. In deconstructive terms, Leontes's suspicion is not simply whim: the absence of "ocular proof" (to use Othello's words) is justifiable in a Sicily in which Apollo's authority is belated, not presented by a *deus ex machina*, uttered secondarily and thus removed from an empirical correlative. Leontes's "fall from verbal innocence" makes gestures—"paddling palms, pinching fingers," or the more sexual "virginalling" of palms—and Delphic utterances equivocal and slippery ("Tongue-tied" 10; see also Knapp). It is not Hermione's "resurrection" that becomes emblematic of a magical truth; Autolycus's ballads[1] and his duplicitous confirmation of their veracity to the Bohemian rustics are "comic or surrealistic" parodies of Leontes's jealous fantasies ("Tongue-tied" 15). Ultimately, Felperin sees the play as dramatizing the capriciousness of a language estranged from ocular proof.

Stanley Cavell follows Felperin in identifying this distrust of language as Leontes's overall problem; but for Cavell, Leontes's specific problem is the sheer existence of a son that he fails to acknowledge as his own. Such an acknowledgment requires Leontes to be an adult and to admit that he has separated and replicated himself into a new form: "Taking the jealousy as derivative of the sense of revenge upon life, upon its issuing, or separating, or replicating, I am taking it as, so to speak, the solution of a problem in computation or economy, one that at a stroke solves a chain of equations, in which sons and brothers are lovers,

1 See ISE website, internetshakespeare.uvic.ca, "Village celebrations" and "Music of the streets and fairs."

and lovers are fathers and sons, and wives and mothers become one another" (213). Leontes, thus, must overcome a skepticism that calls into question all of life's certainties.

PERFORMANCE HISTORY

> But some men will say, "How are the dead raised up?"
> (Knight 76)

In the earliest account of the play's performance, Simon Forman fails to address this question: the dramatic return of Hermione in Act 5. Moreover, he makes no mention of the ferocious bear that does away with Antigonus. The disparity between the text of the First Folio and Forman's account has invited recent critics to conjecture that Shakespeare substantially revised the play between its performance at the Globe in 1611 and its subsequent royal performances at the Banqueting Hall, a space for court pageants and masque entertainments, in 1611 and 1613. The Globe production featured Richard Burbage, who provided a tragic dimension to Leontes's jealousy, and Robert Armin, who invested Autolycus with the roguish qualities highlighted by Forman. It is clear, Forman's observations notwithstanding, that the play's design emphasized the fantastical elements we associate with the "romance" genre. However, the play incorporates two features that suggest the court performance: dances and an iconic bear. The arrival of the "saltiers" for the satyrs' dance in 4.4 to celebrate the Bohemian sheep-shearing festival has been traced to the contemporary performance of Ben Jonson's *Masque of Oberon* on 1 January 1611. (See extended note, p. 154.) The description of the dancers—"not the worst of the three but jumps twelve feet and a half by th' square" (4.4.315–16, TLN 2159–60)—suggests that these "saltiers" were skilled jumpers with "tawny wrists" and "shaggie thigh."[1] Jonson's masque also featured white bears as part of its spectacle; thus, the appearance of a bear to dispatch Antigonus also suggests the influence of the recent masque.[2]

1 Ben Jonson, *Masque of Oberon* <http://www.luminarium.org/editions/oberon.htm>, accessed 17 April 2014.

2 See also ISE website, internetshakespeare.uvic.ca, "Exit pursued by a bear."

The appearance of Hermione as a statue has been attributed to the influence of Anthony Munday's Lord Mayor's show, *Chrusos-thriambus: The Triumphes of Golde*, which features the restoration of a fourteenth-century mayor from a tomb: "Time striketh on the Tombe with his silver wand and then Faringdon ariseth" (Bergeron "Restoration" 128). The presence of Time and the restoration of Hermione have led David Bergeron to conjecture the relevance of these elements for the wedding celebration of Princess Elizabeth in 1613. Two masques were presented at the nuptials, each of which included statues as part of their invention:

> The renewal of Hermione would fit these dramatic events and correspond in the larger sense to the occasion of the wedding. One should recall that the marriage of Elizabeth came just a few months after the sudden and tragic death of her brother, Henry, Prince of Wales, on 6 November 1612. Within a brief period of time we meet on the national scene "with things dying ... [and] with things newborn." ("Restoration" 129–30)

By 1634, the play had been performed at the court six times before disappearing from the stage for a century.

The Eighteenth Century

Eighteenth-century productions were, in Theophilus Cibber's words, "lop'd, hack'd, and dock'd" adaptations that reflected neoclassical taste dismissive of the play's geographical and temporal expansiveness.[1] These adaptations, notably those by Macnamara Morgan and David Garrick, accorded primary attention to the pastoral romance of Florizel and Perdita. The opinions earlier voiced by Sir Philip Sidney in his *Apologie for Poetrie* (c. 1580) emphasized the dramatic unities adhered to in these adaptations:

> For where the stage should always represent but one place, and the uttermost time presupposed in it should be, both by Aristotle's precept and common reason, but one day, then is both many dayes, and many places inartificially imagined ... you shall have Asia of the one

1 Quoted by Dennis Bartholomeusz in his richly informative *The Winter's Tale in Performance in England and America 1611–1976* (Cambridge: Cambridge UP, 1982), 38.

> side, and Afric of the other, and so many under-kingdoms.... Now of time they are more liberal, for ordinary it is that two young princes fall in love. After many traverses, she is got with child, delivered of a fair boy, he is lost, groweth a man, and is ready to get another with child, and all this in two hours space: which how absurd it is in sense, even sense may imagine, and art hath taught, and all ancient examples justified, and at this day the ordinary players in Italy will not err in. (qtd. in Bartholomeusz 21)

The adaptations that were popular during the time—112 performances compared with only 14 of Shakespeare's play—reflect the sentimental drama that hewed closely to the neoclassical unities, especially those of time, place, and character. Both Morgan and Garrick accentuated the pathos of Perdita's and Florizel's plight, at the expense of either eliminating or condensing the reunion of Leontes and Hermione.

Morgan's *The Sheep-Shearing: or Florizel and Perdita* eliminated Leontes and Hermione and the tragic dimensions behind Perdita's story. The focus on Florizel and Perdita, acted by Spranger Barry and Isabella Nossitor at Covent Garden in 1754, was complemented by the comic exuberance of Ned Shuter as Autolycus. The old Shepherd Alcon, Perdita's surrogate father, provided a narrative flashback to the play's omitted Sicilian past. Alcon offers a safe, sanitized account of Perdita's royal lineage that allows her and Florizel to marry according to proper levels of status:

> Then let us all be blithe and gay
> Upon this joyful, bridal day.
> That Florizel weds Perdita,
> That Florizel weds Perdita.
> And let each nymph and shepherd tell
> No happy pair e'er lov'd so well,
> As Perdita and Florizel
> As Perdita and Florizel
> Sing high, sing down, sing ding-dong bell,
> For Perdita and Florizel (102–03);[1]

1 *Florizel and Perdita, or The Sheepshearing: A dramatic pastoral*. 1782. A Google eBook, accessed 4 October, 2013.

David Garrick's *Florizel and Perdita*, a "dramatic pastoral" in three acts, restores Hermione and Leontes at the end in a play confined to Bohemia. More popular than Morgan's adaptation, Garrick's version, sentimental and histrionic, was performed over sixty times between 1756 and 1795. One Drury Lane review captures the truncated version:

> Her [Hermione's] having lived sequestered for many Years might be allowed, if she did not stand for a Statue at last. This Circumstance is certainly childish, as is likewise the pretended Revival of her by Music. Had Hermione been discovered to us in a rational Manner, the Close would have been pathetic, whereas at present, notwithstanding many Strokes of fine Writing, Reason operates too strongly against the Incident, and our Passions subside into Calmness and Inactivity (qtd. in Bartholomeusz 32)

Hermione's resurrection is perfunctory, and all elements of eighteenth-century sentimentality fail to recuperate the loss of Shakespeare's original play. Garrick took the role of Leontes, Hannah Pritchard and Susannah Cibber the roles of Hermione and Perdita respectively, the former saintly and the latter "innocent and blooming," in productions between 1756 and 1765. Theophilus Cibber laments: "*The Winter's Tale* of Shakespeare, thus lop'd, hack'd, and dock'd appears without Head or Tail. In order to curtail it to Three Acts, the story of the three first Acts of the original Play (and which contains some of the noblest Parts) are crowded into a dull Narrative" (qtd. in Bartholomeusz 38). Despite the extreme cutting of Shakespeare's play, these adaptations addressed audience expectations for a spectacle that elicited audience wonder, hence the popularity of Garrick's dramatic fleeing from the resurrected Hermione. It would take the next century for Shakespeare's original design to return to the stage.

The Nineteenth Century

Despite some restructuring—a transposition of 3.1 to follow Paulina's encounter with Emilia at the jail at 2.2 and a division of the trial scene into two parts—and the retention of some of Garrick's melodramatic dialogue and lyrics, John Philip Kemble's 1802 script restored the two halves of the play without the presence of Time to provide a chronological transition. Kemble added additional characters to swell the ranks of judges, scribes, and morris dancers. The production trimmed lines for decency and comprehension (Florizel's description of Perdita's exquisite dance; the debate on art and nature between Polixenes and Perdita) and used a wing-and-flat system of scenic changes to accommodate the shifts from a Sicily defined by Gothic architecture to a Bohemia distinctly set in England. Kemble's Leontes and Sarah Siddons's Hermione embodied the pathos of the play: According to William Hazlitt, Kemble "evinced a perfect knowledge of his author, and displayed a judgement and feeling which justly place it among his most successful parts," while Siddons presented a Hermione with "monumental dignity and noble passion" (qtd. in Hunt, *Critical Essays* 66).

William Charles Macready's production at Drury Lane and Covent Garden that appeared between 1823 and 1843 was distinctive for investing Leontes's jealousy with believability. Indeed, Macready's elevation of Leontes's psychic collapse into a response that was laced with "realism" was a hallmark of this production. Macready's jealousy ripened from his initial doubts over Hermione's fidelity to a devastating hatred that humanized the spectacle of Leontes's and Hermione's restoration, Macready's visible joy measured by his backward movement from the visual center of the scene, Helen Faucit's graceful appearance as Hermione.

Contrasted with Macready's attempts to humanize the story, Charles Kean's 1856 production at the Princess Theatre was a lavish spectacle that stripped away Shakespearean anachronism in favor of a firmly established fourth-century BCE setting. Kean's major achievement was to transform the choric figure of Time into Chronos, the father of Zeus, seated on an iconic globe that was part of an elaborate allegory. Kean's insistence on spectacle, which minimized Shakespeare's characterization of Time in favor of theatrical display, set the tone for most productions that were staged in the latter half of the nineteenth century. Kean's insistence on historical accuracy also led him to relocate seacoast-challenged Bohemia to the Roman colony of Bithynia, seacoast and all, an adaptation first suggested by Thomas Hanmer's 1744 edition of Shakespeare.

The Twentieth Century and the "Shakespearean Revolution"

Productions of the play during the twentieth century sought to resurrect Shakespeare's play as written, avoiding both the excessive trimming that marked the eighteenth-century productions and the lavish spectacle of the great nineteenth-century actor-managers. On 21 September 1912, Harley Granville-Barker's *The Winter's Tale* opened at the Savoy Theatre with minimal textual excisions. The stage, costuming inspired by Giulio Romano (see extended note, p. 188), innovative lighting, and naturalized performances reaffirmed the primacy of a text subjected earlier to neoclassical adaptation and sentimental excess. Stripping away the Victorian veneer of pictorial realism and a framed construction, Granville-Barker paid homage to the play's internal drama and created the template for most modern productions.

His decision to build a thrust stage over the orchestra pit and an interior inset stage created a playing area of depth and space. The imaginative use of white columns and curtains represented the Sicilian court, and the impression of a thatched cottage with leaf-patterned curtains for exterior scenes depicted the arrival in Bohemia. Henry Ainley, Lillah McCarthy, and Cathleen Nesbitt each conveyed realistically the manic abruptness of a jealous Leontes, the dignified repose of the wronged Hermione, and the naive, bucolic youthfulness of a fresh Perdita. English poet John Masefield characterized the significance of Granville-Barker's production in these terms: "The performance seemed to me to be a riper and juster piece of Shakespearean criticism than I have seen hitherto in print" (qtd. in Bartholomeusz 164).

If Barker's 1912 production gave its audience a Leontes with severe psychic disturbance, an insecure and clearly undignified neurotic, Peter Brook's 1951 production at the Phoenix Theatre, London, provided a nuanced performance by John Gielgud, whose Leontes was matched by Diana Wynyard's gentle, gracious Hermione. Gielgud's Leontes demonstrated a jealousy mounting from an initial quietness to reach fever pitch during his query to Camillo, "Is this whispering nothing?" Flora Robson's Paulina was a determined, loyal presence in the play, "Fury-like" (Venezky 338) in her denunciations of Leontes. The play's pastoral elements paled next to the tragic intensity of the scenes in Sicilia. Much of this diminution can be attributed to director Peter Brook's decision to remove the satyr dance from the sheep-shearing festival. (He also excised the opening scene with Camillo and Archidamus and the arrival of Cleomines and Dion from Delphi.) The performances enhanced a production for which the use of multiple performance stages proved "cumbersome" (Venezky 338) and awkward in promoting organic, fluid staging. Despite the omissions and the imbalance between the Sicilian and Bohemian sequences, the production at the Phoenix Theatre ran a spectacular 162 performances.

The Stratford performances at the Shakespeare Memorial Theatre in the latter half of the twentieth century reflect directors who treat the stage as extensions of the psychic state of the play's protagonists. Anthony Quayle's 1948 production transformed the domestic dynamics into a "fairy tale" in which Esmond Knight's Leontes was played as a tyrant devoid of nuance or subtlety. Sicily was treated as a Slavic kingdom and Bohemia transformed into a steppe-like wilderness with Paul Scofield's Clown adopting a Warwickshire dialect. Peter Wood's 1960 production opted to recreate a Renaissance court, replete with Gothic arches and flourishes of courtly magnificence (Tatspaugh 29 ff.). Eric Porter's Leontes was an urbane, passionate husband propelled by his misunderstanding of Hermione's innocent "If you first sinned with us" 1.2.83, TLN 150) to a jealousy that was both reasonable and extreme. His portrait of a man driven to jealousy by the paddling of palms and free expression of Hermione's hospitality was lauded as even superior to Gielgud's highly esteemed performance of a decade earlier. In this production, Time (played by Derek Godfrey) was an elegant, eloquent figure with an hourglass who seemingly supervised the entrances and exits of the play's characters during the transition: summoning forth the arrival and departure in a dumb show of Leontes in his decline and the pastoral meetings of Florizel and Perdita in Bohemia.

Productions in the later twentieth century attempted to design a stage that reflected both Sicilia's upheaval and Bohemia's bucolic spirit. Stratford productions (Trevor Nunn in 1969; John Barton and Nunn in a 1976 joint production) emphasized Leontes's psychic break through the use of a symbolic stage to suggest the emotional tenor of jealousy that overwhelms Sicilia in the first half of the play. Indeed, Nunn's 1969 production marks a change of style and dramatic vision from Wood's 1960 Renaissance spectacle. Nunn deployed a white box set that allowed for an imaginative use of spare symbols:

> ... the figure of Leontes, arms outstretched as if crucified, turning in anguish, appeared in an erect, rectangular box or case with mirrored walls which was placed in the centre of the stage and revealed in flashes of light while a part of Time's speech was heard through the

> darkness: "I that please some, try all ..." (Bartholomeusz 213; see also Tatspaugh 33 ff.)

This mirrored box and the novel use of Time's speech reflected the creative forces that connect Leonte's tortured state, Time's role in human dynamics, and Hermione's statued imprisonment (all three step out of the same Perspex box). The opening scene of a white nursery with toys and a white rocking horse captured both the innocence of Mamillius's world and the more insidious forces that would destroy this innocence: Hermione is a "hobby-horse" 1.2.273, TLN 368), a battered doll capturing the domestic violence that unfolds, and a spinning top the fragile core of Leontes's self-display. The Bohemia of this production was not the Russian steppes or an unspecified pastoral but rather a more contemporary modish community of rock music and contemporary Carnaby Street ambience. More controversial was the decision to have Judi Dench double Perdita and Hermione, which had been done by Mary Anderson a century earlier in the 1877 Lyceum production with Johnston Forbes-Robertson as Leontes. The choice of having Perdita onstage speaking to the statue made for awkward staging as Dench had to move offstage to take her place within the mirrored box while a double occupied the Perdita space that Dench was forced to vacate (see Tatspaugh 191–92).

The joint Nunn and Barton production of 1976 invested the play with even more symbolic use of the stage. The world of Sicily was a Lapland rife with bear imagery characterized by critic Richard David as a bear-"totem" (qtd. in Bartholomeusz 222): Polixenes dons a bearskin blanket and becomes the imaginary bear hunted down by the playful Mamillius, a blanket that will then be later wrapped around Hermione's shoulders. The implicit threat of this Sicily was incarnated in Ian McKellan's Leontes, whose jealousy is unpredictable and rash. Here McKellen followed Macready and Gielgud in establishing an anguish born from deep-seated origins. He rendered as palpable the evil moving within his psyche. John Nettles, who would play Leontes in Nunn's 1992 production, doubled the roles of Time and the bear in this joint production. Antigonus's demise was treated not realistically but mythically: Time held a symbolic bear mask before his face, striking a stick upon the stage to signal Antigonus's forced removal from the stage.

Ronald Eyre's 1981 production eschewed the 1976 symbolism for a spare and minimalist approach, often emphasizing the theatricality of the performance: prop tables visible to the audience, actors visible in the wings waiting for their entrances, the opening of 1.2 in which actors put on their costumes and took props for a masque (Hermione a sheaf of wheat; Polixenes and Leontes crowns and robes from tailors' dummies). Autolycus appeared with a giant bear, and an oversized Father Time entered wearing a giant robe patterned in astronomical figures from the winter sky. Mamillius crept out from beneath Time's robe to begin the scene. Patrick Stewart's Leontes was suspicious at the outset, and his jealousy seemed organic and developed. Stewart's scenes with Gemma Jones's Hermione were thus tinged with a latent tension.

Terry Hands's 1984 and Noble's 1992 Stratford productions avoided the starkness of the Eyre's 1981 production, returning to the symbolism of earlier 1960s versions. Hands adorned the white set with a scrim to demarcate the playing areas, a romantic ambience of dramatic set pieces with nursery toys, lighting and reflective surfaces overhead and below that hinted at distortions of the opening scenes of bliss; Noble's "gauze box" could be warmly lit or darkly opaque, flexibly allowing for still-life vignettes and dynamic action spilling onto the main stage. For Hands, Jeremy Irons made Leontes a sardonic husband to Penny Downie's flirtatious Hermione, a man whose fragile marriage made his jealousy both justifiable and rational. For Noble, John Nettles's Leontes was blissfully in love with Samantha Bond's Hermione, and his jealousy was sudden and violent, reflected in the lighting that turned to a chilly blue against a floor covered with fissures that symbolize the breakage of the romantic promise.

The 1986 production at Stratford, Ontario, was notable for a number of reasons: it was one of the three late plays (including *Pericles* and *Cymbeline*) undertaken by John Neville as the new artistic director of the festival; it excelled in using the vast thrust stage to engender two levels of drama, grand spectacle that contained quiet, intimate characterization. David Williams's production heightened the generic rift in the play's structure by setting Sicilia in a chandelier-rich 1830 court and Bohemia in a "Hardyesque rural community" of 1846 (Warren 166). Novel in this production was the decision to have Susan Wright (Paulina) present Hermione's offstage death with a conviction that she herself embraces as true. Colm Feore's Leontes lay prostrate at this announcement, an image that Williams duplicated in Leontes's reappearance 16 years later when he was discovered prostrate upon the sarcophagi of Mamillius and Hermione. Hermione's restoration was staged as the culmination of Leontes's progressive, cathartic penance undertaken under Paulina's tutelage.

Gregory Doran's 1999 RSC production at the Barbican took place on a perspective stage created by five pairs of sliding panels that narrowed to convey the paranoia and insularity of Leontes (Antony Sher). Doran also used sound to suggest suspicious voices and secrets emanating in the psyche of an increasingly paranoid Leontes. The billowy curtains overhead created a threatening gesture that reflected Leontes's descent into a "psychotic jealousy" that cripples him emotionally, which internalizes the physical handicap of the wheelchair-ridden Mamillius (Emily Bruni, who doubled as Perdita). Unlike Jeremy Irons's ironic Leontes, Anthony Sher's Leontes was pathetic and ultimately brutalized by a vindictive Paulina who physically threw him across the stage following the reading of the oracle. Hermione's eventual restoration to him was a therapeutic necessity for his mental health.

The New Century

The twenty-first century has seen renewed interest in this play after the events of 9/11. In 2009 Carol Chillington Rutter queried its revival: "What accounts for the play's currency today? Is it, since that September, our culture's profoundly adjusted attitude to time, history and loss, the daily acknowledgement of life's fragility? Is it a longing for a return to a place we can't recover...." (350). Rutter alludes to the events of 9/11 and the sense of vulnerability created by acts of terrorism. That sense of a failed nostalgia and abrupt violence marks the productions that occurred later in the first decade of the new millennium: the domestic violence and assertion of feminine prerogative, especially in Paulina's bellicosity toward Leontes, resonated for its audience as especially topical and relevant. Notable productions include a 2005 version by the UK's Propeller company, and high-profile productions in New York 2009 and 2010 by the Bridge Project and Shakespeare in the Park, respectively. The Propeller production, which toured the UK, the US, and China, attempted to replicate the all-male productions of Shakespeare's time and the consequent doubling of parts. In it, one actor played Time, Mamillius, and Perdita, accentuating the temporal shifts occasioned by Mamillius's death and Perdita's birth. The play's emphasis on time was reinforced by the rear-projection of the moon ("the watery star," 1.2.1, TLN 50) that gradually became a full moon following the interval. The Bohemia of this production was headed by a band, "The Bleatles," and Autolycus was garbed as punk rocker à la Iggy Pop. The famous stage direction *Exit pursued by a bear* provided the company with an opportunity to tweak audience expectations: Mamillius arrived on stage dressed in a bear suit an act earlier than the actual bear. When the bear did arrive to devour Antigonus, it turned out to be Mamillius's stuffed bear. Noteworthy is the coda director Edward Hall added to the end of the play: the ghost of Mamillius arrived to blow out a candle cradled in Leontes's hands. The coda provided the play with a proper annunciation of a production for a new world. Increasingly, the play turns its attention to the children, Mamillius especially, and the effect of domestic violence on children.

The Bridge Project at the Brooklyn Academy of Music was a binational production by Sam Mendes that used American and British actors to create the Sicilian and Bohemian realms. Notable in this production was Simon Russell Beale's Leontes, who was credited with making "transparent" Leontes's jealousy while sustaining the enigma of its origins.[1] The power of the first half of the production in Sicilia cast with British actors overwhelmed the Bohemia set in rural Midwest America, an unfortunate imbalance given the restorative demands of the Bohemian idyll. Suffering in comparison is the 2010 Shakespeare in the Park production, in which nuanced performances were undercut by the urban acoustics that required actors to blare out dialogue. The psychological layers provided by the 2009 Mendes production were missing in a production for which the Bohemian pastoral setting promise of comic festivities—heightened by puppets and Eastern European dance music—were welcome relief. The 2011 production of the play in Toronto's "Dream in the Park" summer series trimmed the action to 90 minutes, resulting in an abbreviated Sicilia that further obscured the origins of Leontes's incipient jealousy. The Bohemia of the second half allowed director Estelle Shook to take advantage of

1 Ben Brantley, "Alas, Poor Leontes (That Good King Has Not Been Himself of Late)," *The New York Times* 23 February 2009. <http://theater.nytimes.com/2009/02/23/theater/reviews/23winter.html>, accessed 1 August 2012.

the outdoor setting for the sheep-shearing festivities and revelry. The sun's setting and the darkened stage lent the dramatic restoration of Hermione (Kelly McIntosh) a preternatural aura.

Regional productions in San Diego in 2005 and Minneapolis in 2011 provided the play with elements inspired by regional and thematic tastes. Darko Tresnak's Old Globe production in San Diego, spare of stage but resplendent with special lighting to highlight seasonal changes, gave Leontes's jealousy a complexity that captured his tragic trajectory. The restoration of Hermione was especially heightened by the presence of a female Time, who cradled Hermione in a re-creation of a moving pietà. Tresnak's production ushered in a Bohemia in which a beer-barrel polka and a giant funhouse bear established the festive mood of the regenerative kingdom.

Jonathan Munby's production at the Guthrie Theatre in Minneapolis doubled Time with Antigonus, the actor changing from his military uniform to an all-white spectral garb. While the Old Globe created a carnivalesque atmosphere with a cutout bear's head, the Guthrie production used an actor in a bear suit with special lighting to capture the ominous attack on Antigonus. The Guthrie highlighted its Midwest roots by setting its Bohemia in a northern Minnesota setting, with birch trees and black-eyed susans and Ford Ranchero pickup trucks. Despite the staging idiosyncrasies of these two productions, both directors highlighted the tortured state of Leontes's mind and its incipient jealousy. Munby used a dumbshow to depict Leontes's riven psyche and prerecorded vocal murmurings to create the internal monologue that disrupted his state. Whereas Tresnak's Leontes gained in sympathy through the moving statue scene, in which his Hermione is restored to his side, Munby's production emphasized especially Hermione's anguish during her trial scene, in which she wore a sackcloth dress stenciled with a number, her hair shorn and skin gaunt from the imprisonment.

The RSC's imported production (directed by David Farr) in New York in 2011 gave Leontes's jealousy a "cool ferocity" that revealed a jealousy with an extensive germination period. The Edwardian setting provided the most unsettling of transformations: chandeliers came crashing down and ceiling-high bookcases collapsed, strewing their books with a cataclysmic thunder. The loose pages were given extra power by forming the costumes of the Bohemians and the leaves of the trees. Though the production also created a haunting image of the final reunion of Leontes and Hermione, Farr left Autolycus onstage to challenge the audience's acceptance of the play's promise of a festive reunion and he shrugged to reinforce the ambiguity of the resolution. Does the play conclude "happily ever after?" Perhaps not.

FILM

The 1981 BBC film version is renowned for the influence of producer Jonathan Miller and director Jane Howell in establishing a style that avoided the "realism" of earlier productions in the BBC Shakespeare series. Described as an "economically" adaptive approach to the play for a televised media (Hall 179), Howell's production had a stylized quality more akin to the more experimental theatrical productions (Hall 178–79). The set was a stark wedged-shaped background with a central entrance, two cones and a tree to suggest a nondescript landscape given seasonal change through lighting. Jeremy Kemp was a stern, domineering Leontes to Robert Stephens's more cheery Polixenes. Anna Calder-Marshall and Margaret Tyzack projected, respectively, Hermione's resilience and Paulina's indignant outrage at Leontes's affronts.

The production was also notable for its striking use of television's intimacy to isolate Kemp's whispered asides to the audience from the onstage action and to unite audience and Autolycus in conspiratorial collusion during his dissembling feats. Grouping of actors in the televised frame allowed Howell to control the audience's interpretation and perspective. In Leontes's interruption of Hermione's intimate moments with Mamillius in Act 2, Howell used the camera to shift angles from Hermione and her court dressed in light colors and Leontes with his courtiers dressed in black, pulling back to reveal the growing rift within Sicilia's order. A similar effect is used to isolate Hermione during her trial scene as the camera moves from her isolated close-up to take in the sweep of the court's remoteness from her plight. The Bohemian sheep-shearing scenes were similarly staged, with the swelling of individual to group scenes capturing the festivities as a communal mingling of Perdita, Florizel, and the Bohemian celebrants. As Joan Hall observes (183–84), however, the fluid medium of television failed to deliver the impact of the final statue scene: the close-ups of

Hermione's awakening and Leontes's astonishment deprive the audience of the advantage of the wider perspective as Hermione's return is registered by all the characters onstage.

The theatrical and cinematic productions described above have captured the range of interpretations and staging possibilities presented by Shakespeare's play, a drama that draws attention to its artifice and to the emotional polarities that life presents to all of us. If productions come to different conclusions about the source of Leontes's jealousy, the depth of his depravity or fragile condition, the nature of the bear which sheds blood in the creation of the Bohemian pastoral, and the pathos of the haunting final scene, all theatrical versions exploit the aesthetic demands of this play. *The Winter's Tale* requires both readers and spectators to experience joy and terror as the inexorable consequences of Time's hourglass, as it turns again and again to demarcate this "wide gap" (4.1.7, TLN 1586) of life.

SHAKESPEARE'S LIFE

BY DAVID BEVINGTON

The website of the Internet Shakespeare Editions, in the section "Life & Times," has further information on many topics mentioned here: Shakespeare's education, his religion, the lives and work of his contemporaries, and the rival acting companies in London.

William Shakespeare was baptized on 26 April 1564, in Holy Trinity Church, Stratford-upon-Avon. He is traditionally assumed to have been born three days earlier, on 23 April, the feast day of St. George, England's patron saint. His father, John Shakespeare, prospering for years as a tanner, glover, and dealer in commodities such as wool and grain, rose to become city chamberlain or treasurer, alderman, and high bailiff, the town's highest municipal position. Beginning in 1577, John Shakespeare encountered financial difficulties, with the result that he was obliged to mortgage his wife's property and miss council meetings. Although some scholars argue that he was secretly a Catholic, absenting himself also from Anglican church services for that reason, the greater likelihood is that he stayed at home for fear of being processed for debt. His wife, Mary, did come from a family with ongoing Catholic connections, but most of the evidence suggests that Shakespeare's parents were respected members of the Established Church. John's civic duties involved him in carrying out practices of the Protestant Reformation. John and Mary baptized all their children at the Anglican Holy Trinity Church, and were buried there.

As civic official, John must have sent his son William to the King Edward VI grammar school close by their house on Henley Street. Student records from the period have perished, but information about the program of education is plentifully available. William would have studied Latin grammar and authors, including Ovid, Virgil, Plautus, Seneca, and others that left an indelible print on the plays he wrote in his early years.

Shakespeare did not, however, go to university. The reasons are presumably two: his father's financial difficulties, and, perhaps even more crucially, Shakespeare's own marriage at the age of eighteen to Anne Hathaway. Neither Oxford or Cambridge would ordinarily admit married students. Anne was eight years older than William. She was also three months pregnant when they were married in November 1582. A special license had to be obtained from the Bishop of Worcester to allow them to marry quickly, without the customary readings on three successive Sundays in church of the banns, or announcements of intent to marry. The couple's first child, Susanna, was born in late May 1583. Twins, named Hamnet and Judith, the last of their children, followed in February 1585. Thereafter, evidence is scarce as to Shakespeare's whereabouts or occupation for about seven years. Perhaps he taught school, or was apprenticed to his father, or joined some company of traveling actors. At any event, he turns up in London in 1592. In that year, he was subjected to a vitriolic printed attack by a fellow dramatist, Robert Greene, who seems to have been driven by professional envy to accuse Shakespeare of being an "upstart crow" who had beautified himself with the feathers of other writers for the stage, including Christopher Marlowe, George Peele, Thomas Nashe, and Greene himself.

Shakespeare was indeed well established as a playwright in London by the time of this incident in 1592. In that same year Thomas Nashe paid tribute to the huge success of the tragic death of Lord Talbot in a play, and the only play we know that includes Talbot is Shakespeare's *1 Henry VI*. We do not know for what acting company or companies Shakespeare wrote in the years before 1594, or just how he got started, but he seems to have been an actor as well as dramatist. Two other plays about the reign of Henry VI also belong to those early years, along with his triumphantly successful *Richard III*. These four English history plays, forming his first historical tetralogy, were instrumental in defining the genre of the English history play. Following shortly after the great defeat of the Spanish Armada in 1588, these plays celebrated England's ascent from a century of devastating civil wars to the accession in 1485 of the Tudor Henry VII, grandfather of Queen Elizabeth I. Shakespeare's early work also includes some fine ventures into comedy, including *A Comedy of Errors*, *The Two Gentlemen of Verona*, *Love's Labor's Lost*, and *The Taming of the Shrew*. He wrote only one tragedy at this time, *Titus Andronicus*, a revenge tragedy based on fictional early Roman history. Shakespeare also turned his hand to narrative poetry in these early years. *Venus and Adonis* in 1593 and *The Rape of Lucrece* in 1594, dedicated to the Earl of Southampton, seem to show Shakespeare's interest in becoming a published poet, though ultimately he chose drama as more fulfilling and lucrative. He probably wrote some of his sonnets in these years, perhaps to the Earl of Southampton, though they were not published until 1609 and then without Shakespeare's authorization.

Shakespeare joined the newly-formed Lord Chamberlain's Men, as an actor-sharer and playwright, in 1594, along with Richard Burbage, his leading man. This group quickly became the premier acting company in London, in stiff competition with Edward Alleyn and the Lord Admiral's Men. For the Lord Chamberlain's group, Shakespeare wrote his second and more artistically mature four-play series of English histories, including *Richard II*, the two *Henry IV* plays centered on the Prince who then becomes the monarch and victor at Agincourt in *Henry V* (1599). He also wrote another history play, *King John*, in these years. Concurrently Shakespeare achieved great success in romantic comedy, with *A Midsummer Night's Dream*, *The Merchant of Venice*, and *The Merry Wives of Windsor*. He hit the top of his form in romantic comedy in three plays of 1598–1600 with similar throw-away titles: *Much Ado About Nothing*, *As You Like It*, and *Twelfth Night, or What You Will*. Having fulfilled that amazing task, he set comedy aside until years later.

During these years Shakespeare lived in London, apart from his family in Stratford. He saw to it that they were handsomely housed and provided for; he bought New Place, one of the two finest houses in town. Presumably he went home to Stratford when he could. He was comfortably well off, owning as he did one share among ten in an acting company that enjoyed remarkable success artistically and financially. He suffered a terrible tragedy in 1596 when his only son and heir, Hamnet, died at the age of eleven. In that year, Shakespeare applied successfully for a coat of arms for his father, so that John, and William too, could each style himself as gentleman. John died in 1601, Shakespeare's mother in 1608.

Having set aside romantic comedy and the patriotic English history at the end of the 1590s, Shakespeare turned instead to problematic plays such as *All's Well That Ends Well*, *Measure for Measure*, and *Troilus and Cressida*, the last of which is ambivalently a tragedy (with the death of Hector), a history play about the Trojan War, and a bleak existential drama about a failed love relationship. He also took up writing tragedies in earnest. *Romeo and Juliet*, in 1594–96, is a justly famous play, but in its early acts it is more a comedy than a tragedy, and its central figures are not tragic protagonists of the stature of those he created in

1599 and afterwards: *Julius Caesar*, *Hamlet*, *Othello*, *King Lear*, *Macbeth*, *Timon of Athens*, *Antony and Cleopatra*, and *Coriolanus*, this last play written in about 1608. Whether Shakespeare was moved to write these great tragedies by sad personal experiences, or by a shifting of the national mood in 1603 with the death of Queen Elizabeth and the accession to the throne of James VI of Scotland to become James I of England (when the Lord Chamberlain's Men became the King's Men), or by a growing skepticism and philosophical pessimism on his part, is impossible to say; perhaps he felt invigorated artistically by the challenge of excelling in the relatively new (for him) genre of tragedy.

Equally hard to answer with any certainty is the question of why he then turned, in his late years as a dramatist, to a form of comedy usually called romance, or tragicomedy. The genre was made popular by his contemporaries Beaumont and Fletcher, and it is worth noting that the long indigenous tradition of English drama, comprising the cycles of mystery plays and the morality plays, was essentially tragicomic in form. The plays of this phase, from *Pericles* (c. 1606–08) to *Cymbeline*, *The Winter's Tale*, and *The Tempest* in about 1608–11, would seem to overlap somewhat the late tragedies in dates of composition. These romances are like the early romantic comedies in many ways: young heroines in disguise, plots of adventure and separation leading to tearfully joyful reunions, comic high-jinks, and so on. Yet these late romances are also as tinged with the tragic vision that the dramatist had portrayed so vividly: death threatens or actually occurs in these plays, the emotional struggles of the male protagonists are nearly tragic in their psychic dimensions, and the restored happiness of the endings is apt to seem miraculous.

Shakespeare seems to have retired from London to Stratford-upon-Avon some time around 1611; *The Tempest* may have been designed as his farewell to the theater and his career as dramatist, after which he appears to have collaborated with John Fletcher, his successor at the King's Men, in *Henry VIII* and *The Two Noble Kinsmen* (1613–14). His elder daughter, Susanna, had married the successful physician John Hall in 1607. In his last will and testament Shakespeare left various bequests to friends and colleagues, but to Anne, his wife, nothing other than his "second-best bed." Whether this betokens any estrangement between him and the wife, whom he had married under the necessity of her pregnancy and from whom he then lived apart during the two decades or so when he resided and worked in London, is a matter of hot debate. Divorce was impossible, whether contemplated or not. He did take good care of her and his family, and he did retire to Stratford. Anne lived on with Susanna and John Hall until she died in 1623. Shakespeare was buried on 25 April 1616, having died perhaps on 23 April, fifty-two years to the day after his birth if we accept the tradition that he was born on the Feast of St. George. He lies buried under the altar of Holy Trinity, next to his wife and other family members. A memorial bust, erected some time before 1623, is mounted on the chancel wall.

SHAKESPEARE'S THEATER

BY DAVID BEVINGTON

The website of the Internet Shakespeare Editions includes an extensive discussion of the theaters of Shakespeare's time, and the audiences that attended them: click on "Life & Times" and choose the menu item "Stage."

Where Shakespeare's plays of the early 1590s were performed we do not know. When he joined the newly-formed Lord Chamberlain's Men in 1594, with Richard Burbage as his leading man, most public performances of Shakespeare's plays would have been put on in a building called The Theatre, since, when it was erected in 1576 by Richard Burbage's father James Burbage, it was the only structure in London designed specifically for the performance of plays, and indeed the first such building in the history of English theater. Earlier, plays were staged by itinerant companies in inns and innyards, great houses, churchyards, public squares, and any other place that could be commandeered for dramatic presentation. In Shakespeare's time the professional companies still toured, but to a lesser extent, and several of them also derived part of their income from private performances at court.

The Theatre had been erected in Shoreditch (also called Moorfields), a short walking distance north of London's walls, in order to evade the too-often censorious regulations of the city's governing council. There, spectators might have chosen to see *Romeo and Juliet*, *A Midsummer Night's Dream*, *The Merchant of Venice*, *King John*, or *Richard II*. They would also have seen some earlier Shakespeare plays that he had brought with him (perhaps as the price needed to pay for a share in the company) when he joined the Lord Chamberlain's Men: plays such as *Richard III* and *The Taming of the Shrew*. When in the late 1590s the Puritan-leaning owner of the land on which the building stood, Giles Allen, refused to renew their lease because he wished "to pull down the same, and to convert the wood and timber thereof to some better use," the Lord Chamberlain's Men performed for a while in the nearby Curtain Theatre. Eventually, in 1599, they solved their problem with the landlord by moving lock, stock, and barrel across the River Thames to the shore opposite from London, just to the west of London Bridge, where audiences could reach the new theater—the Globe—by bridge or by water taxi, and where the players were still outside the authority of the city of London. At the time of this move, the River Thames was frozen over solid in an especially harsh winter, so that possibly they slid the timbers of their theater across on the ice.

At any event, the Globe Theatre that they erected in Southwark, not far from the location of today's reconstructed Globe, was in the main the same building they had acted in before. Because timbers were all hand-hewn and fitted, the best plan was to reassemble them as much as was feasible. No doubt the company decided on some modifications, especially in the acting area, based on their theatrical experience, but the house remained essentially as before.

No pictures exist today of the interiors of the Theatre, the Curtain, or the Globe. We do have Visscher's View of London (1616) and other representations showing the exteriors of some theatrical buildings, but for the important matter of the interior design we have only a drawing of the Swan Theatre, copied by a Dutchman, Arend van Buchell, from a lost original by the Dutch Johannes de Witt when he visited London in about 1596–98. In many respects, the Swan seems to have been typical of such buildings. As seen in the accompanying illustration, the building appears to be circular or polygonal, with a thatched roof (called *tectum* in the illustration's labels) over the galleries containing seats and another roof over the stage, but leaving the space for standing spectators open to the heavens. (In the modern Globe, similarly constructed, spectators intending to stand in the yard for a performance can purchase a plastic rain poncho to ward off England's frequent rain showers.) From other kinds of information about Elizabethan playhouses, we can estimate a diameter of about 70 feet for the interior space. A large rectangular stage labeled the *proscaenium* (literally, "that which stands before the scene"), approximately 43 feet wide and 27 feet deep, juts out from one portion of the wall into the yard or *planities siue arena* ("the plain place or arena"). The stage stands about 5½ feet above the surface of the yard. Two pillars support the roof over the stage, which in turn is surmounted by a hut. A flag is flying at the top, while a trumpeter at a door in the hut is presumably announcing the performance of a play. The spectators' seats are arrayed in three tiers of galleries. Stairway entrances (*ingressus*) are provided for spectators to gain access from the yard to the seats, labeled *orchestra* on the first level and nearest the stage, and *porticus* above.

ABOVE, LEFT: This sketch of the Swan is the most complete we have of any theater of the time. The Swan was built in 1596; Shakespeare's company, The Chamberlain's Men, played there in the same year. RIGHT: This view of the first Globe by the Dutch engraver J.C. Visscher was printed in 1625, but must be taken from an earlier drawing, since the first Globe was burnt to the ground in 1613 at the first performance of Shakespeare's *Henry VIII*. There is substantial evidence that Visscher simplified the appearance of the theater by portraying it as octagonal: most scholars now believe that it had twenty sides, thus making it seem more circular than in this engraving.

The stage area is of greatest concern, and here the Swan drawing evidently does not show everything needed for performance in a theater such as the Globe. No trapdoor is provided, though one is needed in a number of Renaissance plays for appearances by ghostly or diabolical visitations from the infernal regions imagined to lie beneath the earth. The underside of the stage roof is not visible in this drawing, but from the plays themselves and other sources of information we gather that this underside above the actors' heads, known as the "heavens," displayed representations of the sun, moon, planets, and stars (as in today's London Globe). The back wall of the stage in the drawing, labeled *mimorum ades* or "housing for the actors," provides a visual barrier between the stage itself and what was commonly known as the "tiring house" or place where the actors could attire themselves and be ready for their entrances. The two doors shown in this wall confirm an arrangement evidently found in other theaters like the Globe, but the absence of any other means of access to the tiring house raises important questions. Many plays, by Shakespeare and others, seem to require some kind of "discovery space," located perhaps between the two doors, to accommodate a London shop, or a place where in *The Tempest* Prospero can pull back a curtain to "discover" Miranda and Ferdinand playing chess, or a place to which Falstaff, in the great tavern scene of *1 Henry IV*, can retire to avoid the Sheriff's visit and then be heard snoring offstage before he exits at scene's end into the tiring house. The modern Globe has such a discovery space.

Above the stage in the Swan drawing is what appears to be a gallery of six bays in which we can see seated figures watching the actors on the main stage, thereby surrounding those actors with spectators on all sides. But did theaters like the Swan or the Globe regularly seat spectators above the stage like this? Were such seats reserved for dignitaries and persons of wealth? Other documents refer to a "lords' room" in such theaters. The problem is complicated by the fact that many Elizabethan plays require some upper acting area for the play itself, as when Juliet, in Act II of *Romeo and Juliet*, appears "*above*" at her "*window*" to be heard by Romeo and then converses with him, or later, when Romeo and Juliet are seen together "*aloft*" at her "window" before Romeo descends, presumably by means of a rope ladder in full view of the audience, to go to banishment (3.5). Richard II appears "*on the walls*" of Flint Castle when he is surrounded by his enemies and is obliged to descend (behind the scenes) and then enter on the main stage to Bolingbroke (*Richard II*, 3.3). Instances are numerous. The gallery above the stage, shown in the Swan drawing, must have provided the necessary acting area "*above*." On those many occasions when the space was needed for action of this sort, seemingly the acting company would not seat spectators there. It is unclear how spectators sitting above would have seen action in the "discovery space" since it may have been beneath them.

On stage, in the drawing, a well-dressed lady, seated on a bench and accompanied perhaps by her lady-in-waiting, receives the addresses of a courtier or soldier with a long-handled weapon or staff of office. Even though the sketch is rough and imperfect, it does suggest the extent to which the plays of Shakespeare and his contemporaries were acted on this broad, open stage with a minimum of scenic effects. The actors would identify their fictional roles and their location by their dialogue, their costumes, and their gestures. On other occasions, when, for example, a throne was needed for a throne scene, extras could bring on such large objects and then remove them when they were no longer needed. Beds, as in the final scene of *Othello*, were apparently thrust on stage from the tiring house. The building itself was handsomely decorated and picturesque, so that the stage picture was by no means unimpressive, yet the visual effects were not designed to inform the audience about setting or time of the action. The play texts and the actors took care of that.

We have a verbal description of the Globe Theatre by Thomas Platter, a visitor to London in 1599, on the occasion of a performance of *Julius Caesar*. The description unfortunately says little about the stage, but it is otherwise very informative about the London playhouses:

> The playhouses are so constructed that they play on a raised platform, so that everyone has a good view. There are different galleries and places, however, where the seating is better and more comfortable and therefore more expensive. For whoever cares to stand below pays only one English penny, but if he wishes to sit, he enters by another door and pays another penny, while if he desires to sit in the most comfortable seats, which are cushioned, where he not only sees everything well but can also be seen, then he pays yet another English penny at another door. And during the performance food and drink are carried around the audience, so that for what one cares to pay one may also have refreshment.

Shakespeare's company may have included ten or so actor/sharers, who owned the company jointly and distributed important roles among themselves. Richard Burbage was Shakespeare's leading man from 1594 until Shakespeare's retirement from the theater. Other actor/sharers, such as John Heminges and Henry Condell, who would edit the First Folio collection of Shakespeare's plays in 1623, were his longtime professional associates. The quality of performance appears to have been high. Hired men generally took minor roles of messengers, soldiers, and servants. The women's parts were played by boys, who were trained by the major actors in a kind of apprenticeship and remained as actors of women's parts until their voices changed. Many went on in later years to be adult actors.

WILLIAM SHAKESPEARE: A BRIEF CHRONOLOGY

(Some dates are approximate, notably those of the plays.)

1558	Elizabeth I proclaimed Queen of England following the death of her sister, Queen Mary I.
1564	c. 23 April, William Shakespeare born in Stratford to a tanner, John Shakespeare, and his wife, Mary Shakespeare. His baptism is recorded at the Holy Trinity Church on 26 April.
1571	Shakespeare begins his formal education at the Stratford Grammar School.
1582	28 November, a 'William Shagspeare' (as written in the marriage bond) weds 'Anne Hathwey'—Anne Hathaway of the village of Shottery, east of Stratford.
1583	26 May, the baptism of the Shakespeares' first child, Susanna, born six months after their wedding.
1585–92	Shakespeare is believed to have left his family in Stratford to join a company of actors as both playwright and performer, starting his career in theater.
1585	The twins Hamnet and Judith born.
1588	The Spanish Armada is defeated as Spain attempts an invasion of England.
1589–90	Shakespeare is believed to have written his first play, *Henry VI, Part One* during this time. He is believed to be a member of the combined players' companies, the Lord Strange's and Lord Admiral's Men.
1592	Shakespeare is criticized in Robert Greene's *Groatsworth of Wit* as an "upstart crow" who plagiarizes from other plays, indicating that Shakespeare is in London.
1592–94	Theaters in London are closed because of the plague.
1592–93	Composition of the narrative poems *Venus and Adonis* and *The Rape of Lucrece*, and the plays *Richard III*, *The Comedy of Errors*, *Titus Andronicus*, and *The Taming of the Shrew*.
1594	The Lord Chamberlain's Men, a theater troupe including distinguished actor Richard Burbage and comic Will Kemp, performs with Shakespeare in their group.

1595	*Richard II*, *A Midsummer Night's Dream*, *Romeo and Juliet*.
1596	11 August, son Hamnet dies. Shakespeare's father is granted a coat of arms.
1597	Shakespeare buys the New Place, one of Stratford's most prominent homes.
1598	Performance in Ben Jonson's *Every Man in His Humor*, which lists Shakespeare as a principal actor in the play.
1599	The Globe Theatre is built on the Bankside from the materials of the demolished Theatre in Shoreditch. *Julius Caesar* is performed at the Globe for the first known time on 21 September, according to the diary of German tourist Thomas Platter.
1600–01	*Hamlet*.
1601	Presumed composition of narrative poem, *The Phoenix and the Turtle*. John Shakespeare dies.
1601–02	*Twelfth Night*, *All's Well That Ends Well*, *Troilus and Cressida*.
1603	24 March, death of Queen Elizabeth I and ascension of James I. The Chamberlain's Men are renamed the King's Men. Shakespeare is recorded as performing in Ben Jonson's *Sejanus*, his last known appearance as an actor.
1604	*Measure for Measure*, *Othello*.
1605	*King Lear*, *Macbeth*.
1607–08	*Timon of Athens*, *Pericles*, *Coriolanus*. Shakespeare's daughter Susanna marries John Hall.
1608	The King's Men take a 21-year lease on London's first permanent indoor playhouse, the Blackfriars Theatre.
1608–10	A new outbreak of the plague forces closure of all theaters from spring 1608 to early 1610.
1609–10	*Cymbeline*.
1610–11	*The Winter's Tale* is written. The play is performed on 15 May 1611 at the Globe and again in November 1611 at the first Banqueting House. The play would also be performed in February 1613 as one of several entertainments to celebrate the wedding of Princess Elizabeth to Frederick V, Elector Palatine and later King of Bohemia.
1611	*The Tempest* is written.

1613	The Globe playhouse burns to the ground during a performance of *Henry VIII*.
1614	Second Globe playhouse opens.
1616	Shakespeare dies, c. April 23. The burial occurs on 25 April at Holy Trinity Church in Stratford.
1623	Death of Shakespeare's wife, Anne Hathaway. Publication of the First Folio, assembled by Shakespeare's fellow actors John Heminge and Henry Condell.

A NOTE ON THE TEXT

This edition is based on the only extant text of *The Winter's Tale*, that of the First Folio, published posthumously in 1623. Despite the "romance" genre by which the play is currently categorized, *The Winter's Tale* is grouped with the Folio's comedies (*The Tempest* being the first and *The Winter's Tale* last in the grouping). The play was entered into the Stationer's Register on 8 November 1623, where it is listed as one of sixteen Folio plays never entered previously for licensing.

We are able to discern some clues from the text as to its placement within the Folio during the initial printing. The "signatures" used at the bottom of the page to indicate the order of the folio sheets to be gathered reveal that *The Winter's Tale* text was not available for the process of "casting off"—the practice of setting the play into copy for printing on folio sheets. *Twelfth Night*, the play which precedes *The Winter's Tale* in the Folio, has one set of signatures and *The Winter's Tale* has another set, suggesting that the copy of the text for printing-house use was not available when the *Twelfth Night* printing had been finished. Typically the plays follow one another without blank pages between them, yet *Twelfth Night* ends on the recto (right-hand page) of one folio sheet with a blank verso page (reverse side of the recto). *The Winter's Tale* begins on the next recto, leaving the preceding verso page blank. Charlton Hinman, a Shakespearean scholar who examined the preparation of the First Folio, concluded that the copy of *The Winter's Tale* arrived too late to be set as part of the Comedies section as it was being prepared (2:521–22).

The clarity of the physical text is often attributed to Ralph Crane, a scribe employed by Shakespeare's company, the King's Men, to prepare copies of plays for the Stationer's Register. Indeed, based on Crane's unique spelling, his punctuation and hyphenation practices, and his tendency to mass the entrance of all characters at the beginning of a scene even if their arrival occurs later in the scene, scholars believe he also prepared the Folio texts of *The Tempest*, *The Two Gentleman of Verona*, *The Merry Wives of Windsor*, and *Measure for Measure*. W.W. Greg surmised that Crane prepared the Folio text from Shakespeare's "foul papers" (his own handwritten copy) rather than from a prompt book used by the players to stage the play, based on the apparent absence of the "allowed" book for licensing on 19 August 1623. T.H. Howard-Hill confirms Greg's suspicions that Crane made one or two transcripts of the play directly from Shakespeare's foul papers to replace the missing prompt book: "Crane made two transcripts from foul papers, one to replace the prompt-book which was missing before a new prompt-book was relicensed ..., and the other as copy for the Folio" (130).

This Broadview edition has modernized the spelling, punctuation and layout of the original text. It also provides the traditional act.scene. line numbers; Through Line Numbers (TLNs), used by the Internet Shakespeare Editions and originally created by Charlton Hinman for *The Norton Facsimile: The First Folio of Shakespeare* (New York: Norton, 1968), appear at the top of each page.

ABBREVIATIONS

DENT	R.W. Dent. *Shakespeare's Proverbial Language: An Index*. Berkeley: U of California P, 1981.
FOLIO OR FIRST FOLIO	*Mr. William Shakespeares Comedies, Histories, & Tragedies*. London: printed by Isaac Jaggard and Ed. Blount, 1623.
GENEVA	The Geneva Bible, complete version first published in 1560. It was the bible Shakespeare used, and the primary Protestant English-language bible prior to the King James Version (1611).
OED	*Oxford English Dictionary*. Web.
ORGEL (ED.)	In playtext citations, refers to an edition of *The Winter's Tale* (see Works Cited, p. 281) as distinct from other works by the same author.
RSC	Royal Shakespeare Company.
SNYDER (ED.)	In playtext citations, refers to an edition of *The Winter's Tale* (see Works Cited, p. 281) as distinct from other works by the same author.
STC	*Short Title Catalogue*, listing titles of early publications from the fifteenth century forward.
TLN	"Through line number(s)," the system of continuous line numbering used in the Internet Shakespeare Editions online texts; see A Note on the Text, p. 64.

THE WINTER'S TALE

[CHARACTERS IN THE PLAY

LEONTES, *King of Sicilia*
HERMIONE, *Queen to Leontes*
MAMILLIUS, *young Prince of Sicilia*
PERDITA, *daughter to Leontes and Hermione*
CAMILLO, ANTIGONUS, CLEOMENES, DION — *four lords of Sicilia*
PAULINA, *wife to Antigonus*
EMILIA, *a lady attending on Hermione*
POLIXENES, *King of Bohemia*
FLORIZEL, *Prince of Bohemia*
ARCHIDAMUS, *a Lord of Bohemia*
SHEPHERD, *reputed father of Perdita*
CLOWN, *his son*
MOPSA, *a shepherdess*
DORCAS, *a shepherdess*
AUTOLYCUS, *a rogue*
A MARINER
A JAILER
Other Lords, Ladies, Gentlemen, Officers, Servants, Shepherds, and Shepherdesses
TIME, *as Chorus*]

[1.1]

Enter Camillo and Archidamus.

ARCHIDAMUS. If you shall chance, Camillo, to visit Bohemia[1] on the like occasion whereon my services are now on-foot,[2] you shall see (as I have said) great difference betwixt our Bohemia and your Sicilia.

CAMILLO. I think this coming summer the King of Sicilia means to pay Bohemia the visitation which he justly owes him.

ARCHIDAMUS. Wherein our entertainment shall shame us, we will be justified in our loves.[3] For indeed—

CAMILLO. Beseech[4] you—

ARCHIDAMUS. Verily, I speak it in the freedom of my knowledge. We cannot with such magnificence[5]—in so rare—I know not what to say. We will give you sleepy drinks, that your senses (unintelligent of our insufficiency)[6] may, though they cannot praise us, as little accuse us.

CAMILLO. You pay a great deal too dear for what's given freely.

ARCHIDAMUS. Believe me, I speak as my understanding instructs me and as mine honesty puts it to utterance.

CAMILLO. Sicilia cannot show himself overkind to Bohemia.[7] They were trained[8] together in their childhoods, and there rooted betwixt them then such an affection which cannot choose but branch now. Since their more mature dignities and royal necessities made separation of their society, their encounters (though not personal) hath been royally attornied[9] with interchange of gifts, letters, loving embassies, that they have seemed to be together, though absent, shook hands as over a vast,[10] and embraced as it

---

1 Polixenes, the King of Bohemia.

2 In the same official capacity as I now visit you.

3 Despite the inadequacy of our hospitality, our love will absolve us from any blame.

4 I beg you.

5 Splendor of display.

6 We will give you sleeping potions to dull your senses as to the inadequacy of our hospitality.

7 Leontes, King of Sicilia ... Polixenes, King of Bohemia.

8 Raised; also in metaphorical sense of "grow" as plants.

9 Undertaken by royal envoys.

10 Great distance.

were from the ends of opposed winds.[1] The heavens continue their loves.

ARCHIDAMUS. I think there is not in the world either malice or matter to alter it. You have an unspeakable comfort of your young Prince Mamillius. It is a gentleman of the greatest promise that ever came into my note.[2]

CAMILLO. I very well agree with you in the hopes of him. It is a gallant child, one that indeed physics[3] the subject, makes old hearts fresh. They that went on crutches ere he was born desire yet their life to see him a man.

ARCHIDAMUS. Would they else be content to die?

CAMILLO. Yes, if there were no other excuse why they should desire to live.

ARCHIDAMUS. If the King had no son, they would desire to live on crutches till he had one.

Exeunt.

[1.2]

Enter Leontes, Hermione, Mamillius, Polixenes, Camillo.

POLIXENES. Nine changes of the watery star[4] hath been
The shepherds' note[5] since we have left our throne
Without a burden. Time as long again
Would be filled up, my brother, with our thanks,
And yet we should for perpetuity
Go hence in debt. And therefore, like a cipher,[6]
Yet standing in rich place I multiply
With one "we thank you" many thousands more
That go before it.

LEONTES. Stay° your thanks a while *delay*
And pay them when you part.

POLIXENES. Sir, that's tomorrow.
I am questioned by my fear of what may chance

1 Opposite ends of the world.

2 To my attention.

3 Restores his subjects to health as if medicine.

4 Nine changes of the moon (i.e., nine months); watery because of the tidal effect of the moon.

5 Observance.

6 A zero that multiplies his "we thank you" a thousand times.

Or breed upon our absence that may blow
No sneaping° winds at home to make us say, *biting*
"This is put forth too truly." Besides, I have stayed
To tire your royalty.

LEONTES. We are tougher, brother,
Than you can put us to it.

POLIXENES. No longer stay.

LEONTES. One seven night° longer. *a week*

POLIXENES. Very sooth, tomorrow.

LEONTES. We'll part[1] the time between's then, and in that
I'll no gainsaying.° *I'll not accept opposition*

POLIXENES. Press me not,[2] beseech you, so.
There is no tongue that moves, none, none i'th' world
So soon as yours could win me. So it should now
Were there necessity in your request, although
'Twere needful I denied it. My affairs
Do even drag me homeward, which to hinder
Were in your love a whip to me;[3] my stay,
To you a charge and trouble. To save both,[4]
Farewell, our brother.

LEONTES. Tongue-tied, our Queen? Speak you.

HERMIONE. I had thought, sir, to have held my peace until
You had drawn oaths from him not to stay. You, sir,
Charge° him too coldly. Tell him you are sure *urge*
All in Bohemia's well. This satisfaction,
The bygone-day proclaimed,[5] say this to him,
He's beat from his best ward.[6]

LEONTES. Well said, Hermione.

HERMIONE. To tell he longs to see his son were strong.
But let him say so then and let him go,
But let him swear so and he shall not stay.
We'll thwack him hence with distaffs.
Yet of your royal presence I'll adventure

---

1 Equally divide.

2 Don't insist on my staying.

3 Which concerns, if I wait in dealing with them, would whip (torture) me should I let your affection keep me here longer.

4 To spare you both the burden and the trouble.

5 Just yesterday we were notified that all was well in Bohemia.

6 Decidedly defeated in his defensive position.

1.2.37: "WE'LL THWACK HIM HENCE WITH DISTAFFS." (TLN 94)

The distaff is a tool emblematic of the domestic life of women during Shakespeare's England. Traditionally the distaff held unspun wool. Women held the distaff under one arm while holding the spindle in the other. The distaff is also emblematic of the feminine sphere of domestic life. This image derives from the proverbial sense that spinning staffs were women's weapons and symbolized chastity. In *King Lear* the image is used to emasculate Goneril's weak husband (4.2.17–18, TLN 2285–86). Here, Hermione imagines the distaff as a cudgel to beat Polixenes away.

"Old Woman with a Distaff" (1642) by Bartolome Esteban Murillo (1617–82). From Wikimedia Commons, <http://commons.wikimedia.org>.

The borrow of a week. When at Bohemia
You take my lord, I'll give him my commission
To let him there a month behind the gest[1]
Prefixed for's parting. Yet, good deed, Leontes,
I love thee not a jar° o'th' clock behind *tick*
What lady she her lord. You'll stay?

POLIXENES. No, madam.

HERMIONE. Nay, but you will?

POLIXENES. I may not, verily.

HERMIONE. Verily?
You put me off with limber vows. But I,
Though you would seek t'unsphere the stars[2] with oaths,
Should yet say "Sir, no going." Verily
You shall not go; a lady's "Verily" is
As potent as a lord's. Will you go yet?
Force me to keep you as a prisoner,
Not like a guest. So, you shall pay your fees

---

1 Beyond the allotted time for the visit.

2 Shatter the stars from their orbits; see also extended note, p. 95.

1.2.45–46: "VERILY? YOU PUT ME OFF WITH LIMBER VOWS." (TLN 105–06)

Hermione's playful return of Polixenes's "Verily" questions its value as a guarantee of his desire to stay. Shakespeare echoes Jesus' "verily" in the New Testment (see John 3:3, John 5:24–25, John 6:47, John 12:2; see also Shaheen 721). Feminist critics turn to this moment in the play to suggest Hermione's playful disposition and her rhetorical agility in transforming one "verily" into a plethora of weak oaths ("limber vows") easily overthrown. David Schwalkwyck (271) notes that Hermione's "verily" is tenuous in a patriarchal society ruled by the emerging tyranny of Leontes and his distrust of his wife's veracity: "the lady's word simply becomes the lord's in a paradoxical, implicit acknowledgement that it is indeed more potent." Within the context of monarchial succession and legitimacy of offspring, the woman's word becomes paramount and—ironically—vulnerable to patriarchal suspicion.

When you depart and save your thanks. How say you?
My prisoner? Or my guest? By your dread "Verily,"
One of them you shall be.

POLIXENES. Your guest then, madam:
To be your prisoner should import offending,[1]
Which is for me less easy to commit
Than you to punish.

HERMIONE. Not your jailer then,
But your kind hostess. Come, I'll question you
Of my lord's tricks and yours when you were boys.
You were pretty lordings° then? *young lords*

POLIXENES. We were, fair Queen.
Two lads that thought there was no more behind° *yet to come*
But such a day tomorrow as today,
And to be boy eternal.

HERMIONE. Was not my lord
The verier wag° o'th' two? *greater mischief maker*

POLIXENES. We were as twinned lambs[2] that did frisk i'th' sun
And bleat the one at th' other. What we changed° *exchanged*
Was innocence for innocence. We knew not
The doctrine of ill-doing nor dreamed
That any did. Had we pursued that life
And our weak spirits ne'er been higher reared
With stronger blood,[3] we should have answered heaven
Boldly, "Not guilty"; the imposition cleared,
Hereditary ours.

HERMIONE. By this we gather
You have tripped since.

POLIXENES. O my most sacred Lady,
Temptations have since then been born to's, for
In those unfledged[4] days was my wife a girl.
Your precious self had then not crossed the eyes
Of my young playfellow.

HERMIONE. Grace to boot!° *heaven help us!*

---

1 Suggest I was guilty of an offense.
2 Biological twins.
3 Had we not matured by the arrival of more adult passions.
4 Immature as with youthful birds.

Of this make no conclusion,[1] lest you say
Your queen and I are devils. Yet go on.
Th' offenses we have made you do we'll answer,
If you first sinned with us and that with us
You did continue fault, and that you slipped not
With any but with us.[2]
LEONTES. Is he won yet?
HERMIONE. He'll stay, my Lord.
LEONTES. At my request, he would not.
Hermione, my dearest, thou never spok'st
To better purpose.
HERMIONE. Never?
LEONTES. Never, but once.
HERMIONE. What? Have I twice said well? When was't before?
I prithee tell me; cram's with praise and make's
As fat as tame things. One good deed dying tongueless
Slaughters a thousand waiting upon that.[3]
Our praises are our wages. You may ride's
With one soft kiss a thousand furlongs[4] ere
With spur we heat an acre.[5] But to th' goal:
My last good deed was to entreat his stay.
What was my first? It has an elder sister,
Or I mistake you. Oh, would her name were Grace![6]
But once before I spoke to th' purpose? When?
Nay, let me have't! I long.
LEONTES. Why, that was when
Three crabbèd months had soured themselves to death
Ere I could make thee open thy white hand:

1 Don't pursue the logical conclusion of your argument, i.e., that your wife and I are responsible for your and Leontes's trip(ping).

2 Your queen and I will be answerable to these charges as long as you have "sinned" only with us spouses.

3 Not praising this one good deed means that a thousand future such deeds will go unperformed.

4 An eighth of a mile.

5 One gentle compliment will enhance our cooperation more than any goading (i.e.,"spur").

6 A pun on "grace" as a gracious act deserving praise.

And clap[1] thyself, my love;[2] then didst thou utter,
"I am yours for ever."

HERMIONE. 'Tis Grace indeed.[3]
Why, lo you now, I have spoke to th' purpose twice:
The one forever earned a royal husband,
Th' other for some while a friend.
[*Takes Polixenes by the hand.*]

LEONTES. [*Aside*] Too hot,[4] too hot!
To mingle friendship far is mingling bloods.[5]
I have *tremor cordis*[6] on me. My heart dances,
But not for joy, not joy. This entertainment
May a free face put on; derive a liberty
From heartiness, from bounty, fertile bosom,
And well become the agent.[7] It may, I grant.
But to be paddling palms[8] and pinching fingers,
As now they are, and making practised smiles
As in a looking-glass, and then to sigh, as 'twere—,
The mort o'th' deer[9]—Oh, that is entertainment
My bosom likes not, nor my brows. Mamillius,
Art thou my boy?

MAMILLIUS. Ay, my good Lord.

LEONTES. I'fecks![10]
Why, that's my bawcock.[11] What? Has't smutched[12] thy nose?
They say it is a copy out of mine. Come, captain,
We must be neat, not neat but cleanly, captain.

---

1 Pledge by grasping my hand.

2 Three bitter (crabbed) months passed before you would open your hand and pledge your love to me.

3 Then my agreeing to marry you was given heaven's blessing.

4 Lascivious, lustful.

5 Mingling with friends excessively leads to an improper mingling of passions.

6 The tremors of my heart (from the Latin).

7 Hermione's hospitality may be innocently intended, reflecting her conviviality, a generosity that compliments her.

8 Playfully fingering the palms.

9 (1) The horn sounding the death of a deer during the hunt (i.e., the slaying of the other "dear," Hermione); (2) the sigh of a dying deer.

10 Truly (a coarsening of "In faith").

11 Fellow.

12 Smudged.

And yet the steer, the heifer, and the calf
Are all called neat—still virginalling
Upon his palm?—[*To Mamillius*] How now, you wanton[1] calf,
Art thou my calf?

MAMILLIUS. Yes, if you will, my Lord.

LEONTES. Thou want'st a rough pash[2] and the shoots that I have
To be full like me, yet they say we are
Almost as like as egg—women say so
That will say anything. But were they false
As o'er-dyed blacks,[3] as wind, as waters? False
As dice are to be wished by one that fixes
No bourne 'twixt his and mine, yet were it true
To say this boy were like me? Come, Sir Page,
Look on me with your welkin[4] eye, sweet villain,
Most dearest, my collop.[5] Can thy dam? May't be?—
Affection, thy intention stabs the center.
Thou dost make possible things not so held,
Communicat'st with dreams (how can this be?)
With what's unreal thou coactive art
And fellowst nothing.[6] Then 'tis very credent,° *credible*
Thou mayst co-join with something and thou dost—
And that beyond commission—and I find it—
And that to the infection of my brains
And hardening of my brows.[7]

POLIXENES. What means Sicilia?[8]

HERMIONE. He something seems unsettled.

POLIXENES. How, my Lord?

---

1 Playful.

2 Coarse head.

3 (1) Fabric made exceedingly fragile because of excessive over-dyeing to achieve a black hue; (2) black fabric achieved by overdyeing black upon other colors, therefore denoting falseness.

4 Sky-blue ("welkin" means sky or heaven).

5 A piece of meat (in this case, of Leontes's flesh).

6 Can thy dam (mother) be an adulteress? Can this affection be caused by her lust? This intention (i.e., either his mental acuity in focusing on Hermione's affection or Hermione's apparent attraction to Polixenes) stabs my soul, going to my very core. You (i.e., lust; his "coactive art") make possible for me the impossible, working with my fantasies ("dreams") and collaborating with the unreal. How is it possible for these fears all to be true?

7 This unauthorized fear infects my thoughts and generates these cuckold's horns.

8 What is troubling Leontes?

1.2.124: "STILL VIRGINALLING" (TLN 200)

The virginal was a popular Renaissance keyboard instrument in the harpsichord family. Smaller than the harpsichord, the virginal was typically portable and placed on a table for playing. The strings of the virginal ran lengthwise in a parallel fashion to the keyboard. The keys struck the strings in the middle, causing a flute-like tone. Leontes describes Hermione's "paddling" of Polixenes's palm as if she were playing his hand like a keyboard; Sonnet 128 also alludes to a keyboard instrument such as the virginal. Blount (1656) offers this definition of virginal: "(Virginalis) Maidenly, Virgin-like; hence the name of that Musical Instrument, called Virginals, because Maids and Virgins do most commonly play on them."

"Man and Woman Sitting at the Virginal" (c. 1660) by Gabriël Metsu (1629–67). From Wikimedia Commons, <http://commons.wikimedia.org>.

LEONTES. What cheer? How is't with you, best brother?
HERMIONE. You look as if you held a brow of much distraction.[1]
Are you moved, my Lord?
LEONTES. No, in good earnest.
How sometimes nature will betray its folly,
Its tenderness and make itself a pastime
To harder bosoms?[2] Looking on the lines
Of my boy's face methoughts I did recoil[3]
Twenty-three years and saw myself unbreeched
In my green velvet coat,[4] my dagger muzzled[5]
Lest it should bite its master and so prove,
As ornaments oft do, too dangerous.
How like, methought, I then was to this kernel,
This squash,[6] this gentleman—[*To Mamillius*] Mine honest friend,
Will you take eggs for money?[7]
MAMILLIUS. No, my Lord, I'll fight.
LEONTES. You will? Why, happy man be's dole![8] [*To Polixenes*] My brother,
Are you so fond of your young prince as we
Do seem to be of ours?
POLIXENES. If at home, sir,
He's all my exercise,[9] my mirth, my matter;
Now my sworn friend and then mine enemy;
My parasite,° my soldier, statesman, all. *flatterer*
He makes a July's day short as December,
And with his varying childness° cures in me *childish humor (OED)*
Thoughts that would thick my blood.° *make me melancholy*

1 You seem anxious about something.
2 Sometimes paternal affection displays its folly and allows itself to become an amusing spectacle to those less prone to sentiment.
3 Go back in my memory.
4 Not yet in pants, wearing my infant skirts.
5 Blunted with a protective tip.
6 Unripe peapod.
7 Proverbially to exchange something of value with something of little value (Dent E90: "To take eggs for money").
8 Good luck. Proverbial, "May your lot be that of a happy man!" (Dent M158).
9 Customary activity (*OED n2*, an obsolete usage, citing *3 Henry VI* but not this play).

LEONTES. So stands this squire
Officed with me.[1] We two will walk, my Lord,
And leave you to your graver steps. Hermione,
How thou lov'st us show in our brother's welcome.
Let what is dear in Sicily be cheap.
Next to thyself and my young rover,[2] he's
Apparent° to my heart. *heir apparent*
HERMIONE. If you would seek us,
We are yours i'th' garden. Shall's° attend you there? *shall we*
LEONTES. To your[3] own bents dispose you. You'll be found,
Be you beneath the sky. [*Aside*] I am angling° now, *fishing*
Though you perceive me not how I give line.
Go to, go to!
How she holds up the neb,° the bill to him, *beak*
And arms her with the boldness of a wife
To her allowing husband.
[*Exeunt Hermione and Polixenes.*]
Gone already![4]
Inch-thick, knee-deep, o'er head and ears a forked one[5]—
[*To Mamillius*] Go play, boy, play. Thy mother plays, and I
Play too, but so disgraced a part, whose issue
Will hiss me to my grave. Contempt and clamor
Will be my knell—[*To Mamillius*] Go play, boy, play—[*Aside*]
There have been,
Or I am much deceived, cuckolds ere now,
And many a man there is, even at this present,
Now, while I speak this, holds his wife by th' arm,
That little thinks she has been sluiced[6] in's absence,
And his pond fished by his next neighbor, by
Sir Smile, his neighbor. Nay, there's comfort in't

---

1 This young squire (i.e., Mamillius) performs a similar function for me.

2 Robber, one who roves (term of endearment for Mamillius).

3 Do as you wish.

4 Hermione couldn't get away fast enough!

5 Leontes characterizes Hermione's loss as "inch-thick" or "without a doubt" (as dependable as a one-inch board and as reliable). The subsequent cuckolding is "knee-deep" and thus irrevocable.

6 Drained (i.e., washed out with seminal fluid, an image picked up in the image of the pond fished by a neighbor).

Whiles other men have gates, and those gates opened
As mine against their will. Should all despair
That have revolted wives, the tenth of mankind
Would hang themselves. Physic for't there's none![1]
It is a bawdy planet° that will strike *the planet Venus*
Where 'tis predominant. And 'tis powerful, think it
From east, west, north, and south. Be it concluded,
No barricado for a belly. Know't,
It will let in and out the enemy,
With bag and baggage.[2] Many thousand on's° *of us*
Have the disease and feel it not. [*To Mamillius*] How now, boy?

MAMILLIUS. I am like you, they say.

LEONTES. Why, that's some comfort.
What? Camillo, there?

CAMILLO. [*Coming forward*] Ay, my good Lord.

LEONTES. Go play, Mamillius, thou'rt an honest man.
[*Exit Mamillius.*]
Camillo, this great sir will yet stay longer.

CAMILLO. You had much ado to make his anchor hold.
When you cast out, it still came home.

LEONTES. Didst note it?

CAMILLO. He would not stay at your petitions, made
His business more material.° *important*

LEONTES. Didst perceive it?
They're[3] here with me already, whispering, rounding,[4]
"Sicilia is a so-forth." 'Tis far gone,
When I shall gust° it last. How cam't, Camillo, *taste*
That he did stay?

CAMILLO. At the good queen's entreaty.

LEONTES. "At the queen's" be't. "Good" should be pertinent,[5]
But so it is,[6] it is not. Was this taken° *comprehended*
By any understanding pate but thine?

---

1 There is no cure for this!
2 An allusion to male sexual organs (scrotum and genitalia).
3 People who know of Hermione's adultery.
4 Discreetly gossiping.
5 Germane.
6 Given the current situation.

For thy conceit is soaking, will draw in
More than the common blocks.[1] Not noted, is't,
But of° the finer natures, by some severals *except by*
Of headpiece extraordinary?[2] Lower messes
Perchance are to this business purblind?[3] Say.
CAMILLO. Business, my lord? I think most understand
Bohemia stays here longer.
LEONTES. Ha?
CAMILLO. Stays here longer.
LEONTES. Ay, but why?
CAMILLO. To satisfy[4] your Highness and the entreaties
Of our most gracious mistress.
LEONTES. "Satisfy"?
"Th' entreaties of your mistress"? "Satisfy"?
Let that suffice. I have trusted thee, Camillo,
With all the nearest things to my heart, as well
My chamber-counsels,[5] wherein, priest-like, thou
Hast cleansed my bosom. I from thee departed
Thy penitent reformed, but we have been
Deceived in thy integrity, deceived
In that which seems so.
CAMILLO. Be it forbid, my lord!
LEONTES. To bide° upon't: thou art not honest, or *insist*
If thou inclin'st that way, thou art a coward,
Which hoxes honesty behind, restraining
From course required,[6] or else thou must be counted
A servant grafted in my serious trust
And therein negligent; or else a fool
That see'st a game played home, the rich stake drawn,

---

1 Your skills of perception are profound and will perceive more than common blockheads

2 By those of great intellect?

3 Lower classes perhaps remain completely blind to this "business" (with a sexual sense, hence Camillo's response in the next line).

4 Please (but Leontes's repetition of "satisfy" in his next speech acquires a sexual sense).

5 Most secret admissions.

6 Which hamstrings (hoxes) honesty, restraining its movement.

And tak'st it all for jest.[1]

CAMILLO. My gracious lord,
I may be negligent, foolish, and fearful.
In every one of these, no man is free,
But that his negligence, his folly, fear,
Among the infinite doings of the world,
Sometime puts forth. In your affairs, my Lord,
If ever I were wilful-negligent,
It was my folly; if industriously° *intentionally*
I played the fool, it was my negligence,
Not weighing well the end; if ever fearful
To do a thing where I the issue doubted,
Whereof the execution did cry out
Against the non-performance, 'twas a fear
Which oft infects the wisest.[2] These, my lord,
Are such allowed infirmities that honesty
Is never free of. But beseech your grace
Be plainer with me; let me know my trespass
By its own visage. If I then deny it,
'Tis none of mine.

LEONTES. Have not you seen, Camillo—
But that's past doubt; you have or your eye-glass
Is thicker than a cuckold's horn—or heard—
For to a vision so apparent, rumor
Cannot be mute—or thought—for cogitation
Resides not in that man that does not think
My wife is slippery?° If thou wilt confess, *unchaste*
Or else be impudently negative
To have nor eyes, nor ears, nor thought, then say
My wife's a hobby-horse,[3] deserves a name
As rank as any flax-wench° that puts to *country girl*
Before her troth-plight.° Say't, and justify't. *betrothal*

CAMILLO. I would not be a stander-by to hear
My sovereign mistress clouded° so without *slandered*

1 That, like a spectator watching a game until the prize is won, considers it only a prank.

2 In which the taking of action clearly underscores the inadequacy of failing to act, a fear of action that frequently affects even the wisest people.

3 Something ridden for pleasure (with sexual connotation).

My present vengeance taken. 'Shrew[1] my heart,
You never spoke what did become you less
Than this, which to reiterate were sin
As deep as that, though true.° *were it true*
LEONTES. Is whispering nothing?
Is leaning cheek to cheek? Is meeting noses?
Kissing with inside lip? Stopping the career° *galloping*
Of laughter with a sigh? A note infallible
Of breaking honesty, horsing foot on foot?[2]
Skulking in corners? Wishing clocks more swift?
Hours, minutes? Noon, midnight? And all eyes
Blind with the pin and web° but theirs, theirs only, *cataracts*
That would unseen be wicked? Is this nothing?
Why, then the world and all that's in't is nothing,
The covering sky is nothing, Bohemia nothing,
My wife is nothing, nor nothing have these nothings,
If this be nothing.
CAMILLO. Good my Lord, be cured
Of this diseased opinion, and betimes,° *soon*
For 'tis most dangerous.
LEONTES. Say it be, 'tis true.
CAMILLO. No, no, my Lord.
LEONTES. It is! You lie, you lie!
I say thou liest, Camillo, and I hate thee,
Pronounce thee a gross lout, a mindless slave,
Or else a hovering temporizer[3] that
Canst with thine eyes at once see good and evil,
Inclining to them both; were my wife's liver
Infected as her life, she would not live
The running of one glass.° *hourglass; thus, one hour*
CAMILLO. Who does infect her?
LEONTES. Why he that wears her like her medal,[4] hanging
About his neck—Bohemia who, if I
Had servants true about me that bare° eyes *bore*
To see alike mine honor as their profits,

1 Beshrew (i.e., place a curse on).
2 "Playing footsie" (Dolan).
3 Irresolute schemer capable of accommodating both good and evil.
4 He who has her hanging upon his neck like a cameo containing her image.

Their own particular thrifts, they would do that
Which should undo more doing. Ay, and thou
His cupbearer,[1] whom I from meaner form
Have benched and reared to worship, who mayst see
Plainly as heaven sees earth and earth sees heaven,
How I am galled, mightst bespice a cup
To give mine enemy a lasting wink,
Which draught to me were cordial.[2]

CAMILLO. Sir, my lord,
I could do this, and that with no rash potion,
But with a lingering dram[3] that should not work
Maliciously like poison, but I cannot
Believe this crack° to be in my dread mistress, *flaw (OED n8)*
So sovereignly being honorable.
I have loved thee—

LEONTES. Make that thy question and go rot![4]
Dost think I am so muddy, so unsettled,
To appoint myself in this vexation?[5]
Sully the purity and whiteness of my sheets—
Which to preserve is sleep; which being spotted
Is goads, thorns, nettles, tails of wasps—
Give scandal to the blood o'th' prince, my son,
Who I do think is mine and love as mine,
Without ripe moving to't?[6] Would I do this?
Could man so blench?[7]

CAMILLO. I must believe you, sir,
I do and will fetch off[8] Bohemia for't,
Provided that when he's removed your Highness
Will take again your Queen as yours at first,
Even for your son's sake, and thereby for sealing
The injury° of tongues in courts and kingdoms *quieting the slander*
Known and allied to yours.

1 Royal officer serving wine.
2 Might poison the cup and produce death, a drink that would comfort me.
3 A small amount (*OED n*13b).
4 If you question Hermione's guilt, go to the devil!
5 To nominate myself as a cuckold.
6 Put Mamillius's legitimacy in question without an adequate cause.
7 Go astray in responding (with a secondary sense of avoiding a situation).
8 Kill (with perhaps an ulterior sense of "rescue").

LEONTES. Thou dost advise me,
Even so as I mine own course have set down;
I'll give no blemish to her honor, none.
CAMILLO. My Lord,
Go then, and with a countenance as clear
As friendship wears at feasts, keep with Bohemia[1]
And with your Queen. I am his cupbearer.
If from me he have wholesome beverage,
Account me not your servant.
LEONTES. This is all.
Do't, and thou hast the one half of my heart;
Do't not, thou splitt'st thine own.[2]
CAMILLO. I'll do't, my Lord.
LEONTES. I will seem friendly, as thou hast advised me.
Exit.
CAMILLO. O miserable lady! But for me,
What case stand I in? I must be the poisoner
Of good Polixenes, and my ground to do't
Is the obedience to a master, one,
Who in rebellion with himself, will have
All that are his so too. To do this deed,
Promotion follows. If I could find example
Of thousands that had struck anointed kings
And flourished after, I'd not do't. But since
Nor brass, nor stone,[3] nor parchment bears not one,
Let villainy itself forswear't. I must
Forsake the court: to do't° or no is certain *kill Polixenes*
To me a breakneck.° Happy star reign now! *death for me*
Here comes Bohemia.

Enter Polixenes.
POLIXENES. [*Aside*] This is strange. Methinks

1 Remain as host for Polixenes.

2 By poisoning Polixenes, you earn my affection; if you refuse to, you divide your own heart between him and me (with the implication of a subsequent death sentence).

3 Since no record survives that testifies to a successful regicide, not even "villainy" would commit such an act. Even were there examples of past successes, I myself would refuse to commit regicide.

My favor here begins to warp.[1] Not speak?
[*To Camillo*] Good day, Camillo.

CAMILLO. Hail, most royal sir.

POLIXENES. What is the news i'th' court?

CAMILLO. None rare, my Lord.

POLIXENES. The King hath on him such a countenance,
As he had lost some province, and a region
Loved as he loves himself; even now I met him
With customary compliment, when he,
Wafting his eyes to th' contrary and falling
A lip of much contempt,[2] speeds from me and
So leaves me to consider what is breeding
That changes thus his manners.

CAMILLO. I dare not know, my Lord.

POLIXENES. How, dare not?[3] Do not? Do you know, and dare not?
Be intelligent[4] to me, 'tis thereabouts;
For to yourself what you do know you must
And cannot say you dare not.[5] Good Camillo,
Your changed complexions are to me a mirror
Which shows me mine changed too, for I must be
A party in this alteration, finding
Myself thus altered with't.[6]

CAMILLO. There is a sickness
Which puts some of us in distemper, but
I cannot name the disease, and it is caught
Of you that yet are well.

POLIXENES. How caught of me?
Make me not sighted like the basilisk.
I have looked on thousands who have sped the better
By my regard, but killed none so. Camillo—
As you are certainly a gentleman, thereto
Clerk-like experienced, which no less adorns

---

1 I feel increasingly unwelcome here in Sicilia (*OED warp v*15b).

2 Turns his head with disdain and allows his lip to droop.

3 Snyder (ed.): "Do you mean that you don't know? Or do you mean you know and don't dare tell me?"

4 Explicit, direct (*OED a*4).

5 Snyder (ed.): "you can't disclaim knowing what you know."

6 I must be the cause of your changed complexion given the fact that I too feel the change.

1.2.385: THE BASILISK (TLN 496)

The basilisk was a mythological reptile in European bestiaries and legends. Reputedly king of the serpents, the basilisk was said to cause death with a single glance. According to Pliny the Elder's *Naturalis Historia*, the basilisk was a small snake, highly venomous and deadly in its gaze. Polixenes rejects the idea that, like a basilisk, his very glance can cause death (see Dent B99.1). Shakespeare also refers to the basilisk in *Cymbeline* 2.4.109–10 (TLN 1279–80).

Detail from "The Basilisk and the Weasel" by Wenceslas Hollar (1607–77). From Wikimedia Commons, <http://commons.wikimedia.org>.

Our gentry than our parents' noble names,
In whose success we are gentle[1]—I beseech you,
If you know aught which does behoove my knowledge
Thereof to be informed,[2] imprisoned not
In ignorant concealment.

CAMILLO. I may not answer.

POLIXENES. A sickness caught of me, and yet I well?
I must be answered. Dost thou hear, Camillo?
I conjure thee, by all the parts of man
Which honor does acknowledge, whereof the least
Is not this suit of mine,[3] that thou declare
What incidency thou dost guess of harm
Is creeping toward me;[4] how far off, how near,
Which way to be prevented, if to be.
If not, how best to bear it.

CAMILLO. Sir, I will tell you,
Since I am charged in honor, and by him
That I think honorable; therefore mark my counsel,
Which must be even as swiftly followed as
I mean to utter it, or both yourself and me,
Cry lost, and so good night![5]

POLIXENES. On, good Camillo.

CAMILLO. I am appointed him° to murder you. *by him*

POLIXENES. By whom, Camillo?

CAMILLO. By the King!

POLIXENES. For what?

CAMILLO. He thinks, nay with all confidence he swears
As he had seen't, or been an instrument
To vice[6] you to't, that you have touched his Queen
Forbiddenly.

---

1 Camillo, because you are a gentleman as clearly reflected in your scholarly learning, qualities that are shared by those of us who inherit their titles and succeed by birthright.

2 If you know anything that should be shared with me.

3 I appeal to you based on the responsibilities that honorable men accept, not the least of which is the obligation to reply to my request.

4 What dangerous situation you suspect is approaching me.

5 If you fail to follow my advice, both of us are finished and we can say farewell to everything.

6 Force, compel (i.e., Leontes has been a complicit force in encouraging the adultery).

POLIXENES. Oh then, my best blood turn
To an infected jelly° and my name *a clotted substance*
Be yoked with his that did betray the best![1]
Turn then my freshest reputation to
A savor° that may strike the dullest nostril *smell*
Where I arrive and my approach be shunned,
Nay, hated too, worse than the greatest infection
That e'er was heard or read.
CAMILLO. Swear his thought over
By each particular star in heaven and
By all their influences; you may as well
Forbid the sea for to° obey the moon *to*
As or° by oath remove or counsel shake *either*
The fabric of his folly, whose foundation
Is piled upon his faith and will continue
The standing of his body.[2]
POLIXENES. How should this grow?
CAMILLO. I know not, but I am sure 'tis safer to
Avoid what's grown than question how 'tis born.
If therefore you dare trust my honesty
That lies enclosèd in this trunk, which you
Shall bear along impawned,[3] away tonight!
Your followers I will whisper to the business,
And will by twos and threes at several posterns[4]
Clear them o'th' city. For myself, I'll put
My fortunes to your service, which are here
By this discovery lost.[5] Be not uncertain,
For, by the honor of my parents, I
Have uttered truth, which, if you seek to prove,
I dare not stand by; nor shall you be safer,
Than one condemned by the king's own mouth

1 That of Judas, who betrayed Christ (clearly an anachronism for a pre-Christian time setting).

2 The edifice of his foolishness is so firmly rooted, and it will endure while his body lives.

3 My body, which you take with you as a promise.

4 Back doors (*OED* *n*1a).

5 My future is endangered in Sicily because I have warned you.

Thereon his execution sworn.[1]

POLIXENES. I do believe thee;
I saw his heart in's face. Give me thy hand,[2]
Be pilot to me, and thy places shall
Still neighbor mine.[3] My ships are ready, and
My people did expect my hence departure
Two days ago. This jealousy
Is for a precious creature; as she's rare,
Must it be great; and, as his person's mighty,
Must it be violent; and, as he does conceive
He is dishonored by a man which ever
Professed to him, why, his revenges must
In that be made more bitter. Fear o'ershades me!
Good expedition be my friend, and comfort
The gracious queen, part of his theme, but nothing
Of his ill-ta'en suspicion.[4] Come, Camillo,
I will respect thee as a father if
Thou bear'st my life off, hence. Let us avoid.° *depart*

CAMILLO. It is in mine authority to command
The keys of all the posterns; please your highness
To take the urgent hour. Come, sir, away.

Exeunt.

[2.1]

Enter Hermione, Mamillius, Ladies. Leontes, Antigonus, Lords [*standing aside*].

HERMIONE. Take the boy to you; he so troubles me,
'Tis past enduring.

1. LADY. Come, my gracious lord.
Shall I be your playfellow?

MAMILLIUS. No, I'll none of you.

---

1 You won't be any safer than the one (Hermione) the king has publicly condemned and ordered executed.

2 Polixenes offers his hand as a pledge.

3 And your position will be near me.

4 "May my hasty departure assist me and bring comfort to the Queen, who is involved in his ill-conceived suspicion, but is not the object of it" (Orgel ed.).

1. LADY. Why, my sweet lord?
MAMILLIUS. [*To 1. Lady*] You'll kiss me hard and speak to me as if
I were a baby still. [*To 2. Lady*] I love you better.
2. LADY. And why so, my lord?
MAMILLIUS. Not for because
Your brows are blacker, yet black brows they say
Become some women best, so that° there be not *as long as*
Too much hair there, but in a semi-circle
Or a half-moon made with a pen.
2 LADY. Who taught this?
MAMILLIUS. I learned it out of[1] women's faces. Pray now,
What color are your eyebrows?
2 LADY. Blue, my lord.
MAMILLIUS. Nay, that's a mock![2] I have seen a lady's nose
That has been blue, but not her eyebrows.
1 LADY. Hark ye,
The Queen your mother rounds[3] apace. We shall
Present our services to a fine new prince
One of these days, and then you'd wanton° with us, *play*
If we would have you.
2 LADY. She is spread of late
Into a goodly bulk—good time encounter her![4]
HERMIONE. What wisdom stirs amongst you? Come, sir, now
I am for you again. Pray you sit by us,
And tell's a tale.
MAMILLIUS. Merry or sad shall't be?
HERMIONE. As merry as you will.
MAMILLIUS. A sad tale's best for winter.
I have one of sprites and goblins.
HERMIONE. Let's have that, good sir.
Come on, sit down, come on, and do your best,
To fright me with your sprites; you're powerful at it.
MAMILLIUS. There was a man—
HERMIONE. Nay, come sit down.

---

1 From.
2 You're making fun of me!
3 Grows rounder in pregnancy.
4 May good fortune follow her in this pregnancy!

[*Gestures Mamillius to sit*] Then on.
MAMILLIUS. —Dwelt by a churchyard. I will tell it softly,
Yond crickets[1] shall not hear it.
HERMIONE. Come on then, and giv't me in mine ear.
[*Leontes, Antigonus, and Lords come forward.*]
LEONTES. Was he[2] met there? His train? Camillo with him?
LORD. Behind the tuft of pines I met them; never
Saw I men scour° so on their way. I eyed them *hurry*
Even to their ships.
LEONTES. How blest am I
In my just censure,° in my true opinion! *true judgment*
Alack, for lesser knowledge! How accursed
In being so blest! There may be in the cup
A spider steeped and one may drink, depart,
And yet partake no venom, for his knowledge
Is not infected, but if one present
Th' abhorred ingredient to his eye make known
How he hath drunk, he cracks his gorge,[3] his sides
With violent hefts.[4] I have drunk and seen the spider.
Camillo was his help in this, his pander.° *pimp*
There is a plot against my life, my crown.
All's true that is mistrusted. That false villain
Whom I employed was pre-employed° by him. *co-opted*
He has discovered my design, and I
Remain a pinched[5] thing, yea, a very trick
For them to play at will. How came the posterns
So easily open?
LORD. By his great authority,
Which often hath no less prevailed than so
On your command.
LEONTES. I know't too well.

---

1 The attending ladies over there.
2 Polixenes.
3 Throat and stomach.
4 There may be a poisonous spider in one's cup, and unless one knows that it is there, one can avoid being poisoned; however, once the spider is brought to his attention, the drinker will heave or vomit so violently that he will damage his throat and stomach, breaking his ribs with these violent tremors.
5 Squeezed (with a secondary meaning of afflicted or tortured).

[*To Hermione*] Give me the boy. I am glad you did not nurse him
Though he does bear some signs of me, yet you
Have too much blood in him.

HERMIONE. What is this? Sport?° *a game?*

LEONTES. [*To the Ladies*] Bear the boy hence. He shall not come about her!
Away with him, [*To Hermione*] and let her sport herself
With that she's big with,[1] for 'tis Polixenes
Has made thee swell thus.

[*Ladies exit with Mamillius.*]

HERMIONE. But I'd say he had not,
And I'll be sworn you would believe my saying,
Howe'er you lean to th' nayward.° *in the denial*

LEONTES. You, my lords,
Look on her, mark her well. Be but about
To say "She is a goodly lady," and
The justice of your hearts will thereto add
"'Tis pity she's not honest" honorable.[2]
Praise her but for this her without-door-form,[3]
Which on my faith deserves high speech, and straight[4]
The shrug, the "Hum," or "ha," these petty-brands
That calumny doth use. Oh, I am out,
That mercy does, for calumny will sear
Virtue itself. These shrugs, these "hum's," and "ha's,"
When you have said she's goodly, come between
Ere you can say she's honest. But be't known
From him that has most cause to grieve it should be,
She's an adulteress!

HERMIONE. Should a villain say so,
The most replenished° villain in the world, *absolute*
He were as much more villain.[5] You, my lord,

---

1 The child she is carrying (for Leontes, rather crudely, Polixenes's baby).

2 Worthy of honor by noble birthright.

3 Outward appearance.

4 Immediately. Leontes imagines that public acceptance of Hermione's virtue is followed by subtle shrugs and skeptical rejoinders that immediately undercut the praise.

5 The worst villain imaginable becomes even more villainous in charging me with adultery.

Do but mistake.
LEONTES. You have mistook,[1] my lady,
Polixenes for Leontes. O thou thing,
Which I'll not call a creature of thy place,
Lest barbarism, making me the precedent,
Should a like language use to all degrees
And mannerly distinguishment leave out
Betwixt the prince and beggar.[2] I have said
She's an adulteress; I have said with whom.
More,° she's a traitor, and Camillo is *moreover*
A federary° with her and one that knows *confederate*
What she should shame° to know herself, *be ashamed*
But with her most vile principal: that she's
A bed-swerver,° even as bad as those *adulteress*
That vulgars give bold'st titles; ay, and privy
To this their late escape.
HERMIONE. No, by my life,
Privy to none of this! How will this grieve you
When you shall come to clearer knowledge that
You thus have published me? Gentle, my Lord,
You scarce can right me throughly than to say
You did mistake.[3]
LEONTES. No, if I mistake
In those foundations which I build upon,
The center is not big enough to bear
A school-boy's top.[4] [*To the Lords*] Away with her to prison!
He who shall speak for her is a far-off guilty,
But that he speaks.

---

1 Hermione, you have made the mistake in unlawfully taking Polixenes for your lover instead of me, your lawful husband "taken" in marriage. (Leontes sarcastically turns Hermione's language against her.)

2 Thou "thing," which I refuse to address by a term unfitting your social stature, since I would then set a precedent for a barbarism that might erode all proper distinctions between princes and beggars.

3 You can barely make complete amends except by saying that you were wrong.

4 If I am mistaken in this and in my grounds for believing so, than the earth itself (the center of the Ptolemaic universe) is so insubstantial that it would not support even a spinning top poised on it.

2.1.101: THE CENTER OF THE UNIVERSE (TLN 708)

Ptolemy's model of the solar system famously placed earth at the center of the universe. This geocentric universe accounted for the movement of the planets by positing their revolution around the earth in distinct epicycles that rotated in a larger orbit called the deferent. The stars moved on a celestial sphere around the outside of these planetary spheres. In 1632 Galileo attacked this view of the cosmology in his *Dialogue Concerning the Two Chief World Systems, Ptolemaic and Copernican*. Aristotle's *On the Heavens* and *Physics* place the earth at the center of the cosmos, the abode of change and corruption. (See <http://microcosmos.uchicago.edu/ptolemy/astronomy.html>.)

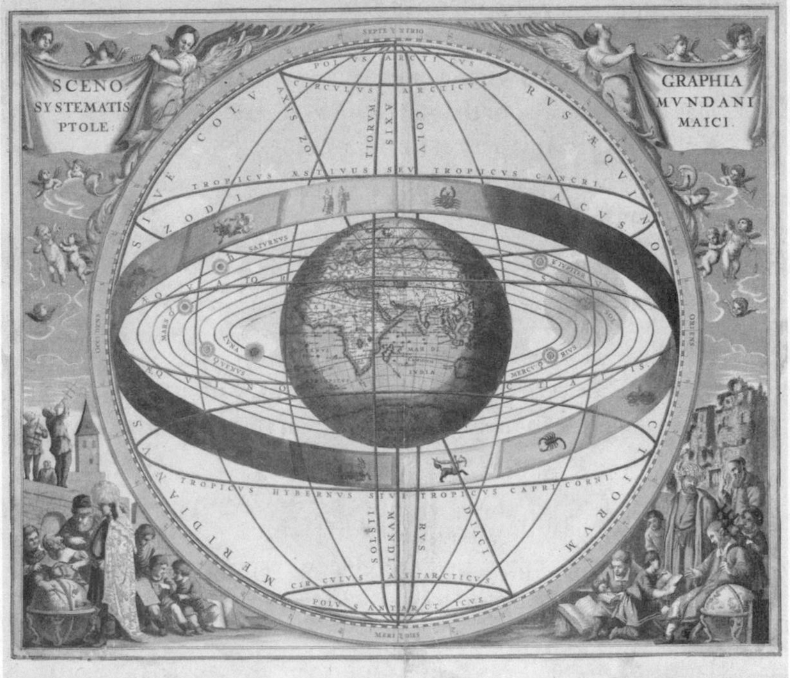

Chart (c. 1660) showing signs of the zodiac and the solar system with earth at the center, as described by Ptolemaic cosmosgraphy. From Wikimedia Commons, <http://commons.wikimedia.org>.

HERMIONE. There's some ill planet[1] reigns.
I must be patient till the heavens look
With an aspect more favorable. Good, my lords,
I am not prone to weeping as our sex
Commonly are, the want of which vain dew
Perchance shall dry your pities,[2] but I have
That honorable grief lodged here which burns
Worse than tears drown. Beseech you all, my lords,
With thoughts so qualified as your charities
Shall best instruct you measure me; and so,
The King's will be performed.

[*The guards delay removing Hermione.*]

LEONTES. Shall I be heard?[3]

HERMIONE. Who is't that goes with me? Beseech your Highness
My women may be with me, for you see
My plight[4] requires it. [*To the women*] Do not weep, good fools,
There is no cause. When you shall know your mistress
Has deserved prison, then abound in tears
As I come out; this action I now go on
Is for my better grace. [*To Leontes*] Adieu, my Lord,
I never wished to see you sorry; now
I trust I shall. My women, come, you have leave.

[*Exit Hermione under guard, with her women.*]

LEONTES. Go, do our bidding. Hence!

LORD. Beseech your Highness, call the Queen again.

ANTIGONUS. Be certain what you do, sir, lest your justice
Prove violence, in the which three great ones suffer:
Yourself, your Queen, your son.

LORD. For her, my Lord,
I dare my life lay down, and will do't, sir,
Please you t' accept it, that the Queen is spotless
I'th' eyes of heaven, and to you—I mean
In this which you accuse her.

ANTIGONUS. If it prove

1 Perhaps Saturn, proverbially a planet of the past and of suffering.
2 The absence of my weeping perhaps would diminish your feelings of pity.
3 Will my orders be followed?
4 Pregnancy.

She's otherwise, I'll keep my stables where
I lodge my wife; I'll go in couples with her.
Than when I feel and see her, no farther trust her;
For every inch of woman in the world,
Ay, every dram° of woman's flesh, is false *the tiniest of amounts*
If she be.

LEONTES. Hold your peaces.

LORD. Good, my lord—

ANTIGONUS. It is for you we speak, not for ourselves.
You are abused, and by some putter-on° *instigator*
That will be damned for't. Would I knew the villain,
I would land-damn° him; be she honor-flawed, *lambaste*
I have three daughters: the eldest is eleven;
The second and the third nine and some five.
If this prove true, they'll pay for't. By mine honor,
I'll geld° 'em all; fourteen they shall not see *spay, make infertile*
To bring false generations. They are co-heirs,
And I had rather glib[1] myself than they
Should not produce fair issue.

LEONTES. Cease, no more!
You smell this business with a sense as cold
As is a dead man's nose;[2] but I do see't and feel't,
As you feel doing thus [*Grabbing Antigonus's beard*] and see withal
The instruments that feel.

ANTIGONUS. If it be so,
We need no grave to bury honesty.
There's not a grain of it the face to sweeten
Of the whole dungy earth.

LEONTES. What? Lack I credit?

LORD. I had rather you did lack than I, my Lord,
Upon this ground, and more it would content me
To have her honor true than your suspicion
Be blamed for't how you might.[3]

LEONTES. Why, what need we
Commune with you of this, but rather follow

1 Castrate myself and deny myself a posterity (see *OED v*2).
2 You do not comprehend this business.
3 Regardless of the blame you receive.

Our forceful instigation? Our prerogative
Calls not your counsels, but our natural goodness
Imparts this, which, if you, or stupefied
Or seeming so in skill, cannot or will not
Relish a truth like us, inform yourselves
We need no more of your advice; the matter,
The loss, the gain, the ordering on't
Is all properly ours.[1]

ANTIGONUS. And I wish, my liege,
You had only in your silent judgement tried° it, *considered*
Without more overture.[2]

LEONTES. How could that be?
Either thou art most ignorant by age,
Or thou wert born a fool. Camillo's flight,
Added to their familiarity—
Which was as gross as ever touched conjecture,
That lacked sight only, naught for approbation
But only seeing, all other circumstances
Made up to th' deed—doth push-on this proceeding.[3]
Yet for a greater confirmation,
For in an act of this importance 'twere
Most piteous to be wild,° I have dispatched in post *rash*
To sacred Delphos[4] to Apollo's temple,
Cleomines and Dion, whom you know
Of stuffed-sufficiency;[5] now, from the oracle
They will bring all whose spiritual counsel had
Shall stop or spur me. Have I done well?

LORD. Well done, my Lord.

LEONTES. Though I am satisfied and need no more

1 Why must I even inform you of this instead of your simply following my own course? My prerogative does not need your permission.

2 Public declaration.

3 Camillo's flight, following the betrayal of Polixenes and Hermione in all of its grossness, an intimacy that is so flagrant that an eyewitness is not needed, compels me to pursue this course of action.

4 The island of Delphos (now Delos), which according to Greek mythology was the birthplace of Apollo. Apollo's oracle was actually at Delphi, on the mainland, but Shakespeare seems to have confused the two locations.

5 More than adequate competency.

Than what I know, yet shall the oracle
Give rest to th' minds of others, such as he[1]
Whose ignorant credulity will not
Come up to th' truth. So have we thought it good
From our free person she should be confined,
Lest that the treachery of the two fled hence
Be left her to perform.[2] Come, follow us.
We are to speak in public; for this business
Will raise° us all. *rouse*

ANTIGONUS. [*Aside*] To laughter, as I take it,
If the good truth were known.

Exeunt.

[2.2]

Enter Paulina, a Gentleman [*and attendants*].

PAULINA. The keeper of the prison, call to him.
Let him have knowledge who I am.

[*Exit Gentleman.*]

Good lady,
No court in Europe is too good for thee.
What dost thou then in prison?

[*Enter Jailer and Gentleman.*]

Now, good sir,
You know me, do you not?

JAILER. For a worthy lady,
And one who much I honor.

PAULINA. Pray you then,
Conduct me to the queen.

JAILER. I may not, madam.
To the contrary I have express commandment.

1 Anyone; Orgel (ed.) notes this might also be aimed at Antigonus.

2 Hermione might carry out this "presumed" treachery on her own. Johnson (ed. 1765) notes that Leontes's paranoia has reached the level of being that Hermione's role as "federary" to Polixenes and Camillo means that she will carry out the assassination conspiracy.

PAULINA. Here's ado,[1] to lock up honesty and honor from
Th' access of gentle visitors. Is't lawful° pray you *allowable*
To see her women? Any of them? Emilia?
JAILER. So please you, madam,
To put apart° these your attendants, I *send away*
Shall bring Emilia forth.
PAULINA. I pray now call her;
Withdraw yourselves.
[*Exeunt Gentleman and attendants.*]
JAILER. And, madam,
I must be present at your conference.
PAULINA. Well, be't so, prithee.
[*Exit Jailer.*]
Here's such ado to make no stain a stain
As passes coloring.[2]

[*Enter Jailer and Emilia.*]
Dear gentlewoman,
How fares our gracious lady?
EMILIA. As well as one so great and so forlorn
May hold together; on° her frights and griefs, *because of*
Which never tender lady hath borne greater,
She is something before her time delivered.[3]
PAULINA. A boy?
EMILIA. A daughter, and a goodly babe,
Lusty and like to live;[4] the Queen receives
Much comfort in't, says, "my poor prisoner,
I am innocent as you."
PAULINA. I dare be sworn,
These dangerous, unsafe lunes[5] i'th' King, beshrew them!
He must be told on't,° and he shall. The office *of this business*
Becomes a woman best. I'll take't upon me.

1 Terrible state of affairs.

2 Here is so much fuss that has allowed purity to be blemished, an act of dyeing that defies the art itself.

3 She gave birth earlier than expected.

4 Healthy and likely to survive.

5 Bouts of madness.

If I prove honey-mouthed, let my tongue blister
And never to my red-looked anger be
The trumpet any more. Pray you, Emilia,
Commend my best obedience to the Queen;
If she dares trust me with her little babe,
I'll show't the King and undertake to be
Her advocate to th' loudest.° We do not know *most forcefully*
How he may soften at the sight o'th' child.
The silence often of pure innocence
Persuades when speaking fails.

EMILIA. Most worthy madam,
Your honor and your goodness is so evident
That your free undertaking cannot miss
A thriving issue; there is no lady living
So meet[1] for this great errand. Please your Ladyship
To visit the next room, I'll presently
Acquaint the Queen of your most noble offer,
Who but today hammered of this design,
But durst not tempt a minister of honor
Lest she should be denied.[2]

PAULINA. Tell her, Emilia,
I'll use that tongue I have; if wit flow from't
As boldness from my bosom, let't not be doubted
I shall do good.[3]

EMILIA. Now be you blest for it!
I'll to the Queen. Please you come something nearer.

JAILER. [*To Paulina*] Madam, if't please the Queen to send the babe,
I know not what I shall incur to pass it,[4]
Having no warrant.

PAULINA. You need not fear it, sir,
This child was prisoner to the womb and is

1 Qualified, appropriate.
2 Who strongly deliberated on this plan but dared not to ask a woman of high rank lest she be turned away.
3 I'll use the rhetorical skills I have; if my wit matches the level of my boldness, I shall accomplish this.
4 Allow the baby to be brought out.

By law and process of great nature thence
Freed and enfranchised, not a party to
The anger of the King, nor guilty of,
If any be, the trespass of the Queen.[1]

JAILER. I do believe it.

PAULINA. Do not you fear! Upon mine honor, I
Will stand betwixt you and danger.

Exeunt.

[2.3]

[*Enter Leontes.*]

LEONTES. Nor night nor day no rest. It is but weakness
To bear the matter thus, mere weakness. If
The cause were not in being—part o'th cause,
She, th' adulteress; for the harlot-king
Is quite beyond mine arm, out of the blank
And level of my brain, plot-proof[2]—but she,
I can hook to me.[3] Say that she were gone,[4]
Given to the fire, a moiety of my rest
Might come to me again.[5] Who's there?

[*Enter Servant.*]

SERVANT. My lord?

LEONTES. How does the boy?

SERVANT. He took good rest tonight. 'Tis hoped
His sickness is discharged.

LEONTES. To see his nobleness
Conceiving the dishonor of his mother!

---

1 This child was yet unborn and thus naturally free from the king's wrath and not guilty of the accusations made against its mother.

2 Out of the grasp of any plot I conceive.

3 If those responsible for this situation were removed (i.e., killed), except for Polixenes who has escaped—I can at least seize her ("she, I can hook to me"). Not to do so would be a sign of bitterness.

4 Say that she were dead.

5 Were Hermione burned at the stake (i.e., as a traitor to the king), a portion of me would be at rest (Polixenes would still be out of my grasp). See *OED moiety* 2a. Bullokar (1616) defines it as *half*.

He straight declined, drooped, took it deeply,
Fastened, and fixed the shame on't° in himself; [*for it*]
Threw off° his spirit, his appetite, his sleep, [*tossed away (like clothing)*]
And downright languished. Leave me solely.° Go, [*alone*]
See how he fares.

[*Exit Servant.*]

Fie, fie, no thought of him.[1]
The very thought of my revenges that way
Recoil upon me: in himself too mighty,
And in his parties, his alliance.[2] Let him be
Until a time may serve. For present vengeance
Take it on her. Camillo and Polixenes
Laugh at me, make their pastime[3] at my sorrow.
They should not laugh if I could reach them, nor
Shall she within my power.

Enter Paulina [with baby], Antigonus, Lords and Servants.

LORD. You must not enter.

PAULINA. Nay, rather, good my lords, be second to me.[4]
Fear you his tyrannous passion more, alas,
Than the Queen's life? A gracious innocent soul,
More free than he is jealous.

ANTIGONUS. That's enough.

SERVANT. Madam, he hath not slept tonight, commanded
None should come at him.

PAULINA. Not so hot,° good sir. [*not so abusive*]
I come to bring him sleep. 'Tis such as you
That creep like shadows[5] by him and do sigh
At each his needless heavings,[6] such as you

---

1 Polixenes; Leontes's fixation on him returns.

2 Polixenes is too strong with allies and alliances for me to seek revenge against him.

3 Get their amusement from.

4 Supportive of my efforts.

5 Insubstantial beings (with suggestion of an accompanying shadow). Perhaps also with a sense of a "parasite." See *OED* *n*8a.

6 Each of his undeserved groans.

Nourish the cause of his awaking.[1] I
Do come with words as medicinal as true—
Honest as either—to purge him of that humor
That presses him[2] from sleep.

LEONTES. [*To Paulina, taking notice of voice*] What noise there, ho?

PAULINA. No noise, my Lord, but needful conference[3]
About some gossips[4] for your Highness.

LEONTES. How?
Away with that audacious lady! Antigonus,
I charged thee that she should not come about me.
I knew she would.

ANTIGONUS. I told her so, my lord,
On your displeasure's peril and on mine
She should not visit you.

LEONTES. What? Canst not rule her?

PAULINA. From all dishonesty he can; in this—
Unless he take the course that you have done,
Commit me for committing honor—trust it,
He shall not rule me.

ANTIGONUS. La[5] you now, you hear.
When she will take the rein I let her run,
But she'll not stumble.

PAULINA. Good my liege, I come,
And I beseech you hear me, who professes
Myself your loyal servant, your physician,
Your most obedient counselor yet that dares
Less appear so in comforting your evils,
Than such as most seem yours.[6] I say, I come
From your good queen.

LEONTES. "Good" queen?

PAULINA. Good queen, my Lord, good queen,

1 It is because of you, you who hang upon him and collude with him, that Leontes remains restive.

2 Weighs upon him and prevents.

3 Necessary conversation.

4 Godparents for your child.

5 A mark of emphasis, like "Listen."

6 Than those superficially loyal advisors on whom you currently depend.

I say "good queen,"
And would by combat make her good, so were I
A man, the worst about you.[1]
LEONTES. Force her hence.
PAULINA. Let him that makes but trifles of his eyes
First hand me;[2] on mine own accord, I'll off,
But first I'll do my errand. The good queen—
For she is good—hath brought you forth a daughter.
Here 'tis. Commends it to your blessing.
[*Laying down the baby.*]
LEONTES. Out!
A mankind witch?[3] Hence with her, out o'door!
A most intelligencing bawd.° *a pimp passing secrets*
PAULINA. Not so!
I am as ignorant in that as you
In so entitling me and no less honest
Than you are mad, which is enough I'll warrant
As this world goes to pass for honest.
LEONTES. Traitors!
Will you not push her out?
[*To Antigonus*] Give her the bastard,
Thou dotard! Thou art woman-tired, unroosted[4]
By thy dame Partlet here. Take up the bastard,
Take't up, I say! Give't to thy crone.
PAULINA. [*To Antigonus*] Forever
Unvenerable[5] be thy hands, if thou
Tak'st up the princess by that forced baseness[6]
Which he has put upon't.

---

1 And would prove her virtue in a combat if I were a man, even the least heroic among you.

2 Let he who places no value on his eyes be the first to lay a hand on me (i.e., I'll claw his eyes out).

3 Virago or masculine witch.

4 Henpecked and displaced from rightful domestic authority, a characterization continued in the next line's "dame Partlet," an allusion to the hen in Chaucer's *Nun's Priest's Tale*, used in derogatory fashion.

5 Unblessed (should Antigonus pick up the baby charged as a "bastard," his hands would lose any degree of respectability).

6 Enforced bastardy (Mowat and Werstine).

LEONTES. He dreads[1] his wife.
PAULINA. So I would you did; then 'twere past all doubt
You'd call your children yours.
LEONTES. A nest of traitors!
ANTIGONUS. I am none, by this good light.[2]
PAULINA. Nor I, nor any
But one that's here, and that's himself. For he
The sacred honor of himself, his queen's,
His hopeful son's, his babe's, betrays to slander,
Whose sting is sharper than the sword's[3] and will not—
For as the case now stands, it is a curse
He cannot be compelled to't—once remove
The root of his opinion, which is rotten,
As ever oak or stone was sound.
LEONTES. A callet[4]
Of boundless tongue, who late hath beat her husband
And now baits me. This brat is none of mine.
It is the issue of Polixenes.
Hence with it, and together with the dam[5]
Commit them to the fire!
PAULINA. It is yours,
And might we lay th' old proverb to your charge,
So like you 'tis the worse. Behold, my lords,
Although the print[6] be little, the whole matter
And copy of the father—eye, nose, lip,
The trick[7] of's frown, his forehead, nay, the valley,
The pretty dimples of his chin, and cheek, his smiles
The very mold and frame of hand, nail, finger.
And thou, good goddess Nature, which hast made it
So like to him that got it, if thou hast
The ordering of the mind too, 'mongst all colors

1 Fears, with a secondary sense of "respects," which Paulina applies in the following line.
2 By my eyesight (a solemn oath).
3 (Slander), as sharp as a sword's blade.
4 A scold, with a sense of lewdness.
5 Mother (with bestial connotation).
6 Image (alluding to the printing process and the infant's details replicating Leontes's original).
7 Characteristic trait (of Leontes).

No yellow in't, lest she suspect, as he does,
Her children not her husband's.[1]

LEONTES. A gross hag!
[*To Antigonus*] And, lozel,[2] thou art worthy to be hanged
That wilt not stay her tongue.

ANTIGONUS. Hang all the husbands
That cannot do that feat, you'll leave yourself
Hardly one subject.

LEONTES. Once more, take her hence!

PAULINA. A most unworthy and unnatural lord
Can do no more.

LEONTES. I'll ha' thee burnt.

PAULINA. I care not.
It is an heretic that makes the fire,
Not she which burns in't. I'll not call you tyrant.
But this most cruel usage of your queen,
Not able to produce more accusation
Than your own weak-hinged[3] fancy, something savors
Of tyranny and will ignoble make you,
Yea, scandalous to the world.

LEONTES. [*To Antigonus*] On your allegiance,
Out of the chamber with her. Were I a tyrant,
Where were her life? She durst not call me so
If she did know me one. Away with her!

PAULINA. [*To Lords*] I pray you do not push me; I'll be gone.
Look to your babe, my Lord, 'tis yours. Jove send her
A better guiding spirit. What needs these hands?[4]
You that are thus so tender o'er his follies[5]
Will never do him good, not one of you.
So, so. Farewell, we are gone.

Exit.

LEONTES. Thou, traitor, hast set on thy wife to this.
My child? Away with't! Even thou that hast

1 Oh Goddess of Nature, responsible for the physical resemblance between the baby girl and Leontes, please vanquish the "yellow" of jealousy from her mind, lest she should some day distrust the paternity of her own children.

2 Wastrel, good-for-nothing.

3 Ungrounded.

4 The Lords who are ushering Paulina out of the room.

5 Enabling of his foolishness.

A heart so tender o'er it, take it hence,
And see it instantly consumed with fire.
Even° thou, and none but thou. Take it up straight; *only*
Within this hour bring me word 'tis done,
And by good testimony, or I'll seize thy life
With what thou else call'st thine. If thou refuse,
And wilt encounter with my wrath, say so.
The bastard-brains with these my proper hands
Shall I dash out. Go, take it to the fire,
For thou set'st on thy wife.[1]

ANTIGONUS. I did not, sir.
These lords, my noble fellows, if they please,
Can clear me in't.

LORDS. We can, my royal liege.
He is not guilty of her coming hither.

LEONTES. You're liars all!

LORDS. Beseech your Highness, give us better credit.
We have always truly served you and beseech
So to esteem of us, and on our knees we beg
As recompense of our dear services
Past[2] and to come that you do change this purpose,
Which being so horrible, so bloody, must
Lead on to some foul issue. We all kneel.

LEONTES. I am a feather for each wind that blows.
Shall I live on to see this bastard kneel
And call me father? Better burn it now
Than curse it then. But be it;° let it live. *so, let it be*
It shall not neither. You sir, come you hither,
You that have been so tenderly officious
With Lady Margerie,° your midwife there, *slang for "hen"*
To save this bastard's life, for 'tis a bastard,
So sure as this beard's gray.[3] What will you adventure
To save this brat's life?

ANTIGONUS. Anything, my lord,
That my ability may undergo

1 For you are responsible for inciting your wife against me.
2 That you give us the respect that we have earned from our past loyalty.
3 Antigonus's gray beard.

And nobleness impose, at least thus much:
I'll pawn the little blood which I have left
To save the innocent. Anything possible.

LEONTES. It shall be possible. Swear by this sword
Thou wilt perform my bidding.

ANTIGONUS. [*Places hand on hilt of sword*] I will, my lord.

LEONTES. Mark, and perform it, seest thou? For the fail° *failure*
Of any point in't shall not only be
Death to thyself, but to thy lewd-tongued wife,
Whom for this time we pardon. We enjoin thee,
As thou art liegeman° to us, that thou carry *loyal follower*
This female bastard hence, and that thou bear it
To some remote and desert place, quite out
Of our dominions; and that there thou leave it
Without more mercy, to it own[1] protection
And favor of the climate. As by strange fortune
It came to us, I do in justice charge thee
On thy soul's peril and thy body's torture
That thou commend it strangely[2] to some place
Where chance may nurse or end it. Take it up.

ANTIGONUS. I swear to do this, though a present death
Had been more merciful. Come on, poor babe,
[*Takes up baby.*]
Some powerful spirit instruct the kites° and ravens *birds of prey*
To be thy nurses. Wolves and bears, they say,
Casting their savageness aside have done
Like offices of pity—[*To Leontes*] Sir, be prosperous
In more than this deed does require—[3] [*To baby*] and blessing
Against this cruelty fight on thy side,
Poor thing, condemned to loss.
Exit [*with child.*]

LEONTES. No, I'll not rear
Another's issue.

---

1 Its own (see p. 100, note 4).
2 As a stranger, outsider (since it was fathered by a foreigner, Polixenes).
3 May you have more prosperity than you deserve for this act of banishment (i.e., Antigonus's sense of the child's being "condemned to loss," exile and subsequent vulnerability to the forces of nature).

Enter a Servant.

SERVANT. Please your Highness, posts
From those you sent to th' oracle are come
An hour since. Cleomines and Dion,
Being well arrived from Delphos, are both landed,
Hasting° to th' court. *speeding*

SERVANT. So please you, sir, their speed
Hath been beyond account.° *unprecedented*

LEONTES. Twenty-three days
They have been absent. 'Tis good speed, foretells
The great Apollo suddenly will have
The truth of this appear.° Prepare you, lords, *made evident*
Summon a session° that we may arraign *court proceeding*
Our most disloyal lady, for as she hath
Been publicly accused, so shall she have
A just and open trial. While she lives,
My heart will be a burden to me. Leave me,
And think upon my bidding.

Exeunt.

[3.1]

Enter Cleomines and Dion.

CLEOMINES. The climate's delicate, the air most sweet,
Fertile the isle,[1] the temple much surpassing
The common praise it bears.

DION. I shall report,
For most it caught me, the celestial habits,° *garments*
Methinks I so should term them, and the reverence
Of the grave wearers. O, the sacrifice,[2]
How ceremonious, solemn, and unearthly
It was i'th' offering!

CLEOMINES. But of all, the burst
And the ear-deafening voice o'th' oracle,
Kin to Jove's thunder, so surprised my sense

---

1 Delphos; see p. 98, note 4.

2 The pagan ritual of burning entrails to the gods as an offering.

That I was nothing.[1]
DION. If th' event° o'th' journey *outcome*
Prove as successful to the queen—O, be't so—
As it hath been to us, rare, pleasant, speedy,
The time is worth the use on't.° *of it*
CLEOMINES. Great Apollo,
Turn all to th' best! These proclamations,
So forcing faults upon Hermione
I little like.
DION. The violent carriage of it
Will clear or end the business[2] when the oracle
Thus by Apollo's great divine sealed up
Shall the contents discover, something rare
Even then will rush to knowledge. Go. Fresh horses!
And gracious be the issue.° *and fortunate be the result*
Exeunt.

[3.2]

Enter Leontes, Lords, [and] Officers.
LEONTES. This sessions[3] to our great grief we pronounce,
Even pushes 'gainst our heart. The party tried,
The daughter of a king, our wife, and one
Of us too much beloved. Let us be cleared
Of being tyrannous, since we so openly
Proceed in justice, which shall have due course,
Even to the guilt or the purgation.° *acquittal*
Produce the prisoner.
OFFICER. It is his Highness' pleasure that the queen
Appear in person, here in court.

[Enter Hermione for trial, with Paulina and Ladies.]
Silence!

1 The oracle's voice is a booming sound that reverberates as Jove's thunder, and it renders Cleomines insignificant in its blast.
2 The hastiness of the trial and the speed to acquire Apollo's judgment will resolve this issue, one way or another.
3 Sitting of the court.

LEONTES. Read the indictment.

OFFICER. [*Reads*] Hermione, queen to the worthy Leontes, King of Sicilia, thou art here accused and arraigned of high treason, in committing adultery with Polixenes, King of Bohemia, and conspiring with Camillo to take away the life of our soveraign lord the king, thy royal husband, the pretence[1] whereof being by circumstances partly laid open, thou, Hermione, contrary to the faith and allegiance of a true subject, didst counsel and aid them, for their better safety, to fly away by night.

HERMIONE. Since what I am to say must be but that
Which contradicts my accusation, and
The testimony on my part no other
But what comes from myself, it shall scarce boot me[2]
To say, "Not guilty." Mine integrity,
Being counted falsehood, shall, as I express it,
Be so received. But thus, if powers divine
Behold our human actions, as they do,
I doubt not then but innocence shall make
False accusation blush and tyranny
Tremble at patience.° You, my lord, best know *stoic suffering*

1 Intention.
2 Benefit me.

3.2.20–52: HERMIONE'S DEFENSE (TLN 1196–1228)

Turner and Haas cite a range of critics who describe the power of Hermione's oration and her elegance in the face of Leontes's slander. She clearly realizes that once Leontes has denigrated her chastity, she is deprived of a language predicated on her integrity as a virtuous wife and mother. Her vows of innocence are themselves rendered suspect. Other critics (Williamson, 12) have found echoes of the Catholic martyr Edmund Campion's own defense at his trial for treason.

Kittredge (433) observes that Hermione's defense is a poetic rendition of Robert Greene's prose, as given in Appendix A1, p. 214 ff.

Whom least will seem to do so[1] my past life
Hath been as continent, as chaste, as true,
As I am now unhappy, which is more
Than history can pattern, though devised
And played to take spectators.[2] For behold me,
A fellow of the royal bed, which owe
A moiety of the throne, a great king's daughter,[3]
The mother to a hopeful prince, here standing
To prate and talk for life and honor fore° *in the presence of*
Who please to come and hear. For life, I prize it
As I weigh grief, which I would spare.[4] For honor,
'Tis a derivative from me to mine,
And only that I stand for.[5] I appeal
To your own conscience, sir, before Polixenes
Came to your court how I was in your grace,
How merited to be so. Since he came,
With what encounter so uncurrent[6] I
Have strained t' appear thus;[7] if one jot beyond
The bound of honor or in act or will
That way inclining, hardened be the hearts
Of all that hear me, and my nearest of kin
Cry fie upon my grave.[8]

LEONTES. I never heard yet
That any of these bolder vices wanted
Less impudence to gainsay what they did
Than to perform it first.

HERMIONE. That's true enough,
Though 'tis a saying, sir, not due to me.

---

1 Who apparently seem to be disinclined.

2 Than any narrative or dramatic story can equal to captivate an audience.

3 The daughter of the Emperor of Russia (see line 116, TLN 1299).

4 My life I value only as I value grief, since my life is now only mourning.

5 I value honor only inasmuch as it will be inherited by my children.

6 Improper conduct. See *OED encounter n*3; *OED uncurrent* 2.

7 Since Polixenes's visit in Sicilia, what unacceptable behavior have I engaged in that makes this appearance in court possible.

8 If I have gone one iota beyond honorable behavior—either by my acts or my thoughts—let all who hear me harden their hearts and may my next of kin cry "Shame" at my grave.

LEONTES. You will not own it.
HERMIONE. More than mistress of
Which comes to me in name of fault I must not
At all acknowledge. For Polixenes,
With whom I am accused, I do confess
I loved him as in honor he required,
With such a kind of love as might become
A lady like me; with a love, even such,
So and no other, as yourself commanded,
Which, not to have done, I think had been in me
Both disobedience and ingratitude
To you and toward your friend, whose love had spoke
Even since it could speak, from an infant, freely,
That it was yours. Now for conspiracy,
I know not how it tastes, though it be dished° *served up*
For me to try how;[1] all I know of it
Is that Camillo was an honest man,
And why he left your court the gods themselves,
Wotting° no more than I, are ignorant.[2] *knowing*
LEONTES. You knew of his departure, as you know
What you have underta'en to do in's absence.
HERMIONE. Sir,
You speak a language that I understand not.
My life stands in the level of your dreams,[3]
Which I'll lay down.
LEONTES. Your actions are my dreams.
You had a bastard by Polixenes,
And I but dreamed it; as you were past all shame,
Those of your fact[4] are so, so past all truth,
Which to deny concerns more than avails;[5] for as

---

1 With respect to conspiracy, I would not know how it tastes, even if it were served to me.

2 I must not acknowledge blame for performing something of which I am not guilty (i.e., I demonstrated an honorable, appropriate love for Polixenes; that I am "mistress of," nothing more).

3 My life stands as the target of your delusions (and thus I forfeit it).

4 Guilty of your crime.

5 Which (denying the shame, the fact of your crime, and all truth) is of more importance to you than the effect of that denial on me.

Thy brat hath been cast out, like to itself,
No father owning it, which is indeed
More criminal in thee than it,[1] so thou
Shalt feel our justice, in whose easiest passage[2]
Look for no less than death.

HERMIONE. Sir, spare your threats.
The bug[3] which you would fright me with I seek;
To me can life be no commodity.° *be of no value*
The crown and comfort of my life, your favor,° *loving regard*
I do give° lost, for I do feel it gone, *consider*
But know not how it went. My second joy
And first fruits° of my body, from his presence *Mamillius*
I am barred, like one infectious. My third comfort[4]
Starred most unluckily, is from my breast—
The innocent milk in it° most innocent mouth— *its*
Hal'd out to murder.[5] Myself on every post
Proclaimed a strumpet, with immodest hatred
The child-bed privilege[6] denied, which longs° *belongs*
To women of all fashion. Lastly, hurried
Here, to this place, i'th' open air, before
I have got strength of limit.[7] Now, my liege,
Tell me what blessings I have here alive
That I should fear to die? Therefore, proceed,
But yet hear this—mistake me not—no life,
I prize it not a straw,[8] but for mine honor,
Which I would free.° If I shall be condemned *vindicate*
Upon surmises, all proofs sleeping else
But what your jealousies awake,[9] I tell you

---

1 Which lack of paternity is more your crime than the baby's.
2 In its least painful form (i.e., death would be the least painful form of our justice; torture is more likely).
3 Bugbear, bogeyman.
4 Her infant daughter.
5 Ill-fated by birth and dragged away from my nursing to be murdered.
6 Bedrest following birth, a rightful treatment for all new mothers.
7 The conclusion of the normal month-long bedrest.
8 My life is as worthless as straw (proverbial; see Dent S917).
9 Based on your jealous suspicions rather than any hard proof.

'Tis rigor and not law.[1] Your honors all,
I do refer me to the oracle:
Apollo be my judge.

LORD. This your request
Is altogether just. Therefore, bring forth,
And in Apollo's name, his oracle.

[*Exeunt certain officers.*]

HERMIONE. The emperor of Russia was my father.
Oh that he were alive and here beholding
His daughter's trial, that he did but see
The flatness° of my misery; yet with eyes *absoluteness*
Of pity, not revenge.

[*Enter Cleomines and Dion with officers.*]

OFFICER. You here shall swear upon this sword of justice,
That you, Cleomines and Dion, have
Been both at Delphos and from thence have brought
This sealed-up oracle by the hand delivered
Of great Apollo's priest; and that since then,
You have not dared to break the holy seal
Nor read the secrets in't.

CLEOMINES AND DION. All this we swear.

LEONTES. Break up the seals and read.

OFFICER. [*Reads*] Hermione is chaste, Polixenes blameless, Camillo a true subject, Leontes a jealous tyrant, his innocent babe truly begotten, and the king shall live without an heir if that which is lost be not found.

LORDS. Now blessed be the great Apollo.

HERMIONE. Praised!

LEONTES. Hast thou read truth?

OFFICER. Ay, my lord, even so
As it is here set down.

LEONTES. There is no truth at all i'th' oracle!
The sessions shall proceed. This is mere falsehood.

1 Severe punishment without the backing of the *law* itself (based on Leontes's "jealousies").

[*Enter Servant.*]

SERVANT. My lord, the King, the King!

LEONTES. What is the business?

SERVANT. O, sir, I shall be hated to report it.
The prince your son, with mere conceit and fear
Of the queen's speed,[1] is gone.

LEONTES. How "gone"?

SERVANT. Is dead!

LEONTES. Apollo's angry, and the heavens themselves
Do strike at my injustice!

[*Hermione falls.*]

How now there?

PAULINA. This news is mortal to the Queen! Look down
And see what death is doing.

LEONTES. Take her hence!
Her heart is but o'er-charged;[2] she will recover.
I have too much believed mine own suspicion.
Beseech you tenderly apply to her
Some remedies for life.

[*Paulina and Ladies exit with Hermione.*]

Apollo, pardon
My great profanenesse 'gainst thine oracle.
I'll reconcile me to Polixenes,
New woo my queen, recall the good Camillo,
Whom I proclaim a man of truth, of mercy;
For being transported by my jealousies
To bloody thoughts and to revenge, I chose
Camillo for the minister to poison
My friend Polixenes, which had been done,
But that the good mind of Camillo tardied[3]
My swift command. Though I with death and with
Reward did threaten and encourage him
Not doing it and being done,[4] he—most humane,

1 Utter fixation on and fear for the queen's fate.

2 Overburdened with anxiety.

3 Delayed in carrying out.

4 Though I threatened him with death should he not fulfill my command and promised a reward should he complete my order.

And filled with honor—to my kingly guest
Unclasped my practice,° quit his fortunes here, *revealed my plot*
Which you knew great, and to the hazard
Of all incertainties himself commended,
No richer than his honor.[1] How he glisters
Through my rust, and how his piety
Does my deeds make the blacker![2]

[*Enter Paulina.*]

PAULINA. Woe the while!
Oh cut my lace,[3] lest my heart, cracking it,
Break too.

LORD. What fit is this? Good lady?

PAULINA. What studied torments,[4] tyrant, hast for me?
What wheels, racks, fires? What flaying? Boiling
In leads or oils? What old or newer torture
Must I receive, whose every word deserves
To taste of thy most worst! Thy tyranny
Together working with thy jealousies—
Fancies too weak for boys, too green and idle
For girls of nine[5]—Oh think what they have done,
And then run mad indeed, stark-mad, for all
Thy bygone fooleries were but spices of it.
That thou betrayedst Polixenes, 'twas nothing.
That did but show thee of a fool, inconstant,
And damnable ingrateful. Nor was't much,
Thou wouldst have poisoned good Camillo's honor
To have him kill a king: poor trespasses,
More monstrous standing by;[6] whereof I reckon

1 And committed himself to the danger of all uncertainties, rich only in his honor.

2 How he shines next to my rust (i.e., his armor glitters next to the corroded state of mine)! How his moral integrity shows up my own immoral actions!

3 The ties of my bodice.

4 Devised tortures (she then describes some: bodies being tied to wheels and broken, stretched on racks, burned; skin flayed or pulled off or placed in molten lead or oil).

5 Childish and immature ("green") fantasies not appropriate for boys or nine-year-old girls.

6 Compared with the even more monstrous actions you have taken.

The casting forth to crows thy baby daughter
To be or none, or little, though a devil
Would have shed water out of fire ere done't.[1]
Nor is't directly laid to thee the death
Of the young prince, whose honorable thoughts,
Thoughts high for one so tender, cleft the heart
That could conceive a gross and foolish sire
Blemished his gracious dam. This is not, no,
Laid to thy answer. But the last—O lords,
When I have said, "Cry woe!"—the Queen, the Queen,
The sweetest, dearest creature's dead, and vengeance for't
Not dropped down yet.

LORD. The higher powers forbid!

PAULINA. I say she's dead! I'll swear't! If word nor oath
Prevail not, go and see. If you can bring
Tincture or luster in her lip, her eye,[2]
Heat outwardly, or breath within, I'll serve you
As I would do the gods. But, O thou tyrant,
Do not repent these things, for they are heavier
Than all thy woes can stir; therefore, betake thee° *commit yourself*
To nothing but despair. A thousand knees[3]
Ten thousand years together, naked, fasting
Upon a barren mountain and still winter
In storm perpetual, could not move the gods
To look that way thou wert.[4]

LEONTES. Go on, go on!
Thou canst not speak too much. I have deserved
All tongues to talk their bitt'rest.

LORD. [*To Paulina*] Say no more.
Howe'er the business goes, you have made fault
I'th' boldness of your speech.

PAULINA. I am sorry for't.
All faults I make, when I shall come to know them,
I do repent. Alas, I have showed too much

1 Even the devil would have shed tears in fiery hell before he banished this baby.
2 Color to her lips, brightness to her eye.
3 Five hundred supplicants on their knees.
4 Take notice or pay heed to you and your prayers.

The rashness of a woman. He is touched° *afflicted*
To th' noble heart. What's gone and what's past help
Should be past grief. [*To Leontes*] Do not receive affliction
At my petition; I beseech you, rather,
Let me be punished that have minded° you *reminded*
Of what you should forget. Now, good my liege,
Sir, royal sir, forgive a foolish woman;
The love I bore your queen—lo, fool again![1]
I'll speak of her no more, nor of your children;
I'll not remember you of my own lord,
Who is lost too. Take your patience to you,
And I'll say nothing.

LEONTES. Thou didst speak but well,[2]
When most the truth which I receive much better
Than to be pitied of thee. Prithee bring me
To the dead bodies of my queen and son;
One grave shall be for both. Upon them shall
The causes of their death appear, unto
Our shame perpetual. Once a day I'll visit
The chapel where they lie, and tears shed there
Shall be my recreation.[3] So long as nature
Will bear up with this exercise, so long
I daily vow to use it. Come and lead me
To these sorrows.[4]

Exeunt.

[3.3]

[*Enter Antigonus carrying baby, followed by a mariner.*]

ANTIGONUS. Thou art perfect, then,[5] our ship hath touched upon
The deserts of Bohemia?

---

1 Addressed, either sincerely or ironically, to herself for continuing to remind Leontes of Hermione's death and of the other deaths attributed to his foolishness.

2 You spoke most appropriately of my wrongs, which I deserve much more than your pity.

3 *OED recreation n*2b. The sense is of "mental or spiritual consolation," but also ironically with a sense of the "pleasurable or interesting pastime."

4 The grave where Hermione and Mamillius are buried.

5 Certain that.

MARINER. Ay, my lord, and fear
We have landed in ill time: the skies look grimly
And threaten present blusters. In my conscience
The heavens with that we have in hand[1] are angry
And frown upon's.

ANTIGONUS. Their sacred wills be done. Go, get aboard,
Look to thy bark.° I'll not be long before *ship*
I call upon thee.

MARINER. Make your best haste, and go not
Too far i'th' land. 'Tis like to be loud[2] weather.
Besides, this place is famous for the creatures
Of prey that keep° upon't. *dwell*

ANTIGONUS. Go thou away,
I'll follow instantly.

MARINER. I am glad at heart
To be so rid o'th' business.

Exit.

ANTIGONUS. Come, poor babe.
I have heard—but not believed—the spirits o'th' dead
May walk again. If such thing be, thy mother
Appeared to me last night, for never was dream
So like a waking. To me comes a creature,
Sometimes her head on one side, some another.
I never saw a vessel of like sorrow,
So filled and so becoming; in pure white robes
Like very sanctity she did approach
My cabin where I lay, thrice bowed before me,
And, gasping to begin some speech, her eyes
Became two spouts;[3] the fury spent, anon° *soon*
Did this break from her: "Good Antigonus,
Since Fate—against thy better disposition—
Hath made thy person for the thrower-out
Of my poor babe according to thine oath,
Places remote enough are in Bohemia.
There weep, and leave it crying; and for° the babe *because*

1 With what we are performing.
2 Blustery, thunderous.
3 Tears gushing from both eyes.

Is counted lost forever, Perdita[1]
I prithee call't. For this ungentle[2] business
Put on thee by my lord, thou never shalt see
Thy wife Paulina more!" And so, with shrieks
She melted into air. Affrighted much,
I did in time collect myself and thought
This was so and no slumber.° Dreams are toys,° *dream; trifles*
Yet for this once, yea superstitiously,
I will be squared° by this. I do believe *ruled*
Hermione hath suffered death, and that
Apollo would, this being indeed the issue
Of King Polixenes, it should here be laid,
Either for life or death, upon the earth
Of its right father. Blossom, speed thee well!
[*Places the baby and a scroll upon the ground.*]
There lie, and there thy character;° there these, *written history*
[*He lays down a bundle.*]
Which may, if Fortune please, both breed thee, pretty,
And still rest thine.[3]

[*Thunder.*]

The storm begins, poor wretch,
That for thy mother's fault art thus exposed
To loss and what may follow. Weep I cannot,
But my heart bleeds, and most accursed am I
To be by oath enjoined to this. Farewell.
The day frowns more and more. Thou'rt like to have
A lullaby too rough. I never saw
The heavens so dim by day.
[*The sound of a storm, with horns and dogs barking.*]
A savage clamor!
Well may I get aboard! This is the chase.[4]
I am gone forever!

Exit pursued by a bear.

1 "Perdita" means one who is lost.

2 Violent (with a secondary sense of "unfitting for one of the gentry").

3 Presumably, jewels and treasure for her breeding (i.e., her rearing) and her inheritance.

4 The bear, being pursued, now also in pursuit of a fleeing Antigonus.

3.3.47: FORTUNA (TLN 1490)

Fortuna (equivalent to the Greek goddess Tyche) was the goddess of fortune, and she is invoked several times in the play (see 4.4.51, TLN 1855; 4.4.475, TLN 2350; 4.4.778, TLN 2712; 5.1.215, TLN 2988). She was frequently depicted as either veiled or blind, producing either good or bad luck indifferently. She came to represent the capriciousness of life. Shakespeare refers to the goddess Fortune in *All's Well That Ends Well*, *Coriolanus*, and Sonnets 29 and 111.

"Fortuna." Engraving of allegorical figure representing Fortune, 1541, by Hans Sebald Beham (1500–50). From Wikimedia Commons, <http:// commons.wikimedia.org>.

[*Enter Old Shepherd.*]

SHEPHERD. I would there were no age between ten and three and twenty, or that youth would sleep out the rest,[1] for there is nothing in the between but getting wenches with child, wronging the ancientry,[2] stealing, fighting—hark you now! Would any but these boiled-brains[3] of nineteen and two-and-twenty hunt this weather? They have scared away two of my best sheep, which I fear the wolf will sooner find than the master. If anywhere I have them, 'tis by the seaside, browsing of ivy. Good luck, an't be thy

1 Sleep through the interval.
2 Elderly.
3 "Muddle-headed" (Orgel ed.).

3.3.57: "I AM GONE FOREVER" (TLN 1500)

Clearly this is Antigonus's statement of his imminent death at the hands of the bear. Pitcher suggests, perhaps tongue-in-cheek, that the actor in the original production, given its history of doubling roles, is signaling his departure from the role of Antigonus and his later reappearance in another role, perhaps that of Autolycus. Interpretations of Antigonus's demise have tended to underplay any tragic dimension in order to read it as a symbolic component of the play's plot. For Randall (90) the appearance of the bear and the end of Antigonus occur equipoised at the very middle of the play, seven scenes having been played and seven subsequent scenes to follow. For Adelman (*Common Liar* 176–77), the romance is the incarnation of King Lear's proverbial observation: "Lear says to Kent in the storm, '... where the greater malady is fixt, / The lesser is scarce felt. Thou'dst shun a Beare, / But if thy flight lay toward the roaring sea, / Thou'dst meete the Beare i'th' mouth' (3.4.8–11, TLN 1788–91) ..." In *The Winter's Tale* precisely this metaphor will become the literal action. Some critics view the scene as itself comic, a "ghastly joke" (Miko 261). Rosalie Colie's interpretive commentary (268–69) is especially convincing: "The absolute rejection of verisimilitude in this episode moves us away from tragic expectation to another mode, one which assumes as its own ground unreality, impossibility, and exaggeration. The horrible

will! What have we here? [*Seeing the baby*] Mercy on's, a bairn?[1] A very pretty bairn! A boy or a child[2] I wonder? A pretty one, a very pretty one, sure some scape.[3] Though I am not bookish, yet I can read waiting-gentlewoman in the scape. This has been some stair-work, some trunk-work, some behind-door work.[4] They were warmer that got this than the poor thing is here. I'll take it up for pity, yet I'll tarry till my son come. He hallooed but even now. Whoa-ho-hoa!

1 Child (dialect).

2 A female child. Quiller-Couch and Wilson characterize it as a "west country" word used in stage productions to suggest "yokels."

3 A child of an illicit affair.

4 Sexual encounters on the stairs, within a clothes trunk, or behind doors.

death, furthermore, is told in the shepherdly clown's rustic malapropisms—turned into a topic for laughter." Other critics find in the presentation a purgation of the tragedy and Sicilian ambience introduced by Leontes's jealousy.

ABOVE: Woodcut from *The History of Four-footed Beasts and Serpents* ... by Edward Topsell (London, 1658). Courtesy of Special Collections, University of Houston Libraries. UH Digital Library.

Enter Clown.

CLOWN. Hilloa, loa!

SHEPHERD. What? Art so near? If thou'lt see a thing to talk on when thou art dead and rotten, come hither.[1] What ailst thou, man?

CLOWN. I have seen two such sights by sea and by land, but I am not to say it is a sea, for it is now the sky; betwixt the firmament and it you cannot thrust a bodkin's point.[2]

SHEPHERD. Why, boy, how is it?

CLOWN. I would you did but see how it chafes, how it rages, how it takes up the shore, but that's not to the point. Oh, the most piteous cry of the poor souls, sometimes to see 'em, and not to see 'em. Now the ship boring the moon with her main mast, and anon swallowed with yeast[3] and froth, as you'd thrust a cork into a hogshead.[4] And then for the land-service,[5] to see how the bear tore out his shoulderbone, how he cried to me for help, and said his name was Antigonus, a nobleman. But to make an end of the ship, to see how the sea flap-dragoned[6] it. But first, how the poor souls roared and the sea mocked them, and how the poor gentleman roared and the bear mocked him, both roaring louder than the sea or weather.

SHEPHERD. Name of mercy,[7] when was this, boy?

CLOWN. Now, now. I have not winked[8] since I saw these sights. The men are not yet cold under water, nor the bear half dined on the gentleman; he's at it now.

SHEPHERD. Would I had been by to have helped the old man.

---

1 If you want to see something that people will still be talking about when you are long dead in your grave, come here. (Proverbial: Dent D126.1.)

2 Dagger's tip (i.e., the raging sea and sky have merged so closely during the storm that no separation can be discerned).

3 Foam.

4 The ship is tossed so high that its mast seems to pierce the moon and then gets swallowed by the foam as if it were a cork thrust into a keg.

5 "Military service on land" (Orgel ed.).

6 Alluding to flaming raisins floating in brandy and swallowed during a winter drinking game. The ship is the raisin drunk by the raging sea.

7 In the name of God's mercy.

8 Blinked (i.e., it only just happened).

CLOWN. I would you had been by the ship side, to have helped her. There your charity would have lacked footing.[1]

SHEPHERD. Heavy[2] matters, heavy matters. But look thee here, boy. Now bless thyself. Thou meet'st with things dying, I with things newborn. Here's a sight for thee! Look thee, a bearing-cloth[3] for a squire's child. Look thee here. Take up, take up, boy. Open't! So, let's see, it was told me I should be rich by the fairies. This is some changeling.[4] Open't! What's within, boy?

CLOWN. [*Opens box*] You're a made[5] old man. If the sins of your youth are forgiven you, you're well to live. Gold, all gold.

SHEPHERD. This is fairy gold boy, and 'twill prove so. Up with't, keep it close. Home, home, the next way. We are lucky, boy, and to be so still requires nothing but secrecy.[6] Let my sheep go. Come, good boy, the next way home.

CLOWN. Go you the next way with your findings. I'll go see if the bear be gone from the gentleman and how much he hath eaten. They are never curst[7] but when they are hungry. If there be any of him left, I'll bury it.

SHEPHERD. That's a good deed. If thou mayst discern by that which is left of him what he is,[8] fetch me to th' sight of him.

CLOWN. Marry, will I, and you shall help to put him i'th' ground.

SHEPHERD. 'Tis a lucky day, boy, and we'll do good deeds on't.

Exeunt.

---

1 Your charity would have been even greater in display given the lack of foundation for your generosity (i.e., the water would offer no foothold for your generous acts).

2 Regrettable, woeful.

3 Baptismal gown.

4 A child left by fairies in place of a human child.

5 Guaranteed wealthy.

6 Treasure left by fairies had to be kept secret; if revealed, misfortune would follow.

7 Vicious, ill-tempered.

8 His identity and social position.

[4.1]

Enter Time, the Chorus.

TIME. I, that please some, try[1] all; both joy and terror
Of good and bad, that makes and unfolds error,
Now take upon me, in the name of Time,
To use my wings. Impute it not a crime
To me or my swift passage that I slide
O'er sixteen years and leave the growth untried
Of that wide gap,[2] since it is in my power

1 Test.
2 Omit the intervening actions and events of the past sixteen years.

4.1.01: ENTER TIME, THE CHORUS (TLN 1580)

The allegorical image of Time is often depicted as an elderly bearded man, dressed in a robe and carrying a scythe and an hourglass or other timekeeping device. The passage of sand through the hourglass (in this painting, held in Time's left hand against the ground) is unidirectional until the hourglass is inverted and life begins anew.

The appearance of the choric Time in *The Winter's Tale* marks a shift in both time and tone of the play. The allegorical personation of the figure Time, alluding to *Pandosto* and its motto that *Truth is the daughter of time*, suggests, as Kittredge observes, that Shakespeare, not an interpolator, is responsible for this figure. Time is traditionally represented as "a doddering, toothless ancient, halting but fluent, senile but self-assured, ridiculous but triumphant" (432). In the painting included here, Time has wings and carries an hourglass.

Early editions of the play (Theobald 1733, Warburton 1747, Johnson 1765) have varied on whether Time appears as a postscript to Act 3 or concluding movement of that act. Not only Time's placement but Time's function has been discussed. Time is either a mere "device" (Panofsky 81) or the "heart of the play's mystery" (Coghill 36) because poised within a chronological gap that spans the tragedy of the first three acts and the comedy of the final two. Time is also seen as Providence's replacement, a *deus ex machina*, or a dramatic means of admitting the play's absurdity

To o'erthrow law, and in one self-born hour
To plant and o'erwhelm custom. Let me pass
The same I am ere ancient'st order was
Or what is now received.[1] I witness to
The times that brought them in. So shall I do
To th' freshest things now reigning and make stale
The glistering of this present, as my tale
Now seems to it.[2] Your patience this allowing,
I turn my glass° and give my scene such growing *hourglass*

1 Time stands outside of time itself and both creates and subverts custom as he wishes.

2 I witness both the past and the present, affecting the glistering (sparkling) of the present and transforming it likewise into the stale past.

in covering over sixteen years of action. For Orgel (ed.), Time is winged and iconographic based on Cesare Ripa's iconographic tradition.

ABOVE: "Father Time Overcome by Love, Hope and Beauty" by Simon Vouet (1590–1649). From Wikimedia Commons, <http://commons.wikimedia.org>.

As you had slept between: Leontes leaving
Th' effects of his fond jealousies, so grieving
That he shuts up himself. Imagine me,° *imagine for my sake*
Gentle spectators, that I now may be
In fair Bohemia. And remember well,
I mentioned a son o'th' king's, which Florizel
I now name to you, and with speed so pace° *proceed*
To speak of Perdita, now grown in grace
Equal with wond'ring.[1] What of her ensues
I list not prophesy,[2] but let Time's news
Be known when 'tis brought forth. A shepherd's daughter
And what to her adheres,° which follows after, *concerns her*
Is th' argument° of Time; of this allow, *subject, theme*
If ever you have spent time worse, ere now.
If never, yet that Time himself doth say
He wishes earnestly you never may.[3]

Exit.

[4.2]

Enter Polixenes and Camillo.

POLIXENES. I pray thee, good Camillo, be no more importunate.[4] 'Tis a sickness denying thee anything, a death to grant this.

CAMILLO. It is fifteen years since I saw my country. Though I have for the most part been aired abroad,[5] I desire to lay my bones there. Besides, the penitent king, my master, hath sent for me, to whose feeling sorrows I might be some allay,[6] or I o'erween[7] to think so, which is another spur to my departure.

1 Perdita's graceful appearance elicits a reciprocal wonder.
2 Do not intend to foreshadow; Time will allow the drama to tell the story, which, however, remains his story.
3 Grant me this passage of sixteen years if you have spent your time in worse fashion than in watching this play; if this play has been your worst experience, Time hopes you never have a worse one.
4 Obstinately persistent in requesting.
5 Breathed foreign air.
6 Relief.
7 Presume.

POLIXENES. As thou lov'st me, Camillo, wipe not out the rest of thy services by leaving me now. The need I have of thee thine own goodness hath made. Better not to have had thee than thus to want[1] thee. Thou, having made me businesses which none without thee can sufficiently manage, must either stay to execute them thyself, or take away with thee the very services thou hast done, which if I have not enough considered—as too much I cannot—to be more thankful to thee shall be my study, and my profit therein the heaping friendships.[2] Of that fatal country Sicilia, prithee speak no more,whose very naming punishes me with the remembrance of that penitent, as thou call'st him, and reconciled king my brother, whose loss of his most precious queen and children are even now to be afresh lamented. Say to me when saw'st thou the prince Florizel, my son? Kings are no less unhappy, their issue not being gracious, than they are in losing them when they have approved their virtues.[3]

CAMILLO. Sir, it is three days since I saw the Prince. What his happier affairs may be are to me unknown, but I have missingly[4] noted he is of late much retired from court and is less frequent to his princely exercises than formerly he hath appeared.

POLIXENES. I have considered so much, Camillo, and with some care, so far that I have eyes under my service[5] which look upon his removedness, from whom I have this intelligence: that he is seldom from the house of a most homely shepherd, a man, they say, that from very nothing and beyond the imagination of his neighbors is grown into an unspeakable estate.[6]

CAMILLO. I have heard, sir, of such a man, who hath a daughter of most rare note: the report of her is extended more than can be thought to begin from such a cottage.[7]

---

1 Lack.

2 You are irreplaceable in the services you have done me; if you leave, the services leave with you.

3 Kermode paraphrases: "It is as hard for kings to bear the disobedience and ill conduct of their children as to lose them when convinced of their virtues."

4 With a sense of loss (*OED*'s only citation).

5 Spies.

6 Amassed a considerable fortune.

7 Perdita's reputation is extraordinary for one who has such a lowly origin.

POLIXENES. That's likewise part of my intelligence, but I fear the angle[1] that plucks our son thither. Thou shalt accompany us to the place where we will, not appearing what we are, have some question with the shepherd, from whose simplicity I think it not uneasy to get the cause of my son's resort thither. Prithee, be my present partner in this business and lay aside the thoughts of Sicilia.

CAMILLO. I willingly obey your command.

POLIXENES. My best Camillo, we must disguise ourselves.

[*Exeunt.*]

[4.3]

Enter Autolycus singing.

When daffodils[2] begin to peer
With heigh, the doxy° over the dale, *a beggar's mistress*
Why then comes in the sweet o'the year,
For the red blood reigns in the winter's pale.[3]
The white sheet bleaching on the hedge,[4]
With heigh, the sweet birds, O how they sing!
Doth set my pugging tooth on edge,[5]
For a quart of ale is a dish for a king.
The lark that tirra lirra[6] chants,
With heigh, with heigh, the thrush and the jay,
Are summer songs for me and my aunts° *mistresses*
While we lie tumbling in the hay. [*Song ends.*]

I have served Prince Florizel, and in my time wore three-pile,[7] but now I am out of service.

But shall I go mourn for that, my dear? [*Singing.*]
The pale moon shines by night,

---

1 Fish hook.

2 The Lent Lily that is a harbinger of spring (*OED n*3).

3 Winter's grip (or, alternatively, winter's conventional pallidness) gives way to the ascendency of blood (fertility) coursing through new life springing from a dormant winter.

4 White sheets drying (and lightening) on the hedge.

5 Whets my appetite for thievery ("pugging tooth") of sheets from the hedge.

6 The onomatopoeic refrain of a skylark.

7 Expensive velvet cloak.

And when I wander here and there
I then do most go right.[1]
If tinkers[2] may have leave to live,
And bear the sow-skin budget,[3]
Then my account I well may give,
And in the stocks avouch it.[4]

My traffic is sheets. When the kite builds, look to lesser linen.[5] My father named me Autolycus, who being as I am littered under Mercury, was likewise a snapper-up of unconsidered trifles. With die and drab,[6] I purchased this caparison,[7] and my revenue is the silly cheat. Gallows and knock[8] are too powerful on the highway. Beating and hanging are terrors to me. For the life to come, I sleep out the thought of it.[9] A prize, a prize!

Enter Clown.

CLOWN. Let me see, every 'leven wether tods, every tod yields pound and odd shilling. Fifteen hundred shorn, what comes the wool to?[10]

AUTOLYCUS. [*Aside*] If the springe[11] hold, the cock's mine.

CLOWN. I cannot do't without counters.[12] [*Taking out a list*] Let me see, what am I to buy for our sheep-shearing feast?[13] Three pound of sugar, five pound of currants, rice. What will this sister of mine do with rice? But my father hath made her mistress of the feast,

1 Wandering takes me in the best possible direction.

2 Traveling tinsmiths who repaired pots and pans.

3 Leather bag made of pigskin which contained the tinsmith's tools (with sexual connotations for male genitals).

4 And attest to my trade while I sit in the stocks as punishment for vagrancy.

5 Though the kite builds its nest from fragments of sheets, (by implication) I traffic in entire sheets stolen from hedges.

6 Playing dice and prostitution.

7 Garment made of rags.

8 Hanging and being beaten.

9 I give no thought to the future.

10 Eleven sheep produce one tod (28 lbs.) of wool; every tod is worth a "pound and odd shilling" (£1.1s.), so the total is approximately £143.

11 Trap for the proverbially stupid woodcock. For a similar allusion, see *Hamlet* 1.3.116 (TLN 581).

12 Metal tokens used in calculations.

13 Rural festival occurring between May and the end of July.

4.3.24: "MY FATHER NAMED ME AUTOLYCUS" (TLN 1692)

Born under the sign of Mercury, the god of thieves, the classical Autolycus was the son of Mercury (Hermes) and thus a prolific thief. Orgel (ed.) gives the etymological origins for the name: "the wolf itself." According to Pausanias, Autolycus wore a helmet to make himself invisible and thus prone to sly insinuations in unlawful situations. Autolycus was adept at the art of trickery and theft and was musically inclined. Shakespeare clearly combines these qualities to invest Autolycus with his artful song and thieving mischief.

"John Fawcett as Autolycus in 'The Winter's Tale'" by Thomas Charles Wageman (1768–1837). From Victoria & Albert Museum.

and she lays it on.[1] She hath made me four-and-twenty nosegays[2] for the shearers—three-man song men,[3] all, and very good ones—but they are most of them means and basses but one puritan amongst them, and he sings psalms to hornpipes.[4] I must have saffron to color the warden pies;[5] mace;[6] dates, none—that's out of my note;[7] nutmegs, seven; a race[8] or two of ginger, but that I may beg; four pound of prunes and as many of raisins o'th' sun.[9]

AUTOLYCUS. [*Groveling on the ground*] Oh, that ever I was born.[10]

CLOWN. I'th' name of me—[11]

AUTOLYCUS. Oh, help me, help me! Pluck but off these rags, and then, death, death!

CLOWN. Alack, poor soul, thou hast need of more rags to lay on thee rather than have these off.

AUTOLYCUS. O sir, the loathsomeness of them offend me more than the stripes I have received, which are mighty ones and millions.

CLOWN. Alas, poor man, a million of beating may come to a great matter.[12]

AUTOLYCUS. I am robbed, sir, and beaten; my money and apparel ta'en from me, and these detestable things put upon me.

CLOWN. What, by a horseman or a footman?[13]

AUTOLYCUS. A footman, sweet sir, a footman.

CLOWN. Indeed, he should be a footman by the garments he has left with thee. If this be a horseman's coat,[14] it hath seen very hot

1 Plans it lavishly.
2 Small floral bouquets.
3 Singers of three-part songs, generally counter-tenor ("mean"), tenor, bass.
4 But the Puritan, singing tenor, sings even his psalms to the secular sounds of the pastoral hornpipe.
5 Pies made from warden pears.
6 Spice derived from a nutmeg.
7 Dates are not on my list.
8 Root.
9 Sun-dried raisins.
10 Proverbial (Dent B140).
11 A mild oath.
12 A million beatings is indeed a great number.
13 A robber on horse or one on foot.
14 The ragged conditions of the garment suggest that your robber was a footman, not a better dressed horseman.

service.[1] Lend me thy hand; I'll help thee. Come, lend me thy hand. [*Helps Autolycus to stand.*]

AUTOLYCUS. Oh, good sir, tenderly. Oh!

CLOWN. Alas, poor soul!

AUTOLYCUS. Oh, good sir, softly, good sir! I fear, sir, my shoulder blade is out.

CLOWN. How now? Canst stand?

AUTOLYCUS. Softly, dear sir! Good sir, softly! [*Picking Clown's pocket*] You have done me a charitable office.

CLOWN. Dost lack any money? I have a little money for thee.

AUTOLYCUS. No, good sweet sir. No, I beseech you, sir. I have a kinsman not past three quarters of a mile hence, unto whom I was going. I shall there have money or anything I want. Offer me no money I pray you; that kills my heart.

CLOWN. What manner of fellow was he that robbed you?

AUTOLYCUS. A fellow, sir, that I have known to go about with troll-my-dames.[2] I knew him once a servant of the prince. I cannot tell, good sir, for which of his virtues it was, but he was certainly whipped out of the court.

CLOWN. His vices you would say. There's no virtue whipped out of the court: they cherish it to make it stay there, and yet it will no more but abide.

AUTOLYCUS. Vices I would say, sir. I know this man well. He hath been since an ape-bearer,[3] then a process-server—a bailiff. Then he compassed a motion of the prodigal son[4] and married a tinker's wife within a mile where my land and living lies, and, having flown over many knavish professions, he settled only in rogue. Some call him Autolycus.

CLOWN. Out upon him! Prig,[5] for my life, prig! He haunts wakes, fairies, and bearbaitings.

AUTOLYCUS. Very true, sir, he, sir, he. That's the rogue that put me into this apparel.

1 Much military action.

2 Trullmadams or prostitutes.

3 A keeper of a circus ape.

4 Obtained a puppet show depicting the famous biblical parable of the prodigal son (Luke 15:11–32).

5 A thief.

CLOWN. Not a more cowardly rogue in all Bohemia. If you had but looked big and spit at him, he'd have run.[1]

AUTOLYCUS. I must confess to you, sir, I am no fighter. I am false of heart that way, and that he knew, I warrant him.

CLOWN. How do you now?

AUTOLYCUS. Sweet sir, much better than I was. I can stand and walk. I will even take my leave of you and pace softly towards my kinsman's.

CLOWN. Shall I bring thee on the way?

AUTOLYCUS. No, good-faced sir, no, sweet sir.

CLOWN. Then fare thee well. I must go buy spices for our sheep-shearing.

Exit.

AUTOLYCUS. Prosper you, sweet sir. Your purse is not hot enough[2] to purchase your spice. I'll be with you at your sheep-shearing too. If I make not this cheat bring out another and the shearers prove[3] sheep, let me be unrolled[4] and my name put in the book of virtue!

[*Sings.*]

Jog on, jog on, the footpath way,
    And merrily hent the stile-a;[5]
A merry heart goes all the day,
    Your sad tires in a mile-a.

Exit.

[4.4]

[*Enter Florizel and Perdita.*]

FLORIZEL. These your unusual weeds[6] to each part of you
    Does give a life—no shepherdess, but Flora
    Peering in April's front.[7] This your sheep-shearing

1 Had you looked threateningly at him and spit, he would run in fear.

2 Empty (thus cold because not "hot" with money).

3 (1) If this trickery fails to produce even more tricks to turn these shearers into sheep for my fleecing; or (2) provide evidence (of further swindling of these sheep).

4 Dismissed from the fraternity of thieves.

5 Grabbing a set of steps to hoist oneself over a fence.

6 A festive costume (because of flower garlands that suggest greater status).

7 Spring's tentative arrival in April. Shakespeare uses a similar phrase, in "summer's front" in Sonnet 102.7.

4.4.2: FLORA (TLN 1799)

Pandosto describes Fawnia (Perdita) thus: "Every day she went forth with her sheep to the field, keeping them with such care and diligence, as all men thought she was very painful, defending her face from the heat of the sun with no other vail, but with a garland made of bows and flowers: which attire became her so gallantly, as she seemed to be the goddess Flora herself for beauty" (see Appendix A1, p. 222).

In Roman mythology, Flora was a goddess of flowers and the season of spring. (Her Greek parallel was the nymph Chloris.) She was a harbinger of spring because of her association with other fertility goddesses. The festival to which she gives her name, the Floralia, held between 28 April and 3 May, celebrated the rebirth of all natural forces. Perdita's costume thus associates her with the rebirth of life, and also the imminent rebirth of the play from its wintry beginning.

The significance of this scene cannot be overstated. Critical commentary has connected it to the influence of the masque genre, in which personified abstract virtues such as grace, justice, and love overcome antimasque oppositions such as corruption and decay. Given the probable use of dancers from Jonson's court masque (see extended note, p. 154) to perform the satyrs' dance here, the scene has the quality of an interlude. Fergusson (298) describes it as a set-piece that pauses the story and interweaves the themes of "winter and spring, age and youth, guilt and innocence" in a series of vignettes that includes echoes of the previous scenes of Sicilia being overcome by the Ovidian power of Perdita as Flora, whose promise of rebirth stifles the potential return of winter in Polixenes's plotting against his son Florizel. Also see Frye ("Romance" 38): "The sense of 'great creating nature' as an integral part of what man's life ought to be comes to a focus in the sheep-shearing festival, a masque scene in which the dance of the twelve satyrs forms the antimasque." For Rabkin (118), the memory of Leontes and Polixenes's childhood of innocence remains firmly etched in these moments between Perdita and Florizel, the process of renewal always retaining a past that makes that renewal necessary.

FACING: Flore (c. 1690) by René Frémin (1672–1744). From Wikimedia Commons, <http://commons.wikimedia.org>.

Is as a meeting of the petty gods,
And you the queen on't.

PERDITA. Sir, my gracious lord,
To chide at your extremes° it not becomes me. *exaggerations*
Oh pardon that I name them! Your high self,
The gracious mark o'th' land,[1] you have obscured
With a swain's wearing, and me, poor lowly maid,
Most goddess-like pranked up![2] But that our feasts
In every mess have folly and the feeders
Digest it with a custom, I should blush
To see you so attired, swoon I think,
To show myself a glass.[3]

FLORIZEL. I bless the time
When my good falcon made her flight across
Thy father's ground.

PERDITA. Now Jove afford you cause![4]
To me the difference[5] forges dread; your greatness
Hath not been used to fear. Even now I tremble
To think your father by some accident
Should pass this way, as you did. Oh, the Fates!
How would he look to see his work, so noble,
Vilely bound up? What would he say? Or how
Should I, in these my borrowed flaunts,° behold *fineries*
The sternness of his presence?

FLORIZEL. Apprehend
Nothing but jollity.[6] The gods themselves,
Humbling their deities to love, have taken
The shapes of beasts upon them. Jupiter

---

1 Object of all attention.

2 Decked out (the implication is that Florizel is responsible not only for his own "swain's wearing" but also for Perdita's "extremes").

3 Were it not necessary that these sheep-shearing feasts (and attendant social groups) require a degree of foolishness and those who love such foolishness devour it, I would blush with embarrassment to see you dressed so rustically and faint to look at myself in a mirror.

4 Give you good reason to so bless this encounter.

5 The social disparity between Florizel's nobility and Perdita's peasant class.

6 Expect nothing but fun! (Florizel won't admit that Perdita voices real concerns in their ability to celebrate their love.)

Became a bull and bellowed; the green Neptune
A ram and bleated; and the fire-robed god
Golden Apollo, a poor humble swain,
As I seem now. Their transformations
Were never for a piece of beauty rarer,
Nor in a way so chaste, since my desires
Run not before mine honor, nor my lusts
Burn hotter than my faith.[1]

PERDITA. O but sir,
Your resolution cannot hold when 'tis
Opposed, as it must be, by th' power of the king.
One of these two must be necessities
Which then will speak that you must change this purpose,
Or I my life.[2]

FLORIZEL. Thou dearest Perdita,
With these forced thoughts I prithee darken not
The mirth o'th' feast, or I'll be thine, my fair,
Or not my father's. For I cannot be
Mine own nor anything to any if
I be not thine. To this I am most constant,
Though destiny say no. Be merry, gentle,° *dearest one*
Strangle° such thoughts as these with anything *keep in check*
That you behold the while. Your guests are coming.
Lift up your countenance as° it were the day *as if*
Of celebration of that nuptial which
We two have sworn shall come.

PERDITA. O Lady Fortune,
Stand you auspicious!

[*Enter the Old Shepherd, Clown, Mopsa, Dorcas, Servants, shepherds and shepherdesses, Polixenes and Camillo both disguised.*]

FLORIZEL. See, your guests approach.

---

1 The metamorphoses of the gods were for less worthy girls (pieces) than you, and their transformations had less chaste, less honorable intentions. ("My faith": my intent to marry you.)

2 Perdita suggests that one of two events will happen if Polixenes discovers Florizel and Perdita's love: either Florizel will be forced to abandon her, or she will lose her life.

Address yourself to entertain them sprightly,
And let's be red with mirth.

SHEPHERD. Fie,[1] daughter, when my old wife lived, upon
This day she was both pantler,[2] butler, cook,
Both dame and servant: welcomed all; served all;
Would sing her song, and dance her turn; now here
At upper end o'th' table; now, i'th' middle;
On his shoulder, and his;[3] her face o'fire
With labor, and the thing she took to quench it
She would to each one sip.[4] You are retired[5]
As if you were a feasted one and not
The hostess of the meeting. Pray you, bid
These unknown friends[6] to's welcome, for it is
A way to make us better friends, more known.
Come, quench your blushes and present yourself
That which you are, mistress o'th' feast. Come on,
And bid us welcome to your sheep-shearing,
As your good flock shall prosper.

PERDITA. [*To Polixenes*] Sir, welcome.
It is my father's will I should take on me
The hostess-ship o'th' day;
[*To Camillo*] You're welcome, sir.
Give me those flowers there, Dorcas. Reverend sirs,
For you, there's rosemary and rue; these keep
Seeming and savor all the winter long.
Grace and remembrance be to you both
And welcome to our shearing.

POLIXENES. Shepherdess,
A fair one are you. Well you fit our ages
With flowers of winter.

---

1 An expression of a mild annoyance.

2 Keeper of the pantry.

3 Serving from the head to the middle of the table, first at one shoulder and then at another.

4 And the drink taken to quench her thirst and put out the fire of exertion, she would offer in turn as a toast to each of her guests.

5 Withdrawn (i.e., the old shepherd instructs Perdita to step forward and begin hosting the feast as the recognized *mistress* of the feast).

6 Polixenes and Camillo in disguise.

PERDITA. Sir, the year growing ancient,[1]
Not yet on summer's death nor on the birth
Of trembling winter, the fairest flowers o'th' season
Are our carnations and streaked gillyvors,[2]
Which some call nature's bastards. Of that kind
Our rustic garden's barren, and I care not
To get slips° of them. *cuttings*

POLIXENES. Wherefore, gentle maiden,
Do you neglect them?

PERDITA. For I have heard it said
There is an art which in their piedness shares
With great creating nature.

POLIXENES. Say there be,
Yet nature is made better by no mean° *method*
But nature makes that mean. So over that art
Which you say adds to nature is an art
That nature makes; you see, sweet maid, we marry
A gentler scion to the wildest stock,
And make conceive a bark of baser kind
By bud of nobler race.[3] This is an art
Which does mend nature; change it rather, but
The art itself is nature.

PERDITA. So it is.

POLIXENES. Then make your garden rich in gillyvors,
And do not call them bastards.

PERDITA. I'll not put
The dibble[4] in earth to set one slip of them,
No more than, were I painted, I would wish
This youth should say 'twere well, and only therefore
Desire to breed by me. Here's flowers for you:
Hot lavender, mints, savory, marjoram,
The marigold that goes to bed wi'th' sun,
And with him rises, weeping. These are flowers

---

1 Sir, the year is half over (sheep-shearing occurs in early summer).

2 "Both cultivated forms of dianthus" (Orgel ed.).

3 We hybridize plants by cultivating a "gentler scion" to the "wildest stock" to create a "nobler" plant.

4 A pronged gardening tool for planting.

Of middle summer, and I think they are given
To men of middle age.[1] You're very welcome.

CAMILLO. I should leave grazing were I of your flock,
And only live by gazing.

PERDITA. Out, alas!
You'd be so lean that blasts of January
Would blow you through and through.
[*To Florizel*] Now, my fair'st friend,
I would I had some flowers o'th' spring that might
Become your time of day; [*To the sheperdesses*] and yours, and yours,
That wear upon your virgin branches yet
Your maidenheads growing[2]—O Proserpina,[3]
For the flowers now that frighted, thou let'st fall
From Dis's wagon! Daffodils,
That come before the swallow dares, and take
The winds of March with beauty; violets dim,
But sweeter than the lids of Juno's eyes
Or Cytherea's breath;[4] pale primroses
That die unmarried ere they can behold
Bright Phoebus in his strength,[5] a malady
Most incident to maids; bold oxlips, and
The crown imperial; lilies of all kinds,
The flower-de-luce being one. Oh, these I lack
To make you garlands of, and my sweet friend,
To strew him o'er and o'er.

FLORIZEL. What? like a corpse?

PERDITA. No, like a bank for love to lie and play on,
Not like a corpse; or if, not to be buried,
But quick,° and in mine arms. Come, take your flowers. *living*
Methinks I play as I have seen them do

1 Perdita corrects her previous distribution of winter flowers to old men with mature flowers reflective of men of middle age.

2 Perdita laments the lack of flowers for the virginal Mopsa and Dorcas ("virgin branches yet ... maidenheads growing").

3 See Appendix A2b.

4 Violets, not as striking as daffodils, remain more sweet and aromatic than Juno's eyes or Cytherea's (Venus's) breath.

5 Primroses fade before the peak of summer ("Bright Phoebus").

In Whitson pastorals. Sure this robe of mine
Does change my disposition.

FLORIZEL. What you do
Still betters what is done. When you speak, sweet,
I'd have you do it ever; when you sing,
I'd have you buy and sell so; so give alms,
Pray so, and for the ordering your affairs,
To sing them too. When you do dance, I wish you
A wave o'th' sea that you might ever do
Nothing but that; move still, still so,
And own no other function.[1] Each your doing,
So singular in each particular,
Crowns what you are doing in the present deeds,
That all your acts are queen's.

PERDITA. O Doricles,[2]
Your praises are too large, but that[3] your youth
And the true blood which peeps fairly through't
Do plainly give you out an unstained shepherd,
With wisdom I might fear, my Doricles,
You wooed me the false way.

FLORIZEL. I think you have
As little skill to fear as I have purpose
To put you to't. But come, our dance I pray.
Your hand, my Perdita—so turtles[4] pair
That never mean to part.

PERDITA. I'll swear for 'em.

[*Perdita and Florizel dance.*]

POLIXENES. [*To Camillo*] This is the prettiest low-born lass that ever
Ran on the greensward.° Nothing she does or seems *grassy turf*
But smacks of something greater than herself,
Too noble for this place.

CAMILLO. He tells her something

---

1 Florizel's lines capture the movement of a wave that rises, pauses, before falling again, a movement that reflects for him Perdita's dance, a "function" that defines her perfection.

2 Florizel's pastoral name.

3 Were it not for the fact that.

4 Turtledoves (emblematic of love and faithfulness).

4.4.134: WHITSON PASTORALS (TLN 1949)

In this drawing, masque designer Inigo Jones presents the costume of Chloris for Queen Henrietta Maria, who performed the role of Chloris (Spring) in the 1631 masque *Chloridia* by Ben Jonson. This masque was written for Shrovetide, a carnival period preceding Lent. It depicts the transformation of Chloris into Flora, goddess of flowers, following the arrival of Zephyrus, the west wind, who drives out the antimasque of wintry discord. This design is presumably the conventional depiction of Spring captured by Perdita in the play.

In England, the term Whitsun (for White Sunday) signifies the day of Pentecost, the seventh Sunday after Easter. Celebrations might include church parades, in which girls dressed in white.

Queen Henrietta Maria as Chloris in 1631 masque *Chloridia*. © Devonshire Collection, Chatsworth. Reproduced by permission of Chatsworth Settlement Trustees.

That makes her blood look on't.[1] Good sooth, she is
The queen of curds and cream.

CLOWN. [*To musicians*] Come on! Strike up!

DORCAS. Mopsa must be your mistress? Marry, garlic to mend her kissing with!

MOPSA. Now, in good time!

CLOWN. Not a word, a word; we stand upon our manners.[2] Come, strike up!

Here a dance of shepherds and shepherdesses.

POLIXENES. Pray, good shepherd, what fair swain is this
Which dances with your daughter?

SHEPHERD. They call him Doricles and boasts himself
To have a worthy feeding.[3] But I have it
Upon his own report, and I believe it;
He looks like sooth.° He says he loves my daughter. *truthful*
I think so too; for never gazed the moon
Upon the water as he'll stand and read
As 'twere my daughter's eyes;[4] And to be plain,
I think there is not half a kiss to choose
Who loves another best.

POLIXENES. She dances featly.° *elegantly*

SHEPHERD. So she does anything, though I report it
That should be silent.[5] If young Doricles
Do light upon her, she shall bring him that
Which he not dreams of.[6]

Enter Servant.

SERVANT. O Master, if you did but hear the peddler at the door, you would never dance again after a tabor and pipe; no, the bagpipe could not move you. He sings several tunes, faster than you'll tell[7]

---

1 That makes her blush.

2 We act according to our principles.

3 Sizeable estate (measured in terms of pasturage).

4 Florizel studies Perdita's eyes with a devotion and constancy that rival the moon's fixed reflection in the water.

5 She does everything elegantly, if I, her father, may be so bold in proclaiming.

6 If Doricles is fortunate in marrying her, she will give him more than he can dream of (i.e., both good fortune and sizable dowry).

7 Count.

money. He utters them as he had eaten ballads,[1] and all men's ears grew[2] to his tunes.

CLOWN. He could never come better; he shall come in. I love a ballad but even too well, if it be doleful matter merrily set down, or a very pleasant thing indeed and sung lamentably.

SERVANT. He hath songs for man or woman of all sizes. No milliner[3] can so fit his customers with gloves. He has the prettiest love songs for maids, so without bawdry, which is strange, with such delicate burdens of dildos and fadings,[4] "Jump her and thump her." And where some stretch-mouthed rascal[5] would, as it were,

1 Autolycus must have eaten the broadside sheet music because of how fluent he is in singing the ballads.

2 All listeners were drawn to or enchanted by his melodies.

3 Haberdasher, tailor.

4 Obscene refrains, alluding to male sexual organs and orgasms.

5 Indecent scoundrel.

4.4.181: TABOR AND PIPE (TLN 2009)

The tabor and pipe were musical instruments commonly used in rustic entertainments. The tabor was a portable drum often used as a marching instrument. It had a wood shell with skin heads stretched over each end. A strap would attach the tabor to the player, who struck the tabor's end with a stick.

"The Minstrels of Beverley," woodcut of sixteenth-century English musicians. The figure on the left is playing a tabor and pipe. Printed in The Homes of Other Days (1871) by Thomas Wright. From The British Library.

mean mischief and break a foul gap into the matter, he makes the maid to answer, "Whoop, do me no harm, good man"; put's him off, slights him with "Whoop, do me no harm, good man."[1]

POLIXENES. This is a brave[2] fellow.

CLOWN. Believe me, thou talkst of an admirable conceited fellow. Has he any unbraided wares?[3]

SERVANT. He hath ribbons of all the colors i'th' rainbow; points,[4] more than all the lawyers in Bohemia can learnedly handle, though they come to him by th' gross; inkles, caddises, cambrics, lawn; why he sings 'em over as they were gods or goddesses. You would think a smock were a she-angel, he so chants to the sleeve-hand and the work about the square on't.

CLOWN. Prithee bring him in, and let him approach singing.

PERDITA. Forewarn him that he use no scurrilous words in's tunes.

[*Exit Servant.*]

CLOWN. You have of these peddlers that have more in them than you'd think, sister.

PERDITA. Ay, good brother, or go about[5] to think.

Enter Autolycus [in disguise] singing.

Lawn as white as driven snow,
Cypress black as ere was crow,
Gloves as sweet as damask roses,
Masks for faces and for noses,
Bugle-bracelet, necklace amber;
Perfume for a lady's chamber,
Golden coifs[6] and stomachers[7]
For my lads to give their dears;

---

1 Wherever the song's "rascal" might attempt an obscene interruption, the refrain allows the maid to cut short the interruption with "Whoop, do me no harm, good man" and disrupt the lyric's swerve towards potential obscenities.

2 Excellent (used ironically by Polixenes to describe Autolycus, the servant, or the song's "rascal").

3 Fresh, new items ("braided" indicates second-hand inventory).

4 Pieces of threaded lace (with a pun on legalistic points or articles).

5 Or desire to think—Perdita finds her brother's defense of Autolycus and peddlers dubious.

6 Small caps worn indoors as a headdress.

7 Stiff shields worn over the abdomen and under the doublet.

Pins and poking-sticks of steel,
What maids lack from head to heel.
Come buy of me, come. Come buy, come buy,
Buy, lads, or else your lasses cry. Come buy.

CLOWN. If I were not in love with Mopsa, thou shouldst take no money of me, but being enthralled as I am, it will also be the bondage of certain ribbons and gloves.[1]

MOPSA. I was promised them against[2] the feast, but they come not too late now.

DORCAS. He hath promised you more than that, or there be liars.

MOPSA. He hath paid you all he promised you. Maybe he has paid you more,[3] which will shame you to give him again.

CLOWN. Is there no manners left among maids? Will they wear their plackets where they should bear their faces? Is there not milking-time, when you are going to bed, or kiln-hole,[4] to whistle[5] of these secrets, but you must be tittle-tattling before all our guests? 'tis well they are whispering. Clamor[6] your tongues and not a word more.

MOPSA. I have done. Come, you promised me a tawdry-lace[7] and a pair of sweet gloves.

CLOWN. Have I not told thee how I was cozened[8] by the way and lost all my money?

AUTOLYCUS. And, indeed sir, there are cozeners abroad. Therefore, it behooves men to be wary.

CLOWN. Fear not, thou man. Thou shalt lose nothing here.

AUTOLYCUS. I hope so, sir, for I have about me many parcels of charge.[9]

CLOWN. What hast here? Ballads?

1 The bound and packaged ribbons and gloves (with wordplay on "bondage" and the previous "enthralled").

2 In time for.

3 Got you pregnant.

4 Kiln-hole, an opening in an oven large enough to allow gossipers to sit (also hinting sexually at female genitalia).

5 Whisper.

6 Stifle (*OED clamour v2*: An image from the muffling of ringing bells. This is the first citation).

7 Silken neckerchief.

8 Cheated.

9 Valuable goods.

MOPSA. Pray now, buy some. I love a ballet in print, a-life,[1] for then we are sure they are true.

AUTOLYCUS. Here's one to a very doleful tune, how a usurer's[2] wife was brought to bed of twenty money bags at a burden,[3] and how she longed to eat adder's heads and toads carbonadoed.[4]

MOPSA. Is it true, think you?

---

1 On my life (a mild oath).
2 Moneylender's.
3 In childbirth.
4 Scored with a knife and then grilled on coals.

4.4.231: PLACKETS (TLN 2067)

The Clown asks if these maids will reveal what should be secret, with a sexual pun on revealing their plackets.

The placket is a slit or opening in skirts or trousers that enables the wearer to put on or remove the piece of clothing. Given the location of the placket in the garment, the Clown's criticism of Mopsa and Dorcas indicates his disapproval at their lack of discretion in keeping their plackets open for ease of access. Autolycus, by implication, also has easy access.

Illustration of a placket, or opening, made in the upper part of a petticoat or skirt for convenience in putting it on. Source: Home and School Sewing by Frances Patton (New York: Newson and Company, 1901). From Wikimedia Commons, <http://commons.wikimedia.org>.

AUTOLYCUS. Very true, and but a month old.

DORCAS. Bless me from marrying a usurer!

AUTOLYCUS. Here's the midwife's name to't, one Mistress Taleporter,[1] and five or six honest wives that were present. Why should I carry lies abroad?

MOPSA. Pray you now, buy it.

CLOWN. Come on, lay it by, and let's first see more ballads. We'll buy the other things anon.

AUTOLYCUS. Here's another ballad of a fish that appeared upon the coast on Wednesday the fourscore of April[2] forty thousand fathom above water,[3] and sung this ballad against the hard hearts of maids. It was thought she was a woman and was turned into a cold fish,[4] for she would not exchange flesh[5] with one that loved her. The ballad is very pitiful and as true.

DORCAS. Is it true too, think you?

AUTOLYCUS. Five justices' hands at it, and witnesses more than my pack will hold.

CLOWN. Lay it by, too. Another.

AUTOLYCUS. This is a merry ballad, but a very pretty one.

MOPSA. Let's have some merry ones.

AUTOLYCUS. Why, this is a passing merry one, and goes to[6] the tune of "Two Maids Wooing a Man." There's scarce a maid westward but she sings it; 'tis in request I can tell you.

MOPSA. We can both sing it. If thou'lt bear a part thou shalt hear; 'tis in three parts.

DORCAS. We had the tune on't[7] a month ago.

AUTOLYCUS. I can bear my part. You must know 'tis my occupation. Have at it with you.

Song

Get you hence, for I must go

---

1 A tale-bearer or gossip.
2 The 80th of April.
3 45.5 miles above sea level.
4 A person lacking emotion.
5 Engage in sexual intercourse.
6 Is set to.
7 Of it.

AUTOLYCUS. Where it fits not you to know.
DORCAS. Whither?
MOPSA. Oh whither?
DORCAS. Whither?
MOPSA. It becomes thy oath full well,
Thou to me thy secrets tell.
DORCAS. Me too. Let me go thither.
MOPSA. Or thou goest to th' grange or mill,
DORCAS. If to either thou dost ill.
AUTOLYCUS. Neither.
DORCAS. What neither?
AUTOLYCUS. Neither.
DORCAS. Thou hast sworn my love to be.
MOPSA. Thou hast sworn it more to me.
Then whither goest? Say whither?[1]

CLOWN. We'll have this song out[2] anon by ourselves. My father and the gentlemen are in sad talk, and we'll not trouble them. Come, bring away thy pack after me. Wenches, I'll buy for you both. Peddler, let's have the first choice. Follow me, girls.

[*Exit Clown with Dorcas and Mopsa.*]

AUTOLYCUS. And you shall pay well for 'em.

Song

Will you buy any tape, or lace for your cape?
My dainty duck, my dear-a?
Any silk, any thread, any toys for your head
Of the newest, and finest, finest wear-a.
Come to the peddler, money's a meddler,[3]
That doth utter[4] all men's ware-a.

Exit.

[*Enter a Servant.*]

---

1 An appropriate song of two maids wooing a man, as Dorcas and Mopsa have demonstrated previously with their wooing of the Clown.

2 In its entirety.

3 Money is a means of exchanging (and interfering) that makes everything marketable.

4 Put up for transaction.

4.4.305: SALTIERS (TLN 2147)

This is evidently the servant's malapropism for satyrs—half-goat half-man creatures from Greek mythology that were associated with drunkenness and fertility. They were also representative of typical antimasque characters in court masques, as in this illustration by the celebrated architect and stage designer Inigo Jones. "Saltiers" might also suggest that he thinks they are leapers or dancers (*Fr.* saultiers = vaulters).

Satyrs © Devonshire Collection, Chatsworth. Reproduced by permission of Chatsworth Settlement Trustees.

SERVANT. [*To Shepherd*] Master, there is three carters,[1] three shepherds, three neatherds,[2] three swineherds that have made themselves all men of hair.[3] They call themselves saltiers, and they have a dance which the wenches say is a gallimaufry of gambols[4] because they are not in't; but they themselves are o'th' mind, if it be not too rough for some that know little but bowling,[5] it will please plentifully.

SHEPHERD. Away! We'll none on't. Here has been too much homely foolery already. I know, sir, we weary you.

POLIXENES. You weary those that refresh us. Pray, let's see these four threes[6] of herdsmen.

SERVANT. One three of them, by their own report, sir, hath danced before the king; and not the worst of the three but jumps twelve foot and a half by th' square.[7]

SHEPHERD. Leave your prating. Since these good men are pleased, let them come in, but quickly now.

SERVANT. Why, they stay at door, sir.

[*He brings in the dancers.*]
Here a dance of twelve satyrs.

POLIXENES. [*To the Old Shepherd*] O father, you'll know more of
that hereafter.[8]
[*To Camillo*] Is it not too far gone? 'tis time to part them.
He's simple and tells much.[9] [*To Florizel*] How now, fair
shepherd?
Your heart is full of something that does take
Your mind from feasting. Sooth, when I was young
And handed love,° as you do, I was wont *dealt in love*

---

1 Drivers of farm wagons.

2 Herders of cows.

3 Dressed in animal skins, perhaps suggestive of disorder and chaos.

4 A hodgepodge medley of dance leaps.

5 The more gentle sport of lawn bowling.

6 Twelve.

7 One group of three has danced before the king, and even the worst of these three jumps twelve and a half feet by the square (precisely).

8 Polixenes addresses the old shepherd (father) as they are engaged in a conversation captured in progress, a conversation apparently addressing the courtship of Florizel and Perdita.

9 Referring to the old shepherd who knowingly has transmitted information gleaned by Polixenes regarding Florizel and Perdita.

To load my she with knacks.[1] I would have ransacked
The peddler's silken treasury and have poured it
To her acceptance. You have let him go
And nothing marted° with him. If your lass *bargained*
Interpretation should abuse[2] and call this
Your lack of love or bounty, you were straited° *hard-pressed*
For a reply, at least, if you make a care
Of happy holding her.

FLORIZEL. Old sir, I know
She prizes not such trifles as these are.
The gifts she looks from me are packed and locked
Up in my heart, which I have given already,
But not delivered.[3] [*To Perdita*] Oh hear me breathe my life
Before this ancient sir, who, it should seem,
Hath sometime loved. I take thy hand, this hand,
As soft as dove's down, and as white as it,
Or Ethiopian's tooth, or the fanned snow that's bolted
By th' northern blasts twice o'er[4]—

POLIXENES. What follows this?
[*To Camillo*] How prettily th' young swain seems to wash
The hand was fair before! [*To Florizel*] I have put you out.
But to your protestation. Let me hear
What you profess.

FLORIZEL. Do, and be witness to't.

POLIXENES. And this my neighbor too?

FLORIZEL. And he, and more
Than he and men—the earth, the heavens, and all—
That were I crowned the most imperial monarch,
Thereof most worthy, were I the fairest youth
That ever made eye swerve, had force and knowledge
More than was ever man's, I would not prize them

---

1 Trifling tokens.

2 Should misconstrue this lack of trinket-buying.

3 Perdita values what I have packed and locked away in my heart, promised to her but as yet unbestowed.

4 Florizel's professed love for Perdita's purity is drawn from proverbial images of a dove's white down (Dent D573.2), the whiteness of an Ethiopian tooth, and "fanned" (drifted) snow blown by wind (Dent S591).

Without her love; for her, employ them all,
Commend them and condemn them to her service
Or to their own perdition.[1]

POLIXENES. Fairly offered.

CAMILLO. This shows a sound affection.

SHEPHERD. But, my daughter,
Say you the like to him?

PERDITA. I cannot speak
So well, nothing so well, no, nor mean better.
By th' pattern of mine own thoughts I cut out
The purity of his.[2]

SHEPHERD. Take hands, a bargain[3]—
And friends unknown, you shall bear witness to't;
I give my daughter to him and will make
Her portion equal his.

FLORIZEL. Oh, that must be
I'th' virtue of your daughter. One being dead,[4]
I shall have more than you can dream of yet,
Enough then for your wonder. But come on,
Contract us 'fore these witnesses.[5]

SHEPHERD. Come, your hand—
And daughter, yours.

POLIXENES. Soft, swain, awhile, beseech you.
Have you a father?

FLORIZEL. I have, but what of him?

POLIXENES. Knows he of this?

FLORIZEL. He neither does nor shall.

POLIXENES. Methinks a father

---

1 Commend them all (Florizel's conjectured "force and knowledge" were he "the most imperial monarch") only to Perdita's service or condemn them to their own destruction ("perdition," perhaps a wordplay on Perdita).

2 Perdita, using the imagery drawn from tailors, finds that the purity of Florizel's love for her is an exact pattern of her own love for him.

3 A proverbial expression (Dent H109.1) of a deal being made, in this case, the sheperd's intent for the betrothal of Perdita and Florizel in a love match.

4 Florizel alludes to the wealth he will inherit following his father's death: More than you can dream of now and so much that will amaze you when I have it.

5 Either a promise of marriage or a formal declaration of marriage to be witnessed by those in attendance.

Is at the nuptial of his son a guest
That best becomes the table. Pray you once more,
Is not your father grown incapable
Of reasonable affairs? Is he not stupid
With age and altering rheums?[1] Can he speak? Hear?
Know man from man? Dispute his own estate?
Lies he not bed-rid, and again does nothing
But what he did being childish?

FLORIZEL. No, good sir.
He has his health and ampler strength indeed
Than most have of his age.

POLIXENES. By my white beard,[2]
You offer him, if this be so, a wrong
Something unfilial. Reason,[3] my son,
Should choose himself a wife, but as good reason
The father, all whose joy is nothing else
But fair posterity, should hold some counsel
In such a business.

FLORIZEL. I yield all this;
But for some other reasons, my grave sir,
Which 'tis not fit you know, I not acquaint
My father of this business.

POLIXENES. Let him know't.

FLORIZEL. He shall not.

POLIXENES. Prithee let him.

FLORIZEL. No, he must not.

SHEPHERD. Let him, my son; he shall not need to grieve
At knowing of thy choice.

FLORIZEL. Come, come, he must not.
Mark our contract.[4]

POLIXENES. [*Removing disguise*] Mark your divorce, young sir,
Whom son I dare not call. Thou art too base
To be acknowledged. Thou a scepter's heir

1 Degenerative condition brought on by injurious humors.
2 Polixenes's disguise.
3 It is reasonable that.
4 Witness our marriage contract.

That thus affects a sheep-hook?[1] Thou, old traitor,
I am sorry that by hanging thee I can
But shorten thy life one week. And thou, fresh piece
Of excellent witchcraft, whom of force must know
The royal fool thou cop'st[2] with—

SHEPHERD. Oh, my heart!

POLIXENES. I'll have thy beauty scratched with briers and made
More homely than thy state. [*To Florizel*] For thee, fond[3] boy,
If I may ever know thou dost but sigh,
That thou no more shalt never see this knack,[4] as never
I mean thou shalt, we'll bar thee from succession,
Not hold thee of our blood, no, not our kin,
Far than Deucalion off.[5] Mark thou my words.
Follow us to the court. [*To Old Shepherd*] Thou, churl,° for this time,
peasant OED (n4,5)
Though full of our displeasure, yet we free thee
From the dead blow of it. [*To Perdita*] And you, enchantment,
Worthy enough a herdsman—yea, him too
That makes himself but for our honor therein
Unworthy thee[6]—if ever henceforth thou
These rural latches to his entrance open,
Or hoop his body more with thy embraces,
I will devise a death as cruel for thee
As thou art tender to't.[7]

Exit.

PERDITA. Even here undone!
I was not much afeared, for once or twice
I was about to speak and tell him plainly,

---

1 Polixenes's anger stems in part from Florizel's disguising of his own royal nature with the pastoral garb of a shepherd.

2 Are involved with.

3 Foolish.

4 Deceitful toy.

5 Farther in the past than Deucalion was. (In Greek mythology, Deucalion and his wife Pyrrha were the only human survivors of a great flood.)

6 Polixenes characterizes Perdita as worthy enough for her social class, that of the herdsman, and more than worthy for a disgraced Florizel, who were it not for his inherited nobility, would be unworthy of her.

7 Comparable to your tenderness in enduring it.

The selfsame sun that shines upon his court
Hides not his visage from our cottage, but
Looks on alike.[1] [*To Florizel*] Wilt please you, sir, be gone?
I told you what would come of this. Beseech you,
Of your own state take care. This dream of mine,
Being now awake, I'll queen it no inch farther,[2]
But milk my ewes and weep.

CAMILLO. Why, how now, father?
Speak ere thou diest.

SHEPHERD. I cannot speak, nor think,
Nor dare to know that which I know. [*To Florizel*] O sir,
You have undone a man of fourscore-three,° *83 years of age*
That thought to fill his grave in quiet, yea,
To die upon the bed my father died,
To lie close by his honest bones; but now
Some hangman must put on my shroud and lay me
Where no priest shovels in dust. [*To Perdita*] O, cursèd wretch,
That knew'st this was the prince and wouldst adventure[3]
To mingle faith with him! Undone, undone!
If I might die within this hour, I have lived
To die when I desire.

Exit.

FLORIZEL. [*To Camillo*] Why look you so upon me?
I am but sorry, not afeared;° delayed, *afraid*
But nothing altered. What I was, I am,
More straining on for plucking back, not following
My leash unwillingly.[4]

CAMILLO. Gracious, my lord,
You know your father's temper; at this time
He will allow no speech, which I do guess
You do not purpose to him, and as hardly

---

1 See Ecclesiasticus 42:16: "The sunne that shineth, looketh vpon all thinges." Ecclesiasticus was one of the Apocrypha, books which are no longer included in English bibles.

2 This illusion of queenship (being queen of the sheep-shearing) is now dashed, and I will stop pretending to be a queen.

3 Dare.

4 Florizel compares himself to a hound straining on the master's lease that pulls him back, refusing to be led away by his father's commands.

Will he endure your sight as yet, I fear.
Then, till the fury of his highness settle,
Come not before him.

FLORIZEL. I not purpose it.
I think, Camillo?[1]

CAMILLO. [*removing disguise*] Even he, my lord.

PERDITA. How often have I told you 'twould be thus?
How often said my dignity would last
But till 'twere known?

FLORIZEL. It cannot fail but by
The violation of my faith, and then
Let nature crush the sides o'th' earth together
And mar the seeds within. Lift up thy looks.
From my succession wipe me, father! I
Am heir to my affection.[2]

CAMILLO. Be advised.

FLORIZEL. I am, and by my fancy; if my reason
Will thereto be obedient, I have reason.
If not, my senses, better pleased with madness,
Do bid it welcome.[3]

CAMILLO. This is desperate, sir.

FLORIZEL. So call it, but it does fulfill my vow.
I needs must think it honesty. Camillo,
Not for Bohemia, nor the pomp that may
Be thereat gleaned, for all the sun sees or
The close earth wombs or the profound seas hides
In unknown fathoms, will I break my oath
To this my fair beloved.[4] Therefore, I pray you,

---

1 Florizel now recognizes Camillo in disguise.

2 Florizel threatens the end of the world and of Nature's creative powers should he violate his oath of love to Perdita. An allusion to Jeremiah (Geneva) 6:22.

3 Florizel suggests that fancy (i.e., imaginative power) governs his reason, a violation of the traditional hierarchy in which reason responsibly holds irrational behavior in check. Florizel believes that his love is properly the governor of his reason, and if it fails in this, he prefers the madness of love to a reason without Perdita.

4 Florizel reiterates the integrity of his "vow" to marry Perdita: not even the grandeur of his noble title to Bohemia nor the expanse of the sun's rays nor the earth's fertility and the sea's unmeasured depths can change his desire to marry her. Florizel's love is not circumscribed by Time.

As you have ever been my father's honored friend,
When he shall miss me, as in faith I mean not
To see him any more, cast your good counsels
Upon his passion. Let myself and Fortune
Tug[1] for the time to come. This you may know
And so deliver: I am put to sea
With her who here I cannot hold on shore,
And most opportune to her need, I have
A vessel rides fast by, but not prepared
For this design. What course I mean to hold
Shall nothing benefit your knowledge nor
Concern me the reporting.

CAMILLO. O my lord,
I would your spirit were easier for advice
Or stronger for your need.[2]

FLORIZEL. Hark, Perdita—
[*To Camillo*] I'll hear you by and by.
[*Florizel and Perdita walk together.*]

CAMILLO. He's irremoveable,° *adamant*
Resolved for flight. Now were I happy if
His going I could frame to serve my turn,
Save him from danger, do him love and honor,
Purchase the sight again of dear Sicilia,
And that unhappy king, my master, whom
I so much thirst to see.

FLORIZEL. [*Florizel steps forward*] Now, good Camillo,
I am so fraught with curious business that
I leave out ceremony.[3]

CAMILLO. Sir, I think
You have heard of my poor services i'th' love
That I have borne your father?

FLORIZEL. Very nobly
Have you deserved. It is my father's music

1 Contend (allow me and chance to wage a battle for my future).

2 I wish you were more prone to take advice and be resolute about securing your needs.

3 I am so overwhelmed with complex ("curious") affairs that I have not been courteous (in interrupting our conversation to talk with Perdita).

To speak your deeds, not little of his care
To have them recompensed as thought on.[1]

CAMILLO. Well, my lord,
If you may please to think I love the king
And through him, what's nearest to him, which is
Your gracious self, embrace but my direction,
If your more ponderous and settled project
May suffer alteration.[2] On mine honor,
I'll point you where you shall have such receiving
As shall become your highness, where you may
Enjoy your mistress, from the whom I see
There's no disjunction to be made but by—
As heavens forfend—your ruin. Marry her,
And, with my best endeavors in your absence,
Your discontenting father strive to qualify
And bring him up to liking.[3]

FLORIZEL. How, Camillo,
May this, almost a miracle, be done,
That I may call thee something more than man,
And after that trust to thee?

CAMILLO. Have you thought on
A place whereto you'll go?

FLORIZEL. Not any yet.
But as th' unthought-on accident is guilty
To what we wildly do,[4] so we profess
Ourselves to be the slaves of chance and flies
Of every wind that blows.

CAMILLO. Then list to me!
This follows, if you will not change your purpose
But undergo this flight; make for Sicilia
And there present yourself and your fair princess,

---

1 My father sings your praises and strives to repay them as he dwells on them.

2 Accept my suggestion if you are willing to change the plans which you have formulated with great care (said ironically by Camillo).

3 And, striving in your absence, I will intercede with your discontented father and attempt to gain his approval of your proposed marriage to Perdita.

4 Because the accidental discovery by Polixenes of Florizel's and Perdita's mutual love ("unthought-on accident") is responsible for our present rashness.

For so I see she must be, 'fore Leontes
She shall be habited° as it becomes *dressed*
The partner of your bed. Methinks I see
Leontes opening his free arms and weeping
His welcomes forth; asks thee there, "Son, forgiveness"
As 'twere i'th' father's person; kisses the hands
Of your fresh princess; o'er and o'er divides him
'Twixt his unkindness and his kindness. Th' one
He chides to hell and bids the other grow
Faster than thought or time.[1]

FLORIZEL. Worthy Camillo,
What color for my visitation[2] shall I
Hold up before him?

CAMILLO. Sent by the king your father
To greet him, and to give him comforts. Sir,
The manner of your bearing towards him, with
What you, as from your father, shall deliver—
Things known betwixt us three[3]—I'll write you down,
The which shall point you forth at every sitting[4]
What you must say, that he shall not perceive
But that you have your father's bosom there
And speak his very heart.[5]

FLORIZEL. I am bound to you.
There is some sap[6] in this.

CAMILLO. A course more promising
Than a wild dedication of yourselves
To unpathed waters, undreamed shores; most certain
To miseries enough; no hope to help you,
But as you shake off one to take another;

---

1 Leontes divides his attention between his past unkindness (to Hermione and Polixenes), which he condemns, and his current kindness (to Florizel and Perdita), which he strives to multiply.

2 Pretext for my visit to Sicilia.

3 Among Leontes, Polixenes, and Camillo.

4 Guide you at every instance.

5 What things you can say that convey that you and your father are of like minds and share the same thoughts.

6 Substance, some promise of success; see *Antony and Cleopatra* 3.13.195 (TLN 2379), where Antony uses it in a similar sense.

Nothing so certain as your anchors, who
Do their best office if they can but stay you
Where you'll be loath to be.[1] Besides, you know
Prosperity's the very bond of love,
Whose fresh complexion and whose heart together
Affliction alters.[2]

PERDITA. One of these is true:
I think affliction may subdue the cheek
But not take in the mind.[3]

CAMILLO. Yea? Say you so?
There shall not at your father's house these seven years
Be born another such.[4]

FLORIZEL. My good Camillo,
She's as forward of her breeding as
She is i'th' rear our birth.[5]

CAMILLO. I cannot say 'tis pity
She lacks instructions, for she seems a mistress
To most that teach.

PERDITA. Your pardon, sir. For this,
I'll blush you thanks.[6]

FLORIZEL. My prettiest Perdita!
But oh, the thorns we stand upon! Camillo,
Preserver of my father—now of me—
The medicine of our house, how shall we do?
We are not furnished like Bohemia's son
Nor shall appear in Sicilia.

---

1 (I am giving you) a course of action more promising than your rash departure to lands unknown and ill-prepared for, which will promise you only an exchange of one misery for another, anchored in a place you don't want to be in.

2 Proverbial expression: "Prosperity gets friends but adversity tries them" (Dent P611, T301).

3 Perdita believes that affliction's effects may touch only the surface (the *cheek*) of a lover but not reach into the soul (mind) of one truly moved by "the very bond of love."

4 Camillo pays Perdita and her character high praise: Polixenes's house will not see born for a long time anyone with such wisdom as Perdita possesses.

5 She is as superior to her breeding (i.e., her humble origins) as her breeding is beneath ours.

6 Perdita appears to apologize for not thanking Camillo for this compliment; she offers a blush as a token of gratitude.

CAMILLO. My lord,
Fear none of this. I think you know my fortunes
Do all lie there. It shall be so my care
To have you royally appointed, as if
The scene you play were mine.[1] For instance, sir,
That you may know you shall not want, one word—
[*Camillo, Florizel, and Perdita talk together.*]

Enter Autolycus.

AUTOLYCUS. Ha, ha! What a fool honesty is![2] And trust, his sworn brother, a very simple gentleman. I have sold all my trumpery.[3] Not a counterfeit stone, not a ribbon, glass, pomander,[4] brooch, table-book, ballad, knife, tape, glove, shoe-tie, bracelet, horn-ring,[5] to keep my pack from fasting.[6] They throng who should buy first, as if my trinkets had been hallowed and brought a benediction to the buyer, by which means I saw whose purse was best in picture,[7] and what I saw, to my good use I remembered. My clown, who wants but something to be a reasonable man, grew so in love with the wenches' song that he would not stir his pettitoes[8] till he had both tune and words, which so drew the rest of the herd to me that all their other senses stuck in ears.[9] You might have pinched a placket, it was senseless; 'twas nothing to geld a codpiece of a purse.[10] I would have filed keys off that hung in chains. No hearing, no feeling, but my sir's song, and admiring the nothing of it. So that in this time of lethargy, I picked and

---

1 Equipped like royalty and performing the lines as if you were me.

2 A proverbial sentiment: "Honesty is a fool" (Dent H539.1).

3 Worthless merchandise.

4 Ornamental scented ball worn about the wrist or neck.

5 A ring made of horn.

6 Being empty.

7 Snyder (ed.): "best in prospect or appearance because of plumpness and position for picking."

8 Pig's feet or toes, Autolycus's contemptuous dismissal of the Clown.

9 To be so enchanted by what they heard that they became oblivious to their other senses.

10 Autolycus celebrates his pickpocket skills with sexual allusions (*placket* and *keys*). Dolan: "it was easy to cut off a purse hanging from the pouch men wore covering their genitals (i.e., to castrate men of their purses)." For "placket," see extended note, p. 151.

4.4.587: **CODPIECE (TLN 2487)**

Autolycus celebrates his pickpocket skills with sexual allusions (placket and codpiece). The codpiece (derived from the Middle English *cod*, meaning "scrotum") is typically a decorative pouch in men's trousers that accentuates the genital area. It was held closed by string ties or buttons. For placket, see extended note, p. 151.

Portrait of Archduke Rudolf, later the Holy Roman Emperor Rudolf II of Austria (1567), by Martino Rota (1520–83). From Wikimedia Commons, <http://commons.wikimedia.org>.

cut most of their festival purses, and had not the old man come in with a hubbub against his daughter and the king's son, and scared my choughs from the chaff,[1] I had not left a purse alive in the whole army.

[*Camillo, Florizel, and Perdita come forward.*]

CAMILLO. [*To Florizel and Perdita*] Nay, but my letters, by this means being there
So soon as you arrive, shall clear that doubt.

FLORIZEL. And those that you'll procure from King Leontes?

CAMILLO. Shall satisfy your father.

PERDITA. Happy be you!
All that you speak shows fair.

CAMILLO. [*Noticing Autolycus*] Who have we here?
We'll make an instrument of this; omit
Nothing may give us aid.

AUTOLYCUS. [*Aside*] If they have overheard me now—why, hanging!

CAMILLO. How now, good fellow! Why shak'st thou so?
Fear not, man, here's no harm intended to thee.

AUTOLYCUS. I am a poor fellow, sir.

CAMILLO. Why, be so still! Here's nobody will steal that from thee. Yet for the outside of thy poverty,[2] we must make an exchange. Therefore, discase[3] thee instantly—thou must think there's a necessity in't—and change garments with this gentleman. Though the penny-worth on his side be the worst, yet hold thee, there's some boot.[4] [*Gives him money.*]

AUTOLYCUS. I am a poor fellow, sir; [*Aside*] I know ye well enough.[5]

CAMILLO. Nay, prithee, dispatch[6]—the gentleman is half flayed[7] already.

AUTOLYCUS. Are you in earnest, sir? [*Aside*] I smell the trick on't.

---

1 Jackdaws (also rustics, *OED chuff n*1) from my worthless merchandise.

2 For the poor condition of your clothing.

3 Undress (used elsewhere only in *The Tempest* 5.1.85, TLN 2041).

4 Despite the fact that Florizel gets the worst end of the bargain (the clothes he gives to Autolycus are better than the ones he receives from him), here's additional money as a tip.

5 A conventional expression to signal the speaker's awareness of a villain. Here, the villain ironically voices it to express his awareness that something is suspicious in these proceedings.

6 Hurry.

7 Half undressed.

FLORIZEL. Dispatch, I prithee.

AUTOLYCUS. Indeed, I have had earnest,[1] but I cannot with conscience take it.

CAMILLO. Unbuckle, unbuckle.

[*Florizel and Autolycus exchange clothes.*]

Fortunate mistress—let my prophecy
Come home to ye!—you must retire yourself
Into some covert.° Take your sweetheart's hat *hiding place*
And pluck it o'er your brows, muffle your face,
Dismantle you, and—as you can—disliken
The truth of your own seeming that you may,
For I do fear eyes over, to shipboard
Get undescried.[2]

PERDITA. I see the play so lies
That I must bear a part.

CAMILLO. No remedy.
[*To Florizel*] Have you done there?

FLORIZEL. Should I now meet my father,
He would not call me son.

CAMILLO. Nay, you shall have no hat. [*Giving hat to Perdita*]
Come, lady, come. Farewell, my friend.

AUTOLYCUS. Adieu, sir.

FLORIZEL. O Perdita! What have we twain forgot?
Pray you a word.

[*The two talk together.*]

CAMILLO. What I do next shall be to tell the king
Of this escape and whither they are bound;
Wherein my hope is I shall so prevail
To force him after, in whose company
I shall review Sicilia, for whose sight
I have a woman's longing.

FLORIZEL. Fortune speed us!
Thus we set on, Camillo, to th' seaside.

CAMILLO. The swifter speed the better.

Exeunt [*Florizel, Perdita, and Camillo.*]

1 Financial compensation.

2 Disguise your true appearance, for there are spies about, and get aboard the ship unrecognized.

AUTOLYCUS. I understand the business; I hear it. To have an open ear, a quick eye, and a nimble hand is necessary for a cutpurse; a good nose is requisite also to smell out work for th' other senses. I see this is the time that the unjust man doth thrive. What an exchange had this been without boot? What a boot is here with this exchange![1] Sure the gods do this year connive at us, and we may do anything extempore.[2] The prince himself is about a piece of iniquity,[3] stealing away from his father with his clog[4] at his heels. If I thought it were a piece of honesty to acquaint the king withal, I would not do't. I hold it the more knavery to conceal it, and therein am I constant to my profession.

Enter Clown and Old Shepherd [*carrying a bundle and a box.*]

Aside, aside—here is more matter for a hot brain; every lane's end, every shop, church, session, hanging, yields a careful man work.[5]

CLOWN. See, see! What a man you are now! There is no other way but to tell the king she's a changeling,[6] and none of your flesh and blood.

SHEPHERD. Nay, but hear me—

CLOWN. Nay, but hear me!

SHEPHERD. Go to, then.

CLOWN. She being none of your flesh and blood, your flesh and blood has not offended the king, and so your flesh and blood is not to be punished by him. Show those things you found about her, those secret things, all but what she has with her. This being done, let the law go whistle,[7] I warrant you.

---

1 What exchange (i.e., of garments and of words) I have experienced, the former with extra payment and now additionally with this overheard conversation that provides unexpected compensation.

2 With no effort, at a spur of the moment (*OED v*3a).

3 Up to no good.

4 Obstacle (i.e., Perdita).

5 Here is opportunity for a clever mind: at every street, market, church, court-house, hanging, I can find more pockets to pick.

6 See 3.3.105, TLN 1558.

7 Proverbial expression, in this instance noting the futility of the law's case against the old shepherd (i.e., Perdita isn't his child, therefore he's not legally responsible for her offenses against the king).

SHEPHERD. I will tell the king all, every word, yea, and his son's pranks[1] too, who—I may say—is no honest man, neither to his father nor to me, to go about to make me the king's brother-in-law.

CLOWN. Indeed, brother-in-law was the farthest off you could have been to him, and then your blood had been the dearer by I know how much an ounce.

AUTOLYCUS. [*Aside*] Very wisely, puppies![2]

SHEPHERD. Well! Let us to the king. There is that in this fardel[3] will make him scratch his beard.

AUTOLYCUS. [*Aside*] I know not what impediment this complaint may be to the flight of my master.[4]

CLOWN. Pray heartily he be at palace.

AUTOLYCUS. [*Aside*] Though I am not naturally honest, I am so sometimes by chance. Let me pocket up my peddler's excrement.[5] [*Removing false beard*]
[*To the Clown and Shepherd*] How now, rustics! Whither are you bound?

SHEPHERD. To th' palace, an[6] it like your worship.

AUTOLYCUS. Your affairs there? What? With whom? The condition of that fardel? The place of your dwelling? Your names? Your ages? Of what having, breeding, and anything that is fitting to be known, discover![7]

CLOWN. We are but plain fellows, sir.

AUTOLYCUS. A lie! You are rough and hairy! Let me have no lying; it becomes none but tradesmen, and they often give us soldiers the lie, but we pay them for it with stamped coin, not stabbing steel; therefore, they do not give us the lie.

CLOWN. Your worship had like to have given us one if you had not taken yourself with the manner.

SHEPHERD. Are you a courtier, an't like you, sir?

---

1 Deception.

2 Very wise, foolish knaves (*OED puppy n*2a: a young, naive man).

3 Bundle (cloak, blanket, jewels found with the infant Perdita).

4 Florizel (Autolycus now envisions himself returning to Florizel's service; see 4.3.13–14, TLN 1681–82).

5 Autolycus's false beard.

6 If.

7 Reveal.

AUTOLYCUS. Whether it like me or no, I am a courtier. See'st thou not the air of the court in these enfoldings? Hath not my gait in it the measure of the court? Receives not thy nose court odor from me? Reflect I not on thy baseness court-contempt?[1] Think'st thou for that I insinuate to toze from thee thy business, I am therefore no courtier?[2] I am courtier cap-à-pie, and one that will either push on or pluck back thy business there, whereupon I command thee to open thy affair.

SHEPHERD. My business, sir, is to the king.

AUTOLYCUS. What advocate hast thou to him?

SHEPHERD. I know not, an't like you.[3]

CLOWN. "Advocate"'s the court word for a pheasant.[4] Say you have none.

SHEPHERD. None, sir. I have no pheasant, cock, nor hen.

AUTOLYCUS. How blessed are we that are not simple men! Yet nature might have made me as these are. Therefore I will not disdain.

CLOWN. This cannot be but a great courtier.

SHEPHERD. His garments are rich, but he wears them not handsomely.[5]

CLOWN. He seems to be the more noble in being fantastical.[6] A great man, I'll warrant. I know by the picking on's teeth.

AUTOLYCUS. The fardel there? What's i'th' fardel? Wherefore that box?[7]

SHEPHERD. Sir, there lies such secrets in this fardel and box which none must know but the king, and which he shall know within this hour, if I may come to th' speech of him.

AUTOLYCUS. Age, thou hast lost thy labor.[8]

SHEPHERD. Why, sir?

---

1 The courtly gait of my walk, my courtly aroma, the courtly contempt in how I regard you.

2 Do you think because I strive to tease out (*OED toze*) from you your business, that I am no courtier? I am a courtier head to toe (cap-à-pie).

3 If you please.

4 Pheasants as bribes or advocates for getting one's case heard in court.

5 As befits a courtier.

6 Nobly eccentric in his dress and behavior (fashionably picking his teeth).

7 Autolycus observes the infant clothing and the box (fardel) which were deposited with Perdita by Antigonus.

8 Old man, your efforts are wasted (proverbial, Tilley L9 and V5).

AUTOLYCUS. The king is not at the palace; he is gone aboard a new ship to purge melancholy and air himself; for if thou be'st capable of things serious, thou must know the king is full of grief.

SHEPHERD. So, 'tis said, sir, about his son that should have married a shepherd's daughter.

AUTOLYCUS. If that shepherd be not in handfast,[1] let him fly. The curses he shall have, the tortures he shall feel, will break the back of man, the heart of monster.[2]

CLOWN. Think you so, sir?

AUTOLYCUS. Not he alone shall suffer what wit can make heavy and vengeance bitter; but those that are germane to him, though removed fifty times, shall all come under the hangman,[3] which, though it be great pity, yet it is necessary. An old sheep-whistling rogue, a ram-tender,[4] to offer to have his daughter come into grace! Some say he shall be stoned, but that death is too soft for him, say I. Draw our throne into a sheepcote? All deaths are too few, the sharpest too easy.

CLOWN. Has the old man e'er a son, sir, do you hear, an't like you, sir?

AUTOLYCUS. He has a son, who shall be flayed alive; then 'nointed over with honey, set on the head of a wasp's nest; then stand till he be three quarters and a dram dead, then recovered again with aquavitae or some other hot infusion; then, raw as he is, and in the hottest day prognostication proclaims, shall he be set against a brick wall, the sun looking with a southward eye upon him,[5] where he is to behold him with flies blown to death. But what talk we of these traitorly-rascals, whose miseries are to be smiled at, their offenses being so capital? Tell me—for you seem to be

---

1 In custody.

2 The insensate feelings of an unnatural beast.

3 Autolycus pretends that all people related (germane) to the Shepherd and his son will face punishment for dragging the royal family down "into a sheepcote" (through Florizel marrying Perdita).

4 A scandalous shepherd, a keeper of sheep.

5 Autolycus's list of punishments (taken from Boccaccio's *Decameron*, c. 1350) are explicit and hyperbolic: the son shall have his skin stripped from him, placed on a wasp's nest, be covered in honey, and brought close to death; he'll then be resuscitated on the hottest day the almanac predicts and placed against a wall until stung to death.

honest plain men—what you have to the king;[1] being something gently considered,[2] I'll bring you where he is aboard, tender your persons to his presence, whisper him in your behalfs; and if it be in man besides the king to effect your suits, here is man shall do it.

CLOWN. [*To the Shepherd*] He seems to be of great authority. Close with him,[3] give him gold, and though authority be a stubborn bear, yet he is oft led by the nose with gold.[4] Show the inside of your purse to the outside of his hand, and no more ado. Remember "stoned," and "flayed alive."

SHEPHERD. An't please you, sir, to undertake the business for us, here is that gold I have. I'll make it as much more and leave this young man in pawn till I bring it you.

AUTOLYCUS. After I have done what I promised?

SHEPHERD. Ay, sir.

AUTOLYCUS. Well, give me the moiety.[5] [*To the Clown*] Are you a party in this business?

CLOWN. In some sort, sir, but though my case[6] be a pitiful one, I hope I shall not be flayed out of it.

AUTOLYCUS. Oh, that's the case of the shepherd's son! Hang him, he'll be made an example.

CLOWN. Comfort, good comfort! [*To the Shepherd*] We must to the king and show our strange sights. He must know 'tis none of your daughter, nor my sister.[7] We are gone else. Sir, I will give you as much as this old man does when the business is performed, and remain, as he says, your pawn till it be brought you.

AUTOLYCUS. I will trust you. Walk before toward the seaside. Go on the right hand. I will but look upon the hedge[8] and follow you.

CLOWN. We are blessed in this man, as I may say, even blessed.

---

1 Have to do with the king.

2 Being offered a sufficient bribe.

3 Accept his offer.

4 Proverbial: bribery is a successful way of leading even authority by the nose (Tilley N233).

5 Half the amount.

6 The Clown and Autolycus play with the notion of "case" as his very flesh, now threatened with flaying, and the "case" (situation) to be brought to Polixenes's attention. See also *Romeo and Juliet* 4.5.98–99 (TLN 2678–79).

7 Polixenes must be made aware that Perdita is not your daughter nor my sister.

8 A proverbial expression for urination, an excuse that Autolycus uses to allow the Clown and Shepherd to flee.

SHEPHERD. Let's before, as he bids us; he was provided to do us good.

[*Exeunt Clown and Shepherd.*]

AUTOLYCUS. If I had a mind to be honest, I see Fortune would not suffer me. She drops booties[1] in my mouth. I am courted now with a double occasion; gold and a means to do the prince my master good, which who knows how that may turn back to my advancement? I will bring these two moles,[2] these blind ones, aboard him. If he think it fit to shore them again, and that the complaint they have to the king concerns him nothing, let him call me rogue for being so far officious, for I am proof against that title and what shame else belongs to't.[3] To him will I present them; there may be matter in it.

Exit.

[5.1]

Enter Leontes, Cleomines, Dion, Paulina, and Servants.

CLEOMINES. Sir, you have done enough and have performed
A saint-like sorrow. No fault could you make
Which you have not redeemed, indeed, paid down
More penitence than done trespass.[4] At the last,
Do as the heavens have done, forget your evil;
With them, forgive yourself.[5]

LEONTES. Whilst I remember
Her and her virtues, I cannot forget
My blemishes in them,[6] and so still think of
The wrong I did myself, which was so much
That heirless it hath made my kingdom, and
Destroyed the sweet'st companion that e'er man
Bred his hopes out of. True?

1 Extra treasure.

2 Proverbially blind animals (Dent M1034).

3 For I am impervious to the insult in being called a rogue.

4 You have performed more penance than you would need for any sin that you have performed or would ever perform.

5 Proverbially, "forgive and forget" (Dent F597).

6 My faults regarding them (her virtues).

PAULINA. Too true, my lord.
If one by one, you wedded all the world,
Or from the all that are took something good
To make a perfect woman, she you killed
Would be unparalleled.

LEONTES. I think so. Killed?
She I killed? I did so, but thou strik'st me
Sorely to say I did;[1] it is as bitter
Upon thy tongue as in my thought. Now, good now,
Say so but seldom.

CLEOMINES. Not at all, good lady.
You might have spoken a thousand things that would
Have done the time more benefit and graced
Your kindness better.

PAULINA. You are one of those
Would have him wed again.

DION. If you would not so,
You pity not the state nor the remembrance
Of his most sovereign name, consider little[2]
What dangers by his highness fail of issue
May drop upon his kingdom and devour
Incertain lookers-on.[3] What were more holy
Than to rejoice the former queen is well?[4]
What holier than, for royalty's repair
For present comfort and for future good,
To bless the bed of majesty again
With a sweet fellow to't?

PAULINA. There is none worthy,
Respecting° her that's gone. Besides, the gods *compared with.*
Will have fulfilled their secret purposes.
For has not the divine Apollo said?

---

1 I am injured by your charges.

2 (You) give little thought to.

3 (You) fail to take into account how the *dangers* posed by the lack of a royal successor ("his highness fail of issue") will, like a predator, fall on his kingdom and devour apprehensive court observers ("Incertain lookers-on").

4 Hermione is in heaven. Proverbial: "He is well since he is in heaven" (Dent H347).

Is't not the tenor of his oracle
That King Leontes shall not have an heir
Till his lost child be found? Which that it shall
Is all as monstrous to our humane reason
As my Antigonus to break his grave
And come again to me, who, on my life,
Did perish with the infant.[1] 'Tis your counsel
My lord should to the heavens be contrary,
Oppose against their wills. [*To Leontes*] Care not for issue.
The crown will find an heir. Great Alexander
Left his to th' worthiest, so his successor
Was like to be the best.

LEONTES. Good Paulina,
Who hast the memory of Hermione,
I know, in honor. Oh, that ever I
Had squared me to° thy counsel! Then, even now, *followed*
I might have looked upon my queen's full eyes,
Have taken treasure from her lips—

PAULINA. And left them
More rich for what they yielded.

LEONTES. Thou speak'st truth!
No more such wives, therefore no wife. One worse
And better used would make her sainted spirit
Again possess her corpse, and on this stage,
Where we offenders now appear, soul-vexed,
And begin, "Why to me?"[2]

PAULINA. Had she such power,
She had just cause.

LEONTES. She had, and would incense me
To murder her I married.[3]

PAULINA. I should so.
Were I the ghost that walked, I'd bid you mark

1 Paulina suggests that Leontes cannot think of marrying again until the oracle's prophecy comes true: his lost daughter returns. Paulina considers this as incredible (monstrous) a notion as the resurrection of Antigonus, whom she believes died with the infant.

2 Why abuse me in death (by remarrying) as you did in life (by mistrusting me)?

3 She would provoke me to murder my new wife.

Her eye and tell me for what dull part in't
You chose her. Then I'd shriek that even your ears
Should rift° to hear me, and the words that followed   *open*
Should be, "Remember mine."[1]

LEONTES. Stars, stars,
And all eyes else, dead coals! Fear thou no wife;
I'll have no wife, Paulina.

PAULINA. Will you swear
Never to marry but by my free leave?

LEONTES. Never, Paulina, so be blessed my spirit.

PAULINA. Then, good my lords, bear witness to his oath.

CLEOMINES. You tempt him over-much.[2]

PAULINA. Unless another
As like Hermione as is her picture,[3]
Affront[4] his eye—

CLEOMINES. Good madam, I have done.

PAULINA. Yet if my lord will marry—if you will, sir,
No remedy but you will—give me the office
To choose you a queen. She shall not be so young
As was your former, but she shall be such
As, walked your first queen's ghost, it should take joy
To see her in your arms.[5]

LEONTES. My true Paulina,
We shall not marry till thou bidd'st us.

PAULINA. That
Shall be when your first queen's again in breath.
Never till then.

Enter a [*Gentleman*].

GENTLEMAN. One that gives out himself Prince Florizel,
Son of Polixenes, with his princess—she

---

1 My eyes (elliptically referring to her eye, line 64). Leontes's next speech compares Hermione's "stars" to the dead coals of others' eyes.

2 You goad him more than you should.

3 Representation (such as painting, statue, or other artistic form).

4 Confront (*OED v*4.).

5 Countering her earlier criticism that Hermione's ghost would rebuke Leontes from ever marrying again, Paulina provides Leontes with the promise of a partner who would bring joy even to Hermione's ghost.

The fairest I have yet beheld—desires access
To your high presence.
LEONTES. What with him?[1] He comes not
Like to his father's greatness. His approach,
So out of circumstance and sudden, tells us
'Tis not a visitation framed,° but forced *planned*
By need and accident. What train?° *retinue*
GENTLEMAN. But few,
And those but mean.
LEONTES. His princess, say you, with him?
GENTLEMAN. Ay, the most peerless piece of earth,[2] I think,
That ere the sun shone bright on.
PAULINA. O Hermione,
As every present time doth boast itself
Above a better, gone, so must thy grave
Give way to what's seen now.[3] [*To the Gentleman*] Sir, you yourself
Have said and writ so, but your writing now
Is colder than that theme: she[4] had not been,
Nor was not to be equaled; thus your verse
Flowed with her beauty once. 'Tis shrewdly ebbed[5]
To say you have seen a better.
GENTLEMAN. Pardon, madam,
The one I have almost forgot—your pardon;
The other,[6] when she has obtained your eye,
Will have your tongue too. This is a creature,
Would she begin a sect, might quench the zeal
Of all professors else, make proselytes

---

1 Schanzer: "What are those with him?" Leontes goes on to question the absence of a royal retinue: "He comes not like to his father's greatness."

2 Proverbial expression (Dent P289.1). The sense is that Perdita is the epitome of human beauty.

3 Each age proclaims its superiority over the better times of the past, and you, Hermione, in your grave must give way to a new paragon.

4 Hermione and, in the subsequent lines, her beauty. Paulina questions the Gentleman's judgment ("his theme") in esteeming Perdita's beauty as greater than Hermione's, given his earlier celebration of Hermione's unparalleled reputation.

5 Hermione's beauty is appallingly diminished (as the tide ebbs in diminution) if the Gentleman claims that it is now surpassed.

6 Hermione ... the now disguised Perdita.

Of who she but bid follow.[1]

PAULINA. How? Not women![2]

GENTLEMAN. Women will love her that she is a woman
More worth than any man; men, that she is
The rarest of all women.

LEONTES. Go, Cleomines,
Yourself, assisted with your honored friends,
Bring them to our embracement. Still 'tis strange
He thus should steal upon us.

[*Exeunt Cleomines with others.*]

PAULINA. Had our prince,° [*Mamillius*]
Jewel of children, seen this hour, he had paired
Well with this lord. There was not full a month
Between their births.

LEONTES. Prithee no more; cease! thou know'st
He dies to me again when talked of. Sure
When I shall see this gentleman, thy speeches
Will bring me to consider that which may
Unfurnish me of reason.[3] They are come.

Enter Florizel, Perdita, Cleomines, and others.

Your mother was most true to wedlock, prince,
For she did print your royal father off,
Conceiving you.[4] Were I but twenty-one,
Your father's image is so hit° in you, [*perfectly made*]
His very air, that I should call you brother,
As I did him, and speak of something wildly
By us performed before. Most dearly welcome,
And your fair princess—goddess! Oh, alas!

1 Perdita's beauty befits that of a goddess of a new religion, which would attract those who currently profess other creeds.

2 Paulina's "women" is both exclamatory and ironic: women would not follow a creature more beautiful than they.

3 Your memories of Mamillius, paired with the arrival of one who could have been he, will only intensify my anguish over Mamillius's death and my responsibility for its occurrence.

4 Your mother, true to her marriage vows, made a perfect copy of your father, Polixenes, when she conceived you.

I lost a couple[1] that 'twixt heaven and earth
Might thus have stood, begetting wonder, as
You, gracious couple, do; and then I lost—
All mine own folly—the society,
Amity too of your brave father, whom,
Though bearing misery, I desire my life
Once more to look on him.

FLORIZEL. By his command
Have I here touched Sicilia, and from him
Give you all greetings that a king at friend° *in friendship*
Can send his brother; and but infirmity,
Which waits upon worn times[2] hath something seized
His wished ability, he had himself
The lands and waters 'twixt your throne and his
Measured° to look upon you, whom he loves— *traversed*
He bade me say so—more than all the scepters,
And those that bear them, living.

LEONTES. O my brother!
Good gentleman, the wrongs I have done thee stir
Afresh within me, and these thy offices,
So rarely kind,[3] are as interpreters
Of my behind-hand slackness.[4] Welcome hither,
As is the spring to th' earth. And hath he too[5]
Exposed this paragon to th' fearful usage
At least ungentle, of the dreadful Neptune,
To greet a man not worth her pains, much less
Th' adventure° of her person? *risk*

FLORIZEL. Good my Lord,
She came from Libya.

LEONTES. Where the warlike Smalus,[6]

---

1 Hermione and Mamillius.

2 Age, that has made him less mobile.

3 Exceptionally kind (i.e., Florizel's courtesies [offices] are generous).

4 Show up my own inadequate attention ("behind-hand slackness") to Polixenes.

5 Polixenes. Leontes asks, perhaps incredulously, whether Polixenes had indeed exposed Perdita ("this paragon") to Neptune's ocean; it is an echo of his own treatment of her.

6 A warlike figure Shakespeare derived from a misreading of Synalos, Punic governor, in Plutarch's *Dion*.

That noble honored lord, is feared and loved?
FLORIZEL. Most royal sir, from thence; from him whose daughter
His tears proclaimed his, parting with her. Thence,
A prosperous south-wind friendly, we have crossed
To execute the charge my father gave me
For visiting your Highness. My best train
I have from your Sicilian shores dismissed,
Who for Bohemia bend to signify
Not only my success in Libya, sir,
But my arrival and my wife's in safety
Here where we are.
LEONTES. The blessèd gods
Purge all infection from our air whilst you
Do climate° here! You have a holy father, *reside*
A graceful gentleman, against whose person,
So sacred as it is, I have done sin,
For which the heavens, taking angry note,
Have left me issueless. And your father's blessed,
As he from heaven merits it, with you,
Worthy his goodness. What might I have been
Might I a son and daughter[1] now have looked on,
Such goodly things as you?

Enter a Lord.

LORD. Most noble sir,
That which I shall report will bear no credit° *belief*
Were not the proof so nigh. Please you, great sir,
Bohemia greets you from himself by me,
Desires you to attach° his son, who has *arrest*
His dignity and duty both cast off,
Fled from his father, from his hopes, and with
A shepherd's daughter.
LEONTES. Where's Bohemia? Speak!
LORD. Here, in your city I now came from him.
I speak amazedly, and it becomes

1 Leontes refers to the children he has lost, Mamillius and Perdita.

My marvel and my message.[1] To your court
Whiles he was hastening—in the chase, it seems,
Of this fair couple—meets he on the way
The father of this seeming lady and
Her brother,[2] having both their country quitted
With this young prince.

FLORIZEL. Camillo has betrayed me,
Whose honor and whose honesty till now
Endured all weathers.

LORD. Lay't so to his charge.
He's with the king your father.

LEONTES. Who? Camillo?

LORD. Camillo, sir. I spake with him, who now
Has these poor men in question. Never saw I
Wretches so quake. They kneel, they kiss the earth,
Forswear themselves as often as they speak.
Bohemia stops his ears and threatens them
With diverse deaths in death.[3]

PERDITA. O my poor father!
The heaven sets spies upon us, will not have
Our contract celebrated.[4]

LEONTES. You are married?

FLORIZEL. We are not, sir, nor are we like to be.
The stars, I see, will kiss the valleys first;
The odds for high and low's alike.[5]

LEONTES. My lord,
Is this the daughter of a king?

FLORIZEL. She is,
When once she is my wife.

LEONTES. That "once," I see, by your good father's speed

---

1 With astonishment, yet an astonishment quite in keeping with my incredible message.

2 The Shepherd and the Clown.

3 Multiple tortures that lead to death.

4 Perdita sees the arrival of Polixenes and Camillo as a sign that the gods are repudiating her betrothal to Florizel.

5 Two images capture the unlikelihood for Florizel of his successful marriage: playing dice with someone who has loaded dice (high and low) and the likelihood of the stars and valleys ever converging.

Will come on very slowly. I am sorry,
Most sorry, you have broken from his liking,
Where you were tied in duty, and as sorry
Your choice is not so rich in worth[1] as beauty,
That you might well enjoy her.

FLORIZEL. Dear, look up,
Though Fortune, visible an enemy,[2]
Should chase us with my father, power no jot
Hath she to change our loves. Beseech you, sir,
Remember since you owed no more to time
Than I do now. With thought of such affections,
Step forth mine advocate.[3] At your request,
My father will grant precious things as trifles.

LEONTES. Would he do so, I'd beg your precious mistress,
Which he counts but a trifle.

PAULINA. Sir, my liege,
Your eye hath too much youth in't. Not a month
'Fore your queen died, she was more worth such gazes
Than what you look on now.

LEONTES. I thought of her,
Even in these looks I made. [*To Florizel*] But your petition
Is yet unanswered. I will to your father.
Your honor not o'erthrown by your desires,[4]
I am friend to them and you; upon which errand
I now go toward him. Therefore follow me,
And mark what way I make. Come, good my lord.

Exeunt.

1 Social rank.

2 Fortune, visibly embodied as our enemy.

3 Florizel asks Leontes to think back to his own youth and his youthful love and asks him to be his advocate before Polixenes.

4 Provided that you have behaved honorably with respect to your affection for Perdita.

[5.2]

Enter Autolycus and a Gentleman.

AUTOLYCUS. Beseech you, sir, were you present at this relation?[1]

FIRST GENTLEMAN. I was by at the opening of the fardel, heard the old shepherd deliver the manner how he found it; whereupon, after a little amazedness, we were all commanded out of the chamber. Only this, methought I heard the shepherd say he found the child.

AUTOLYCUS. I would most gladly know the issue of it.

FIRST GENTLEMAN. I make a broken delivery[2] of the business, but the changes I perceived in the King and Camillo were very notes of admiration; they seemed almost, with staring on one another, to tear the cases[3] of their eyes. There was speech in their dumbness, language in their very gesture. They looked as they had heard of a world ransomed, or one destroyed. A notable passion of wonder appeared in them, but the wisest beholder that knew no more but seeing could not say if th' importance were joy or sorrow. But in the extremity of the one, it must needs be.[4]

Enter another Gentleman [Ruggiero].

Here comes a gentleman that happily knows more. The news, Ruggiero?

SECOND GENTLEMAN. Nothing but bonfires, the oracle is fulfilled: the king's daughter is found! Such a deal of wonder is broken out within this hour that ballad makers cannot be able to express it.

Enter another Gentleman.

Here comes the Lady Paulina's steward. He can deliver you more. How goes it now, sir? This news which is called true is so like an

1 Narration.

2 Incomplete account.

3 The eyelids (i.e., they were staring so intently that their eyes almost popped out of their heads).

4 The King and Camillo were visibly moved by either joy at the return of the "dead" Perdita or sorrow over the loss of Hermione and Mamillius, there can be no mistaking that fact.

old tale, that the verity of it is in strong suspicion. Has the king found his heir?

THIRD GENTLEMAN. Most true, if ever truth were pregnant by circumstance.[1] That which you hear you'll swear you see; there is such unity in the proofs.[2] The mantle of Queen Hermione's, her jewel about the neck of it, the letters of Antigonus found with it, which they know to be his character;[3] the majesty of the creature in resemblance of the mother; the affection of nobleness, which nature shows above her breeding; and many other evidences proclaim her with all certainty to be the king's daughter. Did you see the meeting of the two kings?

SECOND GENTLEMAN. No.

THIRD GENTLEMAN. Then have you lost a sight which was to be seen, cannot be spoken of. There might you have beheld one joy crown another, so and in such manner that it seemed sorrow wept to take leave of them for their joy waded in tears.[4] There was casting up of eyes, holding up of hands, with countenance of such distraction that they were to be known by garment, not by favor. Our king, being ready to leap out of himself for joy[5] of his found daughter, as if that joy were now become a loss, cries, "Oh, thy mother, thy mother," then asks Bohemia forgiveness; then embraces his son-in-law; then again worries he his daughter with clipping[6] her. Now he thanks the old shepherd, which stands by like a weather-bitten conduit[7] of many kings' reigns. I never heard of such another encounter, which lames report to follow it, and undoes description to do it.

SECOND GENTLEMAN. What, pray you, became of Antigonus, that carried hence the child?

1 If ever truth could be confirmed by facts (with the image of "pregnancy" and the late arrival of Perdita to fulfill the play's ending).

2 Confirmation affirmed by the evidence (i.e., the blanket, the jewel, the letters).

3 Handwriting.

4 One joy was surpassed by yet another joy such that Sorrow itself wept in sorrow to leave the two kings wading in tears they had shed.

5 Proverbial: "He is ready to leap out of his skin for joy" (Tilley S507).

6 Embracing.

7 Weathered, weeping fountain.

THIRD GENTLEMAN. Like an old tale still, which will have matter to rehearse, though credit be asleep and not an ear open[1]—he was torn to pieces with a bear. This avouches the shepherd's son, who has not only his innocence, which seems much to justify him, but a handkerchief and rings of his that Paulina knows.

FIRST GENTLEMAN. What became of his bark and his followers?

THIRD GENTLEMAN. Wrecked the same instant of their master's death, and in the view of the shepherd, so that all the instruments which aided to expose the child were even then lost when it was found.[2] But oh, the noble combat that 'twixt joy and sorrow was fought in Paulina! She had one eye declined for the loss of her husband, another elevated that the oracle was fulfilled. She lifted the princess from the earth and so locks her in embracing, as if she would pin her to her heart, that she might no more be in danger of losing.

FIRST GENTLEMAN. The dignity of this act was worth the audience of kings and princes, for by such was it acted.[3]

THIRD GENTLEMAN. One of the prettiest touches of all, and that which angled for mine eyes—caught the water, though not the fish—was, when at the relation of the queen's death, with the manner how she came to't, bravely confessed and lamented by the king, how attentiveness wounded his daughter, till, from one sign of dolor to another, she did, with an "Alas!" I would fain say, bleed tears,[4] for I am sure my heart wept blood. Who was most marble there changed color. Some swooned, all sorrowed. If all the world could have seen't, the woe had been universal.

FIRST GENTLEMAN. Are they returned to the court?

THIRD GENTLEMAN. No. The princess, hearing of her mother's statue which is in the keeping of Paulina, a piece many year's in

---

1 The story of Antigonus is like an old tale that has much substance to be narrated but which none believes in the hearing.

2 All aboard who had brought Perdita to Bohemia and would bear witness to this died at sea the very moment Perdita was discovered.

3 The solemnity of this performed narrative was appropriately played out by royality, who were also the audience for this spectacle.

4 Perdita was so affected by her rapt attention to the account that she uttered an *alas* for each moment of experienced grief and seemed to bleed tears in a heartfelt display of grief.

doing and now newly performed[1] by that rare Italian master, Julio Romano, who—had he himself eternity and could put breath into his work—would beguile nature of her custom, so perfectly he is her ape.[2] He so near to Hermione hath done Hermione that they say one would speak to her and stand in hope of answer.

1 Completed.

2 Had he Nature's immortal breath, Romano could create art so vital that he could appropriate Nature's profession; this continues the debate of Perdita and Polixenes at 4.4.86–102 (TLN 1894–1916).

5.2.82: JULIO ROMANO (TLN 3105)

Julio Romano was a famous sixteenth-century artist, student of Raphael, known for his statues, paintings, and architecture. The presence of this historical artist in the play has raised a host of interpretations. Early editors such as Theobald (1733) and Warburton (1747) question Shakespeare's decision in anachronistically including a sixteenth-century painter as a creator of statues. It is assumed that Romano "performed" or painted the statue, a common sixteenth-century aesthetic practice of adding color to marble for the ruddiness of life (Smith 21). The expression that Romano "could put breath into his work" could be an Anglicized version of *videbat Juppiter corpora spirare*, Giorgio Vasari's epitaph celebrating Romano's art. Muir (*Sources* 7) conjectures Shakespeare's ability to read some Italian, thus a possible exposure to Vasari's *Lives*. Turner and Haas cite another possible source: the presence of Romano paintings in Whitehall which Shakespeare may have seen. Also see Barkan (57): "The most important link between Shakespeare's lines and Vasari's appears in the references to the whole combative spirit of the paragone (comparison).... To a reader of Vasari—especially one who had never seen any of the artist's work—Giulio Romano would appear as a great and godlike creator, master of many arts and worthy opponent of Nature herself as a creator.... Shakespeare required such a figure with whom he could credit the creation of a work of art that was ... both sculpted and painted and which finally proves to be not a work of art at all."

Thither, with all greediness of affection are they gone, and there they intend to sup.[1]

SECOND GENTLEMAN. I thought she had some great matter there in hand, for she hath privately twice or thrice a day ever since the death of Hermione, visited that removed house. Shall we thither and with our company piece[2] the rejoicing?

FIRST GENTLEMAN. Who would be thence that has the benefit of access?[3] Every wink of an eye, some new grace will be born.[4] Our absence makes us unthrifty to our knowledge.[5] Let's along.

[*Exeunt the Gentlemen.*]

AUTOLYCUS. Now, had I not the dash[6] of my former life in me, would preferment drop on my head. I brought the old man and his son aboard the prince,[7] told him I heard them talk of a fardel and I know not what, but he at that time overfond of the shepherd's daughter—so he then took her to be—who began to be much seasick and himself little better, extremity of weather continuing, this mystery remained undiscovered.[8] But 'tis all one to me, for had I been the finder-out of this secret, it would not have relished among my other discredits.[9]

Enter Shepherd and Clown [*ornately dressed.*]

Here come those I have done good to against my will and already appearing in the blossoms of their fortune.

SHEPHERD. Come, boy, I am past more children, but thy sons and daughters will be all gentlemen born.[10]

CLOWN. [*To Autolycus*] You are well met, sir. You denied to fight with me this other day because I was no gentleman born. See you these

1 They are so eager to satisfy their desires to see this statue that they have left for Paulina's remote house to feast on it with their eyes.

2 Add to.

3 Who wouldn't want to be there (to see this)?

4 Each blink of the eye will produce yet additional grace.

5 Remaining here deprives us of additional news.

6 Stain.

7 The prince's ship.

8 Autolycus told Florizel about the bundle and other details, but Florizel's emotional concern for Perdita and her seasickness, and his own queasiness, didn't allow for the full disclosure of this mystery.

9 The information about Perdita's true identity would not have redeemed me from my unsavory reputation as a thief.

10 The shepherd, now past the time for producing more children, believes that the Clown will be able to produce "gentlemen" because of his newfound nobility.

clothes? Say you see them not and think me still no gentleman born; you were best say these robes are not gentlemen born. Give me the lie, do,[1] and try whether I am not now a gentleman born.

AUTOLYCUS. I know you are now, sir, a gentleman born.

CLOWN. Ay, and have been so any time these four hours.

SHEPHERD. And so have I, boy.

CLOWN. So you have, but I was a gentleman born before my father, for the king's son took me by the hand and called me "brother"; and then the two kings called my father "brother" and then the prince my brother and the princess my sister called my father "father," and so we wept, and there was the first gentleman-like tears that ever we shed.

SHEPHERD. We may live, son, to shed many more.

CLOWN. Ay, or else 'twere hard luck being in so preposterous[2] estate as we are.

AUTOLYCUS. I humbly beseech you, sir, to pardon me all the faults I have committed to your worship, and to give me your good report to the prince my master.

SHEPHERD. Prithee, son, do, for we must be gentle now we are gentlemen.

CLOWN. Thou wilt amend thy life?

AUTOLYCUS. Ay, and it like[3] your good worship.

CLOWN. Give me thy hand. I will swear to the prince thou art as honest a true fellow as any is in Bohemia.

SHEPHERD. You may say it, but not swear it.

CLOWN. Not swear it, now I am a gentleman? Let boors and franklins[4] say it. I'll swear it.

SHEPHERD. How if it be false, son?

CLOWN. If it be ne'er so false, a true gentleman may swear it in the behalf of his friend. And I'll swear to the prince thou art a tall fellow of thy hands,[5] and that thou wilt not be drunk, but I know thou art no tall fellow of thy hands and that thou wilt be drunk,

---

1 The Clown returns Autolycus's earlier condescension with his own: call me a liar and see if I won't fight to defend my honor as a gentleman (reflected in the new robes he now wears).

2 The Clown's malapropism for prosperous.

3 If it please.

4 Peasants and yeoman (both socially beneath the rank of gentleman).

5 Valorous man, formidable in the use of arms.

but I'll swear it, and I would thou wouldst be a tall fellow of thy hands.

AUTOLYCUS. I will prove so, sir, to my power.[1]

CLOWN. Ay, by any means prove a tall fellow. If I do not wonder how thou dar'st venture to be drunk, not being a tall fellow, trust me not. Hark, the kings and princes, our kindred, are going to see the queen's picture. Come, follow us. We'll be thy good masters.

Exeunt.

[5.3]

Enter Leontes, Polixenes, Florizel, Perdita, Camillo, Paulina, Lords, etc.

LEONTES. O grave and good Paulina, the great comfort
That I have had of thee!

PAULINA. What, sovereign sir,
I did not well, I meant well. All my services
You have paid home,[2] but that you have vouchsafed
With your crowned brother and these your contracted
Heirs of your kingdoms, my poor house to visit,
It is a surplus of your grace which never
My life may last to answer.

LEONTES. O Paulina,
We honor you with trouble,[3] but we came
To see the statue of our queen. Your gallery
Have we passed through, not without much content
In many singularities,[4] but we saw not
That which my daughter came to look upon,
The statue of her mother.

PAULINA. As she lived peerless,
So her dead[5] likeness I do well believe
Excels whatever yet you looked upon,
Or hand of man hath done. Therefore I keep it
Lonely, apart. But here it is; prepare

1 Autolycus secretly pledges to be valiant with his hands (as a cutpurse and thief).

2 Repaid (proverbial; see Dent H535.1).

3 Our honor to you results in more trouble for you.

4 Rarities (*OED n*9b).

5 Precise (*OED dead a*31c); but also lifeless. Leontes will soon discover the validity of the first meaning and the falseness of the second.

To see the life as lively mocked[1] as ever
Still sleep mocked death.
[*Drawing aside curtain to reveal Hermione as a statue.*]
Behold, and say 'tis well.
I like your silence; it the more shows off
Your wonder, but yet speak. First you, my liege,
Comes it not something near?[2]

LEONTES. Her natural posture.
Chide me, dear stone, that I may say indeed
Thou art Hermione—or rather, thou art she
In thy not chiding, for she was as tender
As infancy and grace.[3] But yet, Paulina,
Hermione was not so much wrinkled, nothing
So aged as this seems.

POLIXENES. O, not by much.

PAULINA. So much the more our carver's excellence,
Which lets go by some sixteen years[4] and makes her
As she lived now.

LEONTES. As now she might have done,
So much to my good comfort as it is
Now piercing to my soul. O, thus she stood,
Even with such life of majesty—warm life,
As now it coldly stands—when first I wooed her.
I am ashamed; does not the stone rebuke me
For being more stone than it? O royal piece![5]
There's magic in thy majesty, which has
My evils conjured to remembrance and
From thy admiring daughter took the spirits,
Standing like stone with thee.

---

1 Imitated (as a quiet sleep imitates in form death itself). Proverbial (Dent S527).

2 Doesn't it resemble her closely?

3 The statue's resemblance to Hermione would be more exact if it accused him of his folly, which he deserves; at the same time, the statue's reticence to chide or scold is appropriate for Hermione, whose gentleness would not allow her to chide him.

4 Ages her sixteen years to capture her as she would be today.

5 Leontes wonders if his earlier hardness of feelings is being rebuked in the stony surface of the statue (the "royal piece"), whose surface brings to life the coldness he demonstrated towards Hermione in life.

PERDITA. And give me leave,
And do not say 'tis superstition° that *magic*
I kneel and then implore her blessing. Lady,
Dear Queen, that ended when I but began,
Give me that hand of yours to kiss.

PAULINA. O, patience!
The statue is but newly fixed;[1] the color's
Not dry.

CAMILLO. My Lord, your sorrow was too sore laid on,
Which sixteen winters cannot blow away,
So many summers dry; scarce any joy
Did ever so long live; no sorrow,
But killed itself much sooner.[2]

POLIXENES. Dear my brother,
Let him that was the cause of this have power
To take off so much grief from you as he
Will piece up[3] in himself.

PAULINA. Indeed, my lord,
If I had thought the sight of my poor image
Would thus have wrought you—for the stone is mine—
I'd not have showed it.

[*Moves to draw curtain.*]

LEONTES. Do not draw the curtain.

PAULINA. No longer shall you gaze on't, lest your fancy
May think anon it moves.

LEONTES. Let be, let be!
Would I were dead but that me thinks already—
What was he that did make it? See, my lord,
Would you not deem it breathed? And that those veins
Did verily bear blood?

POLIXENES. Masterly done.
The very life seems warm upon her lip.

LEONTES. The fixure of her eye has motion in't,

1 Set. Renaissance statues were frequently painted; thus, Paulina's excuse is not without reason, as the paint has not dried.
2 Camillo chides Leontes for allowing a sorrow to endure for sixteen years: no joy has lasted so long, and a reasonable sorrow would have been long over.
3 Assume, take on. Polixenes offers to take over Leontes's grief.

5.3.20: HERMIONE AS A STATUE (TLN 3208)

This painting captures both the celebrity of Elizabeth Farren, a popular eighteenth-century actress at the Drury Lane who played a range of Shakespearean characters (Juliet, Olivia in *Twelfth Night*, Portia in *Merchant of Venice*), and the popularity of Shakespearean productions as subjects for a genre of paintings known as conversational pieces. Johann Zoffany is equally important as a recorder of London society and the London stage, and particularly of David Garrick in variety of Shakespearean personas. In this painting, Zoffany, a founder member of the Royal Academy (in 1769), captures Hermione in the final scene before her statue moves before the astounded Leontes, Perdita, and other court members.

This transformation, which makes Paulina into a masque director who brings to life a statue as masque writers such as Jonson and Thomas Campion did, is accompanied by music to further enhance the effect. The gradual acceleration from here to Hermione's resurrection is powerfully choreographed. For Garber (*Ghost Writers* 139) it is the achievement of prosopopeia, the incarnation and speaking of an inanimate presence. Critics such as Frye ("Romance" 36) see Shakespeare modulating this effect from *Pericles* 5.1 and *Cymbeline* 4.2. Adelman (*Common Liar* 167), similarly: In the romances "the impossible is no longer a matter of poetic assertion: it actually takes place on the stage. When Hermione steps down from her pedestal ..., the impossible has been achieved.... No one would think of questioning Hermione about her perverse sadomasochistic desire to torment Leontes by remaining hidden until Perdita is found or about her living arrangements during that period; nor in fact do we take the rationalization that she has remained hidden very seriously. We know that she has come back to life. We do not, that is to say, seek to explain the impossible away. Instead, we gladly accept the impossibility for the sake of the symbolic pattern: she must remain hidden until her daughter has grown up and returned; only thus can the validity of the natural process of regeneration be asserted."

FACING: Edward Fisher, 1871. Miss Farren in the character of Hermione. Copyright

As we are mocked with art.
PAULINA. I'll draw the curtain.
My Lord's almost so far transported that
He'll think anon it lives.
LEONTES. O sweet Paulina,
Make me to think so twenty year together;
No settled senses of the world can match
The pleasure of that madness.[1] Let't alone.

---

1 No rationality offered by this world can compare with a madness that promotes the illusion of this statue's movement.

5.3.80: "FOR I WILL KISS HER" (TLN 3281)

Shakespeare draws on the myth of Pygmalion, the story of a goldsmith who fashions his ideal bride from ivory. According to Ovid, "The day of Venus's festival came, celebrated throughout Cyprus, and heifers, their curved horns gilded, fell, to the blow on their snowy neck. The incense was smoking, when Pygmalion, having made his offering, stood by the altar, and said, shyly: 'If you can grant all things, you gods, I wish as a bride to have ...' and not daring to say 'the girl of ivory' he said 'one like my ivory girl.' Golden Venus, for she herself was present at the festival, knew what the prayer meant, and as a sign of the gods' fondness for him, the flame flared three times, and shook its crown in the air. When he returned, he sought out the image of his girl, and leaning over the couch, kissed her. She felt warm: he pressed his lips to her again, and also touched her breast with his hand. The ivory yielded to his touch, and lost its hardness, altering under his fingers, as the bees' wax of Hymettus softens in the sun, and is moulded, under the thumb, into many forms, made usable by use. The lover is stupefied, and joyful, but uncertain, and afraid he is wrong, reaffirms the fulfilment of his wishes, with his hand, again, and again" (<http://ovid.lib.virginia.edu/trans/Metamorph10.htm>). See Appendix A2a, p. 251 ff., for a translation popular in Shakespeare's time.

FACING: "Pygmalion Adoring His Statue" by Jean Raoux (1677–1734). From Wikimedia Commons, <http://commons.wikimedia.org>.

PAULINA. I am sorry, sir, I have thus far stirred you, but
I could afflict you farther.
LEONTES. Do, Paulina.
For this affliction has a taste as sweet
As any cordial° comfort. Still methinks *medicinal*
There is an air comes from her. What fine chisel
Could ever yet cut breath? Let no man mock me,
For I will kiss her.
PAULINA. Good, my lord, forbear.
The ruddiness upon her lip is wet;
You'll mar it if you kiss it, stain your own

With oily painting. Shall I draw the curtain?
LEONTES. No, not these twenty years.
PERDITA. So long could I
Stand by, a looker-on.
PAULINA. Either forbear,
Quit presently the chapel, or resolve you
For more amazement; if you can behold it,
I'll make the statue move indeed, descend
And take you by the hand; but then you'll think—
Which I protest against—I am assisted
By wicked powers.
LEONTES. What you can make her do,
I am content to look on; what to speak,
I am content to hear, for 'tis as easy
To make her speak as move.
PAULINA. It is required
You do awake your faith; then, all stand still.
Or those that think it is unlawful business
I am about, let them depart.
LEONTES. Proceed.
No foot shall stir.
PAULINA. Music! Awake her! Strike!
[*Music sounds.*]
[*To Hermione*] 'Tis time! Descend! Be stone no more! Approach!
Strike all that look upon with marvel. Come!
I'll fill your grave up.[1] Stir! Nay, come away;
Bequeath to death your numbness, for from him
Dear life redeems you.
[*To Leontes*] You perceive she stirs.
[*Hermione descends.*]
Start not; her actions shall be holy as
You hear my spell is lawful; [*To Leontes*] do not shun her
Until you see her die again, for then
You kill her double.[2] Nay, present your hand.
When she was young, you wooed her; now, in age,

1 I revoke your death and figuratively fill in your grave.

2 Do not shun her again while she lives; if you do, you will be duplicating your previous treatment of her, killing her again prematurely.

Is she become the suitor?
LEONTES. O, she's warm!
If this be magic, let it be an art
Lawful as eating.
POLIXENES. She embraces him.
CAMILLO. She hangs about his neck—
If she pertain to life, let her speak too.
POLIXENES. Ay, and make it manifest where she has lived,
Or how stolen from the dead?
PAULINA. That she is living,
Were it but told you, should be hooted at
Like an old tale; but it appears she lives,
Though yet she speak not. Mark a little while.
[*To Perdita*] Please you to interpose, fair madam. Kneel,
And pray your mother's blessing. [*To Hermione*] Turn, good lady;
Our Perdita is found!
HERMIONE. You gods, look down,
And from your sacred vials pour your graces
Upon my daughter's head! Tell me, mine own,
Where hast thou been preserved? Where lived? How found
Thy father's court? For thou shalt hear that I,
Knowing by Paulina that the oracle
Gave hope thou wast in being, have preserved
Myself to see the issue.
PAULINA. There's time enough for that,
Lest they desire upon this push[1] to trouble
Your joys with like relation. Go together,
You precious winners all; your exultation
Partake to everyone. I, an old turtle,[2]
Will wing me to some withered bough, and there
My mate—that's never to be found again—
Lament, till I am lost.
LEONTES. O peace, Paulina!
Thou shouldst a husband take by my consent,

1 Critical moment.
2 Turtledove (emblematic of love and faithfulness).

As I by thine a wife. This is a match,
And made between's by vows. Thou hast found mine—
But how is to be questioned; for I saw her,
As I thought, dead, and have in vain said many
A prayer upon her grave. I'll not seek far,
For him I partly know his mind, to find thee
An honorable husband. Come, Camillo,
And take her by the hand, whose worth and honesty
Is richly noted, and here justified
By us, a pair of kings. Let's from this place.
[*To Hermione*] What? Look upon my brother. Both your pardons
That ere I put between your holy looks
My ill suspicion.[1] This your son-in-law,
And son unto the king, whom heavens directing,
Is troth-plight° to your daughter. Good Paulina, *betrothed*
Lead us from hence, where we may leisurely
Each one demand and answer to his part
Performed in this wide gap of time since first
We were dissevered. Hastily lead away.

Exeunt.

1 Leontes asks Hermione to look at Polixenes, and he asks pardons from both for his earlier unfounded suspicions.

APPENDIX A: SOURCES

1. ROBERT GREENE, *PANDOSTO* (1588)

[The principal source for *The Winter's Tale* is Robert Greene's *Pandosto*. It is rich in romantic details and settings, elements that Shakespeare appropriated and adjusted to fit his vision for the play.[1] Published in 1588, *Pandosto* went through at least 24 editions by 1740 and engendered a number of pastoral offshoots focusing on the young lovers, Dorastus and Fawnia. While the novel is considered a "romance," there is a strong cautionary quality to the story. Pandosto, King of Bohemia, and his queen, Bellaria, are victims of the goddess of inconstancy, Fortune, who "turned her wheel and darkened their bright sun of prosperity with the misty clouds of mishap and misery." This turn of the wheel propels the story's elements of mistrust, suspected adultery, fears of illegitimate births, and reunion of parent and child. Despite these broad features, Greene introduces pathos by having the grief-stricken queen die following the news of her son Garinter's death. The restoration of the daughter Fawnia to Pandosto's side fails to endure: Pandosto commits suicide following the onset of a deep melancholy prompted by his guilt.

Greene's moralizing theme can be found in his preface to the prose narrative: "Yea, [jealousy] is such a heavy enemy to that holy estate of matrimony, sowing between the married couples such deadly seeds of secret hatred, as love being once razed out by spiteful distrust, there oft ensueth bloody revenge, as this ensuing history manifest proveth." The text below has been modernized, with spelling and punctuation adjusted for sense and syntax. Source: internetshakespeare.uvic.ca/Annex/DraftTxt/Pandosto/pandosto.html.]

Pandosto: The Triumph of Time

Wherein is discovered by a pleasant history, that although by the means of sinister fortune, truth may be concealed yet by time in spite of fortune it is most manifestly revealed.

1 See Introduction, p. 17, for a table of corresponding characters in *Pandosto* and *The Winter's Tale*.

Pleasant for age to avoid drowsy thoughts, profitable for youth to eschew other wanton pastimes, and bringing to both a desired content.
Temporis filia veritas.[1]
By Robert Greene, Master of Arts in Cambridge.
Omne tulit punctum qui miscuit utile dulci.[2]

Among all the passions wherewith human minds are perplexed, there is none that so galleth with restless despite as the infectious soar of jealousy, for all other griefs are either to be appeased with sensible persuasions, to be cured with wholesome counsel, to be relieved in want, or by tract of time to be worn out—jealousy only excepted—which is so sauced with suspicious doubt and pinching mistrust, that whoso seeks by friendly counsel to raze out this hellish passion, it forthwith suspecteth that he giveth this advice to cover his own guiltiness. Yea, whoso is pained with this restless torment doubteth all, distrusteth himself, is always frozen with fear, and fired with suspicion, having that wherein consists all his joy, to be the breeder of his misery. Yea, it is such a heavy enemy to that holy estate of matrimony, sowing between the married couples such deadly seeds of secret hatred, as love being once razed out by spiteful distrust, there oft ensueth bloody revenge, as this ensuing history manifestly proveth: wherein Pandosto (furiously incensed by causeless jealousy) procured the death of his most loving and loyal wife, and his own endless sorrow and misery.

In the country of Bohemia there reigned a king called Pandosto, whose fortunate success in wars against his foes and bountiful courtesy towards his friends in peace, made him to be greatly feared and loved of all men. This Pandosto had to wife a lady called Bellaria, by birth royal, learned by education, fair by nature, by virtues famous, so that it was hard to judge whether her beauty, fortune, or virtue won the greatest commendations. These two linked together in perfect love, led their lives with such fortunate content that their subjects greatly rejoiced to see their quiet disposition. They had not been married long, but Fortune (willing to increase their happiness) lent them a son, so adorned with the gifts of nature, as the perfection of the child greatly augmented the love of the parents and the joys of their commons; insomuch that

1 Truth is the daughter of time (Latin).
2 He who has blended the useful and the sweet wins each point (Latin).

the Bohemians to show their inward joys by outward actions made bonfires and triumphs throughout all the kingdom, appointing jousts and tourneys for the honor of their young prince; whether resorted not only his nobles, but also divers[1] kings and princes which were his neighbors, willing to show their friendship they ought[2] to Pandosto, and to win fame and glory by their prowess and valor.

Pandosto, whose mind was fraught with princely liberality, entertained the kings, princes, and noblemen with such submiss[3] courtesy and magnifical bounty, that they all saw how willing he was to gratify their good wills, making a general feast for his subjects which continued by the space of twenty days, all which time the jousts and tourneys were kept to the great content both of the lords and ladies there present.

This solemn triumph being once ended, the assembly taking their leave of Pandosto and Bellaria, the young son (who was called Garinter) was nursed up in the house to the great joy and content of the parents. Fortune, envious of such happy success, willing to show some sign of her inconstancy, turned her wheel and darkened their bright sun of prosperity with the misty clouds of mishap and misery. For it so happened that Egistus, King of Sicilia, who in his youth had been brought up with Pandosto, desirous to show that neither tract of time nor distance of place could diminish their former friendship, provided a navy of ship, and sailed into Bohemia to visit his old friend and companion, who hearing of his arrival, went himself in person, and his wife Bellaria, accompanied with a great train of lords and ladies, to meet Egistus; and espying him, alighted from his horse, embraced him very lovingly, protesting that nothing in the world could have happened more acceptable to him than his coming, wishing his wife to welcome his old friend and acquaintance, who (to show how she liked him whom her husband loved) entertained him with such familiar courtesy, as Egistus perceived himself to be very well welcome.

After they had thus saluted and embraced each other, they mounted again on horseback and rode toward the city, devising and recounting how being children they had passed their youth in friendly pastimes, whereby the means of the citizens Egistus was received with triumphs and shows in such sort that he marveled how on so small a warning

1 Various.
2 Owed.
3 Submissive.

they could make such preparation. Passing the streets thus with such rare sights, they rode on to the palace, where Pandosto entertained Egistus and his Sicilians with such banqueting and sumptuous cheer, so royally as they all had cause to commend his princely liberality. Yea, the very basest slave that was known to come from Sicilia was used with such courtesy, that Egistus might easily perceive how both he and his were honored for his friend's sake. Bellaria (who in her time was the flower of courtesy), willing to show how unfeignedly she loved her husband by his friend's entertainment, used him likewise so familiarly that her countenance bewrayed[1] how her mind was affected towards him, oftentimes coming herself into his bedchamber to see that nothing should be amiss to mislike him.

This honest familiarity increased daily more and more betwixt them; for Bellaria, noting in Egistus a princely and bountiful mind adorned with sundry and excellent qualities, and Egistus, finding in her a virtuous and courteous disposition, there grew such a secret uniting of their affections, that the one could not well be without the company of th' other, insomuch that when Pandosto was busied with such urgent affairs that he could not be present with his friend Egistus, Bellaria would walk with him into the garden, where they two in private and pleasant devices would pass away the time to both their contents. This custom still continuing betwixt them, a certain melancholy passion entering the mind of Pandosto, drove him into sundry and doubtful thoughts. First, he called to mind the beauty of his wife Bellaria, the comeliness and bravery of his friend Egistus, thinking that love was above all laws, and therefore to be stayed with no law that it was hard to put fire and flax together without burning that their open pleasures might breed his secret displeasures. He considereth with himself that Egistus was a man and must needs love, that his wife was a woman and therefore subject to love, and that where fancy forced, friendship was of no force.

These and such like doubtful thoughts a long time smothering in his stomach began at last to kindle in his mind a secret mistrust, which increased by suspicion, grew at last to a flaming jealousy, that so tormented him as he could take no rest. He then began to measure all their actions and to misconstrue of their too private familiarity, judging that

1 Divulged.

it was not for honest affection but for disordinate fancy, so as he began to watch them more narrowly, to see if he could get any true or certain proof to confirm his doubtful suspicion.

While thus he noted their looks and gestures and suspected their thoughts and meanings, they two silly[1] souls who doubted nothing of this his treacherous intent frequented daily each other's company, which drove him into such a frantic passion that he began to bear a secret hate to Egistus, and a louring[2] countenance to Bellaria, who, marveling at such unaccustomed frowns, began to cast beyond the moon and to enter into thousand sundry thoughts, which way she should offend her husband; but finding in herself a clear conscience ceased to muse till such time as she might find fit opportunity to demand the cause of his dumps.

In the meantime Pandosto's mind was so far charged with jealousy that he no longer doubted, but was assured (as he thought) that his friend Egistus had entered a wrong point in his tables and so had played him false play;[3] whereupon desirous to revenge so great an injury, he thought best to dissemble the grudge with a fair and friendly countenance, and so under the shape of a friend to show him the trick of a foe. Devising with himself a long time how he might best put away Egistus without suspicion of treacherous murder concluded at last to poison him, which opinion pleasing his humor, he became resolute in his determination, and the better to bring the matter to pass, he called to him his cupbearer, with whom in secret he broke the matter, promising to him for the performance thereof, to give him 1000 crowns of yearly revenues.

His cupbearer, either being of a good conscience or willing for fashion's sake to deny such a bloody request, began with great reasons to persuade Pandosto from his determinate mischief, showing him what an offense murder was to the gods; how such unnatural actions did more displease the heavens than men and that causeless cruelty did seldom or never escape without revenge. He laid before his face that Egistus was his friend, a king, and one that was come into his kingdom to confirm a league of perpetual amity betwixt them, that he had and did show him a most friendly countenance; how Egistus was not

1 Sympathetic.

2 Scowling.

3 Backgammon metaphor for placing one's playing piece in the opponent's place.

only honored of his own people by obedience but also loved of the Bohemians for his courtesy; and that if he now should without any just or manifest cause poison him, it would not only be a great dishonor to his majesty, and a means to sow perpetual enmity between the Sicilians and the Bohemians; but also his own subjects would repine[1] at such treacherous cruelty.

These and such-like persuasions of Franion (for so was his cupbearer called) could no whit[2] prevail to dissuade him from his devilish enterprise, but remaining resolute in his determination, his fury so fired with rage, as it could not be appeased with reason. He began with bitter taunts to take up his man and to lay before him two baits—preferment and death, saying that if he would poison Egistus, he should advance him to high dignities. If he refused to do it of an obstinate mind, no torture should be too great to requite his disobedience. Franion, seeing that to persuade Pandosto any more was but to strive against the stream, consented as soon as opportunity would give him leave to dispatch Egistus, wherewith Pandosto remained somewhat satisfied, hoping now he should be fully revenged of such mistrusted injuries, intending also as soon as Egistus was dead to give his wife a sop of the same sauce, and so be rid of those which were the cause of his restless sorrow. While thus he lived in this hope, Franion, being secret in his chamber, began to meditate with himself in these terms:

> Ah Franion, treason is loved of many, but the traitor hated of all; unjust offenses may for a time escape without danger, but never without revenge. Thou art servant to a king and must obey at command, yet Franion, against law and conscience, it is not good to resist a tyrant with arms nor to please an unjust king with obedience. What shalt thou do? Folly refused gold, and frenzy preferment, wisdom seeketh after dignity, and counsel looketh for gain. Egistus is a stranger to thee and Pandosto thy sovereign. Thou hast little cause to respect the one and oughtest to have great care to obey the other. Think this Franion that a pound of gold is worth a ton of lead, great gifts are little Gods, and preferment to a mean man is a whetstone[3] to courage. There is nothing sweeter than promotion nor lighter than

1 Complain or protest.
2 Not a bit.
3 Sharpener.

> report; care not then though most count thee a traitor, so all call thee rich. Dignity (Franion) advanceth thy posterity, and evil report can hurt but thyself. Know this, where Eagles build, Falcons may prey; where Lions haunt, Foxes may steal. Kings are known to command, servants are blameless to consent; fear not thou then to lift at Egistus. Pandosto shall bear the burthen. Yea, but Franion, conscience is a worm that ever biteth but never ceaseth; that which is rubbed with the stone galactites[1] will never be hot. Flesh dipped in the sea Aegeum will never be sweet; the herb Tragion[2] being once bit with an asp never groweth, and conscience once stained with innocent blood is always tied to a guilty remorse. Prefer thy content before riches and a clear mind before dignity. So being poor, thou shalt have rich peace or else rich, thou shalt enjoy disquiet.

Franion having muttered out these or such like words, seeing either he must die with a clear mind or live with a spotted conscience; he was so cumbered with divers cogitations that he could take no rest, until at last he determined to break the matter to Egistus, but fearing that the king should either suspect or hear of such matters, he concealed the device till opportunity would permit him to reveal it. Lingering thus in doubtful fear, in an evening he went to Egistus's lodging and desirous to break with him of certain affairs that touched the king, after all were commanded out of the chamber. Franion made manifest the whole conspiracy, which Pandosto had devised against him, desiring Egistus not to accompt[3] him a traitor for bewraying his master's counsel, but to think that he did it for conscience, hoping that although his master inflamed with rage or incensed by some sinister reports or slanderous speeches, had imagined such causeless mischief; yet when time should pacify his anger and try those tale bearers but flattering Parasites, then he would count him as a faithful servant, that with such care had kept his master's credit.

Egistus had not fully heard Franion tell forth his tale, but a quaking fear possessed all his limbs, thinking that there was some treason wrought and that Franion did but shadow his craft with these false colors; wherefore he began to wax in choler and said that he doubted

1 White, precious stone.
2 A bitter herb.
3 Account.

not Pandosto, sith[1] he was his friend, and there had never as yet been any breach of amity. He had not sought to invade his lands to conspire with his enemies, to dissuade his subjects from their allegiance; but in word and thought he rested his at all times. He knew not therefore any cause that should move Pandosto to seek his death but suspected it to be a compacted knavery of the Bohemians to bring the King and him at odds.

Frànion, staying him in the midst of his talk, told him that to dally with Princes was with the swans to sing against their death,[2] and that if the Bohemians had intended any such secret mischief, it might have been better brought to pass than by revealing the conspiracy. Therefore his Majesty did ill to misconstrue of his good meaning, sith his intent was to hinder treason, not to become a traitor and to confirm his premises. If it please his Majesty to flee into Sicilia for the safeguard of his life, he would go with him; and if then he found not such a practice to be pretended, let his imagined treachery be repaid with most monstrous torments.

Egistus, hearing the solemn protestation of Franion, began to consider that in love and kingdoms neither faith nor law is to be respected; doubting that Pandosto thought by his death to destroy his men and with speedy war to invade Sicilia, these and such doubts thoroughly weighed, he gave great thanks to Franion, promising if he might with life return to Syracusa,[3] that he would create him a Duke in Sicilia, craving his counsel how he might escape out of the country. Franion, who having some small skill in Navigation, was well acquainted with the Ports and Havens and knew every danger in the Sea, joining in counsel with the Master of Egistus's Navy, rigged all their ships and setting them afloat let them lie at anchor to be in the more readiness when time and wind should serve.

Fortune, although blind yet by chance, favoring this just cause, sent them within six days a good gale of wind, which Franion seeing fit for their purpose to put Pandosto out of suspicion the night before they should sail; he went to him and promised that the next day he would

1 Since.

2 It was a common belief, dating back at least to ancient Greece, that swans sing before they die. Hence the modern term "swan song," meaning final performance or gesture.

3 A province in Sicilia.

put the device in practice, for he had got such a forcible poison as the very smell thereof should procure sudden death. Pandosto was joyful to hear this good news and thought every hour a day till he might be glutted with bloody revenge, but his suit had but ill success; for Egistus, fearing that delay might breed danger and willing that the grass should not be cut from under his feet, taking bag and baggage with the help of Franion, conveyed himself and his men out of a postern[1] gate of the city so secretly and speedily that without any suspicion they got to the seashore, where, with many a bitter curse taking their leave of Bohemia, they went aboard; weighing their anchors and hoisting sail, they passed as fast as wind and sea would permit towards Sicilia, Egistus being a joyful man that he had safely passed such treacherous perils.

But as they were quietly floating on the sea, so Pandosto and his Citizens were in an uproar; for seeing that the Sicilians without taking their leave were fled away by night, the Bohemians feared some treason, and the King thought that without question his suspicion was true, seeing his cupbearer had bewrayed the sum of his secret pretence. Whereupon he began to imagine that Franion and his wife Bellaria had conspired with Egistus and that the fervent affection she bear[2] him was the only means of his secret departure, insomuch that incensed with rage, he commanded that his wife should be carried to strait[3] prison until they heard further of his pleasure. The guard, unwilling to lay their hands on such a virtuous Princess and yet fearing the king's fury, went very sorrowfully to fulfill their charge.

Coming to the Queen's lodging, they found her playing with her young son Garinter, unto whom with tears doing the message, Bellaria astonished at such a hard censure and finding her clear conscience a sure advocate to plead in her case, went to the prison most willingly; where with sighs and tears she past away the time till she might come to her trial.

But Pandosto, whose reason was suppressed with rage and whose unbridled folly was incensed with fury, seeing Franion had bewrayed his secrets and that Egistus might well be railed on but not revenged, determined to wreak all his wrath on poor Bellaria. He therefore caused a general proclamation to be made through all his Realm that

1 Back entrance.
2 Bore.
3 Confined, strict.

the Queen and Egistus had by the help of Franion not only committed most incestuous adultery, but also had conspired the King's death; whereupon the Traitor Franion was fled away with Egistus, and Bellaria was most justly imprisoned.

This Proclamation being once blazed through the country, although the virtuous disposition of the Queen did half discredit the contents, yet the sudden and speedy passage of Egistus and the secret departure of Franion induced them (the circumstances thoroughly considered) to think that both the Proclamation was true and the King greatly injured; yet they pitied her case, as sorrowful that so good a Lady should be crossed with such adverse fortune. But the King, whose restless rage would admit no pity, thought that although he might sufficiently requite his wife's falsehood with the bitter plague of pinching penury, yet his mind should never be glutted with revenge, till he might have fit time and opportunity to repay the treachery [of] Egistus with a fatal injury.

But a curst Cow hath oft times short horns and a willing mind but a weak arm; for Pandosto, although he felt that revenge was a spur to war and that envy always proffereth steel, yet he saw that Egistus was not only of great puissance and prowess to withstand him, but also had many Kings of his alliance to aid him if need should serve. For he [was] married to the Emperor's daughter of Russia. These and the like considerations something daunted Pandosto his courage, so that he was content rather to put up a manifest injury with peace than hunt after revenge [with] dishonor and loss, determining since Egistus had escaped scot free, that Bellaria should pay for all at an unreasonable price.

Remaining thus resolute in his determination, Bellaria continuing still in prison and hearing the contents of the Proclamation, knowing that her mind was never touched with such affection, nor that Egistus had ever offered her such discourtesy, would gladly have come to her answer, that both she might have known her unjust accusers and cleared herself of that guiltless crime. But Pandosto was so inflamed with rage and infected with Jealousy as he would not vouchsafe[1] to hear her nor admit any just excuse, so that she was fain[2] to make a virtue of her need, and with patience to bear these heavy injuries.

1 Allow himself.

2 Willing, eager.

As thus she lay crossed with calamities (a great cause to increase her grief) she found herself quick with child, which as soon as she felt stir in her body, she burst forth into bitter tears, exclaiming against fortune in these terms:

> Alas, Bellaria, how unfortunate art thou because fortunate; better hadst thou been born a beggar than a Prince; so shouldest thou have bridled[1] fortune with want, where now she sporteth herself with thy plenty. Ah happy life, where poor thoughts and mean desires live in secure content, not fearing fortune because too low for fortune! Thou seest now, Bellaria, that care is a companion to honor, not to poverty, that high cedars are frushed[2] with tempests, when low shrubs are not touched with the wind. Precious diamonds are cut with the file, when despised pebbles lie safe in the sand; Delphos is sought to by princes, not beggars;[3] and Fortune's altars smoke with king's presents, not with poor men's gifts. Happy are such, Bellaria, that curse fortune for contempt, not fear, and may wish they were, not sorrow they have been. Thou art a princess, Bellaria, and yet a prisoner, born to the one by dissent, assigned to the other by despite, accused without cause, and therefore oughtest to die without care; for patience is a shield against fortune, and a guiltless mind yielded not to sorrow. Ah, but infamy galleth unto death, and liveth after death. Report is plumed with time's feathers, and envy oftentimes soundeth fame's trumpet. Thy suspected adultery shall fly in the air, and thy known virtues shall lie hid in the earth. One mole staineth a whole face, and what is once spotted with Infamy can hardly be worn out with time. Die then Bellaria, Bellaria die, for if the gods should say thou art guiltless, yet envy would hear the gods, but never believe the gods. Ah hapless wretch! Cease these terms; desperate thoughts are fit for them that fear shame, not for such as hope for credit. Pandosto hath darkened thy fame, but shall never discredit thy virtues. Suspicion may enter a false action, but proof shall never put in his plea. Care not then for envy, sith report hath a blister on her tongue, and let sorrow bite them which offend, not touch thee that art faultless. But alas, poor soul!

1 Constrained.

2 Bruised.

3 I.e., it is the high-born, not low, who seek oracles to allay their worries.

> How canst thou but sorrow? Thou art with child, and by him that in stead of kind pity pincheth thee in cold prison.

And with that such gasping sighs so stopped her breath, that she could not utter any more words, but wringing her hands and gushing forth streams of tears, she passed away the time with bitter complaints.

The jailor, pitying these her heavy passions, thinking that if the king knew she were with child, he would somewhat appease his fury and release her from prison, went in all haste and certified Pandosto what the effect of Bellaria's complaint was; who no sooner heard the jailor say she was with child, but as one possessed with a frenzy he rose up in a rage, swearing that she and the bastard brat she was withal should die, if the Gods themselves said no, thinking that surely by computation of time that Egistus and not he was father to the child. This suspicious thought galled afresh this half-healed sore, insomuch as he could take no rest until he might mitigate his choler with a just revenge, which happened presently after. For Bellaria was brought to bed of a fair and beautiful daughter, which no sooner Pandosto heard, but he determined that both Bellaria and the young infant should be burnt with fire.

His nobles, hearing of the king's cruel sentence, sought by persuasions to divert him from this bloody determination, laying before his face the innocency of the child and virtuous disposition of his wife; how she had continually loved and honored him so tenderly, that without due proof he could not nor ought not to appeach[1] her of that crime. And if she had faulted, yet it were more honorable to pardon with mercy than to punish with extremity, and more kingly to be commended of pity than accused of rigor. And as for the child, if he should punish it for the mother's offense, it were to strive against nature and justice; and that unnatural actions do more offend the gods than men; how causeless cruelty nor innocent blood never scapes without revenge. These and such like reasons could not appease his rage, but he rested resolute in this: that Bellaria being an adulteress, the child was a bastard, and he would not suffer that such an infamous brat should call him father. Yet at last (seeing his noblemen were importunate upon him) he was content to spare the child's life, and yet to put it to a worser death. For he found out this device that seeing (as he thought) it came by fortune,

1 Accuse.

so he would commit it to the charge of fortune, and therefore he caused a little cock-boat[1] to be provided, wherein he meant to put the babe, and then send it to the mercy of the seas and the destinies. From this his peers in no wise could persuade him, but that he sent presently two of his guard to fetch the child, who being come to the prison and with weeping tears recounting their master's message, Bellaria no sooner heard the rigorous resolution of her merciless husband, but she fell down in a sound,[2] so that all thought she had been dead, yet at last being come to herself, she cried and screeched out in this wise:

> Alas, sweet unfortunate babe, scarce born before envied by Fortune. Would the day of thy birth had been the term of thy life; then shouldest thou have made an end to care and prevented thy father's rigor. Thy faults cannot yet deserve such hateful revenge; thy days are too short for so sharp a doom, but thy untimely death must pay thy mother's debts and her guiltless crime must be thy ghastly curse. And shalt thou sweet babe be committed to fortune? When thou art already spited by Fortune? Shall the seas be thy harbor, and the hard boat thy cradle? Shall thy tender mouth instead of sweet kisses be nipped with bitter storms? Shalt thou have the whistling winds for thy lullaby, and the salt sea foam instead of sweet milk? Alas, what destinies would assign such hard hap?[3] What father would be so cruel? Or what gods will not revenge such rigor? Let me kiss thy lips (sweet infant) and wet thy tender cheeks with my tears and put this chain about thy little neck, that if fortune save thee, it may help to succor thee. Thus, since thou must go to surge in the ghastful seas, with a sorrowful kiss I bid thee farewell, and I pray the Gods thou mayst fare well.

Such, and so great was her grief, that her vital spirits being suppressed with sorrow, she fell down again in a trance, having her senses so sotted with care, that after she was revived, yet she lost her memory and lay for a great time without moving, as one in a trance. The guard left her in this perplexities and carried the child to the king, who quite devoid of pity, commanded that without delay it should be put into the boat, having neither sail nor other to guide it, and so to be carried

1 Rowboat.
2 Swoon, faint.
3 Happenstance, fortune.

into the midst of the sea, and there left to the wind and wave as the destinies please to appoint. The very shipmen seeing the sweet countenance of the young babe began to accuse the king of rigor and to pity the child's hard fortune, but fear constrained them to that which their nature did abhor so that they placed it in one of the ends of the boat, and with a few green boughs made a homely cabin to shroud it as they could from wind and weather. Having thus trimmed the boat they tied it to a ship, and so haled it into the main sea, and then cut asunder the cord, which they had no sooner done, but there arose a mighty tempest, which tossed the little boat so vehemently in the waves that the shipmen thought it could not long continue without sinking; yea, the storm grew so great, that with much labor and peril they got to the shore but leaving the child to her fortunes.

Again to Pandosto, who not yet glutted with sufficient revenge, devised which way he should best increase his wife's calamity. But first assembling his nobles and counselors, he called her for the more reproach into open court, where it was objected against her that she had committed adultery with Egistus and conspired with Franion to poison Pandosto her husband, but their pretence being partly spied, she counseled them to fly away by night for their better safety. Bellaria, who standing like a prisoner at the bar, feeling in herself a clear conscience to withstand her false accusers, seeing that no less than death could pacify her husband's wrath, waxed bold, and desired that she might have law and justice, for mercy she neither craved nor hoped, and that those perjured wretches, which had falsely accused her to the king, might be brought before her face to give in evidence. Pandosto, whose rage and jealousy was such no reason nor equity could appease, told her that for her accusers they were of such credit as their words were sufficient witness, and that the sudden and secret flight of Egistus and Franion confirmed that which they had confessed. And as for her, it was her part to deny such a monstrous crime and to be impudent in forswearing the fact, since she had past all shame in committing the fault; but her stale countenance should stand for no coin, for as the bastard which she bare[1] was served, so she should with some cruel death be requited.

Bellaria, no whit dismayed with this rough reply, told her husband Pandosto that he spake upon choler and not conscience, for her virtuous

1 Bore.

life had been ever such, as no spot of suspicion could ever stain. And if she had borne a friendly countenance to Egistus, it was in respect he was his friend, and not for any lusting affection: therefore if she were condemned without any further proof, it was rigor, and not law.

The noblemen which sat in judgment, said that Bellaria spake reason, and entreated the king that the accusers might be openly examined, and sworn, if then the evidence were such, as the jury might find her guilty (for seeing she was a prince) she ought to be tried by her peers, then let her have such punishment as the extremity of the law will assign to such malefactors. The king presently made answer, that in this case he might and would dispense with the law, and that the jury being once paneled they should take his word for sufficient evidence, otherwise he would make the proudest of them repent it.

The noblemen seeing the king in choler were all whist,[1] but Bellaria whose life then hung in the balance, fearing more perpetual infamy than momentary death, told the king if his fury might stand for a law, that it were vain to have the jury yield their verdict; and therefore she fell down upon her knees and desired the king that for the love he bare to his young son Garinter, whom she brought into the world, that he would grant her a request, the which was this: that it would please his majesty to send six of his noblemen whom he best trusted to the isle of Delphos, there to enquire of the oracle of Apollo whether she had committed adultery with Egistus, or conspired to poison with Franion. And if the God Apollo, who by his divine essence knew all secrets, gave answer that she was guilty, she were content to suffer any torment, were it never so terrible. The request was so reasonable, that Pandosto could not for shame deny it, unless he would be counted of all his subjects more willful then wise. He therefore agreed, that with as much speed as might be there should be certain ambassadors dispatched to the isle of Delphos; and in the mean season[2] he commanded that his wife should be kept in close prison. Bellaria, having obtained this grant, was now more careful for her little babe that floated on the seas than sorrowful for her own mishap. For of that she doubted; of herself she was assured, knowing if Apollo should give oracle according to the thoughts of the heart, yet the sentence should go on her side, such was the clearness

1 Silenced.
2 Meantime, interval.

of her mind in this case. But Pandosto (whose suspicious head still remained in one song) chose out six of his nobility, whom he knew were scarce indifferent men in the queen's behalf, and providing all things fit for their journey, sent them to Delphos; they willing to fulfill the king's command and desirous to see the situation and custom of the island dispatched their affairs with as much speed as might be, and embarked themselves to the voyage, which (the wind and weather serving fit for their purpose) was soon ended. For within three weeks they arrived at Delphos, where they were no sooner set on land but with great devotion they went to the temple of Apollo, and there offering sacrifice to the god and gifts to the priest, as the custom was, they humbly craved an answer of their demand. They had not long kneeled at the altar, but Apollo with a loud voice said: "Bohemians, what you find behind the altar take and depart." They forthwith obeying the oracle found a scroll of parchment, wherein was written these words in letters of gold:

> *The Oracle.*
> Suspicion is no proof; jealousy is an unequal Judge; Bellaria is chaste; Egistus blameless; Franion a true subject; Pandosto treacherous; his babe an innocent, and the king shall live without an heir if that which is lost be not found.

As soon as they had taken out this scroll, the priest of the god commanded them that they should not presume to read it before they came in the presence of Pandosto unless they would incur the displeasure of Apollo. The Bohemian lords carefully obeying his command, taking their leave of the priest, with great reverence departed out of the temple and went to their ships, and as soon as wind would permit them, sailed toward Bohemia; whither in short time they safely arrived, and with great triumph issuing out of their ships, went to the king's palace, whom they found in his chamber accompanied with other noblemen. Pandosto no sooner saw them, but with a merry countenance he welcomed them home, asking what news. They told his majesty that they had received an answer of the god written in a scroll, but with this charge, that they should not read the contents before they came in the presence of the king, and with that they delivered him the parchment; but his noblemen entreated him that sith therein was contained either the safety of his wife's life and honesty or her death and perpetual infamy, that he would have his nobles and commons assembled in the judgment hall, where the queen brought in as a prisoner should hear the contents. If she were found guilty by the oracle of the god, then all should have cause to think his rigor proceeded of due desert;[1] if her grace were found faultless, then she should be cleared before all, sith she had been accused openly. This pleased the king so, that he appointed the day and assembled all his lords and commons and caused the queen to be brought in before the judgment seat, commanding that the indictment should be read, wherein she was accused of adultery with Egistus and of conspiracy with Franion. Bellaria hearing the contents, was no whit astonished, but made this cheerful answer:

> If the divine powers be privy to humane actions (as no doubt they are), I hope my patience shall make Fortune blush, and my unspotted life shall stain spitefully discredit. For, although lying report hath sought to appeach mine honor and suspicion hath intended to soil my credit with infamy, yet where virtue keepeth the fort, report and suspicion may assail, but never sack. How I have led my life before Egistus coming, I appeal Pandosto to the gods and to thy conscience. What hath passed between him and me, the gods only know, and I hope will presently reveal; that I loved Egistus I cannot deny; that I honored him I shame not to confess. To the one I was forced by his virtues, to the other for his dignities. But as touching lascivious lust, I say Egistus is honest, and hope myself to be found without spot; for Franion, I can neither accuse him nor excuse him, for I was not privy to his departure, and that this is true which I have here rehearsed, I refer myself to the divine oracle.

Bellaria had no sooner said but the king commanded that one of his dukes should read the contents of the scroll, which after the commons had heard, they gave a great shout, rejoicing and clapping their hands that the queen was clear of that false accusation. But the king whose conscience was a witness against him of his witless fury and false-suspected jealousy was so ashamed of his rash folly that he entreated his nobles to persuade Bellaria to forgive and forget these injuries, promising not only to show himself a loyal and loving husband, but also to reconcile himself to Egistus and Franion; revealing then before them

1 Justifiably.

all the cause of their secret flight, and how treacherously he thought to have practiced his death if the good mind of his cupbearer had not prevented his purpose. As thus he was relating the whole matter, there was word brought him that his young son Garinter was suddenly dead, which news so soon as Bellaria heard, surcharged before with extreme joy and now suppressed with heavy sorrow, her vital spirits were so stopped that she fell down presently dead and could never be revived. This sudden sight so appalled the king's senses that he sunk from his seat in a swoon, so as he was fain to be carried by his nobles to his palace, where he lay by the space of three days without speech. His commons were as men in despair, so diversely distressed; there was nothing but mourning and lamentation to be heard throughout all Bohemia. Their young Prince dead, their virtuous Queen bereaved of her life, and their king and sovereign in great hazard—this tragical discourse of fortune so daunted them as they went like shadows, not men; yet somewhat to comfort their heavy hearts, they heard that Pandosto was come to himself and had recovered his speech, who as in a fury brayed out these bitter speeches.

> O miserable Pandosto, what surer witness than conscience? What thoughts more sour then suspicion? What plague more bad then jealousy? Unnatural actions offend the gods, more than men, and causeless cruelty never scapes[1] without revenge. I have committed such a bloody fact, as repent I may, but recall I cannot. Ah jealousy, a hell to the mind and a horror to the conscience, suppressing reason, and inciting rage; a worse passion than frenzy, a greater plague than madness. Are the gods just? Then let them revenge such brutish cruelty. My innocent babe I have drowned in the seas. My loving wife I have slain with slanderous suspicion. My trusty friend I have sought to betray, and yet the gods are slack to plague such offenses. Ah unjust Apollo, Pandosto is the man that hath committed the fault. Why should Garinter, silly child, abide the pain? Well, sith the gods mean to prolong my days, to increase my dolor,[2] I will offer my guilty blood a sacrifice to those sackless[3] souls, whose lives are lost by my rigorous folly.

1 Escapes.
2 Sorrow.
3 Innocent.

And with that he reached at a rapier to have murdered himself, but his peers being present stayed him from such a bloody act, persuading him to think that the commonwealth consisted on[1] his safety, and that those sheep could not but perish that wanted a shepherd, wishing that if he would not live for himself, yet he should have care of his subjects and to put such fancies out of his mind, sith in sores past help, salves do not heal but hurt; and in things past cure, care is a corrosive. With these and such like persuasions the king was overcome and began somewhat to quiet his mind; so that as soon as he could go abroad, he caused his wife to be embalmed and wrapped in lead with her young son Garinter, erecting a rich and famous sepulcher, wherein he entombed them both, making such solemn obsequies at her funeral, as all Bohemia might perceive he did greatly repent him of his forepassed[2] folly, causing this epitaph to be engraven on her tomb in letters of gold:

The Epitaph.
Here lies entombed Bellaria, fair,
Falsely accused to be unchaste:
Cleared by Apollo's sacred doom,
Yet slain by jealousy at last.
Whate'er thou be that passest by,
Curse him that caused this queen to die.

This Epitaph being engraven, Pandosto would once a day repair to the tomb, and there with watery plaints bewail his misfortune, coveting no other companion but sorrow, nor no other harmony but repentance. But leaving him to his dolorous passions, at last let us come to show the tragical discourse of the young infant.

Who being tossed with wind and wave, floated two whole days without succor, ready at every puff to be drowned in the sea, till at last the tempest ceased, and the little boat was driven with the tide into the coast of Sicilia, where sticking upon the sands, it rested. Fortune minding to be wanton, willing to show that as she hath wrinkles on her brows, so she hath dimples in her cheeks, thought after so many sour looks to lend a feigned smile, and after a puffing storm, to bring a pretty calm; she began thus to dally. It fortuned a poor mercenary shepherd that

1 Depended on.
2 Former.

dwelled in Sicilia, who got his living by other men's flocks, missed one of his sheep, and thinking it had strayed into the covert[1] that was hard by,[2] sought very diligently to find that which he could not see, fearing either that the wolves or eagles had undone him (for he was so poor, as a sheep was half his substance) wandered down toward the sea cliffs to see if perchance the sheep was browsing on the sea ivy; whereon they greatly do feed, but not finding her there, as he was ready to return to his flock he heard a child cry, but knowing there was no house near, thought he had mistaken the sound, and that it was the bleating of his sheep. Wherefore looking more narrowly, as he cast his eye to the sea, he spied a little boat, from whence as he attentively listened, he might hear the cry to come. Standing a good while in a maze[3] at last he went to the shore, and wading to the boat, as he looked in he saw the little babe lying all alone, ready to die for hunger and cold, wrapped in a mantle of scarlet, richly embroidered with gold and having a chain about the neck. The shepherd, who before had never seen so fair a babe nor so rich jewels, thought assuredly that it was some little god and began with great devotion to knock on his breast. The babe, who writhed with the head to seek for the pap, began again to cry afresh, whereby the poor man knew that it was a child, which by some sinister means was driven thither by distress of weather; marveling how such a silly[4] infant, which by the mantle and the chain could not be but born of noble parentage should be so hardly crossed with deadly mishap. The poor shepherd perplexed thus with divers thoughts took pity of the child and determined with himself to carry it to the king, that there it might be brought up, according to the worthiness of birth, for his ability could not afford to foster it, though his mind was willing to further it.

Taking therefore the child in his arms, as he folded the mantle together the better to defend it from cold, there fell down at his foot a very fair and rich purse, wherein he found a great sum of gold, which sight so revived the shepherd's spirits as he was greatly ravished with joy and daunted with fear: joyful to see such a sum in his power; fearful if it should be known, that it might breed his further danger. Necessity wished him at the least to retain the gold, though he would not keep the child. The simplicity of his conscience feared him from such deceitful

1 Hidden place.
2 Nearby.
3 In amazement.
4 Simple.

bribery. Thus was the poor man perplexed with a doubtful dilemma, until at last the covetousness of the coin overcame him; for what will not the greedy desire of gold cause a man to do? So that he was resolved in himself to foster the child, and with the sum to relieve his want. Resting thus resolute in this point, he left seeking of his sheep, and as covertly and secretly as he could went by a byway to his house, lest any of his neighbors should perceive his carriage. As soon as he was got home, entering in at the door, the child began to cry, which his wife hearing and seeing her husband with a young babe in arms, began to be somewhat jealous, yet marveling that her husband should be so wanton abroad sith he was so quiet at home; but as women are naturally given to believe the worst, so his wife, thinking it was some bastard, began to crow against her goodman and taking up a cudgel (for the most master went breechless)[1] swore solemnly that she would make clubs trumps[2] if he brought any bastard brat within her doors. The goodman, seeing his wife in her majesty with her mace in her hand, thought it was time to bow for fear of blows and desired her to be quiet, for there was none such matter; but if she could hold her peace, they were made for ever, and with that he told her the whole matter: how he had found the child in a little boat without any succor, wrapped in that costly mantle, and having that rich chain about the neck. But at last when he showed her the purse full of gold, she began to simper something sweetly and taking her husband about the neck, kissed him after her homely fashion, saying that she hoped god had seen their want and now meant to relieve their poverty; and seeing they could get no children, had sent them this little babe to be their heir.

"Take heed in any case" (quoth the shepherd) "that you be secret, and blab it not out when you meet with your gossips, for if you do, we are like not only to lose the gold and jewels, but our other goods and lives."

"Tush" (quoth his wife) "profit is a good hatch before the door. Fear not, I have other things to talk of than of this, but I pray you let us lay up the money surely and the jewels, least by any mishap it be espied."

After that they had set all things in order, the shepherd went to his sheep with a merry note, and the good wife learned to sing lullaby at home with her young babe, wrapping it in a homely blanket instead of a rich mantle, nourishing it so cleanly and carefully as it began to be a jolly girl, insomuch that they began both of them to be very fond of it,

1 I.e., his wife wore the pants in the family.

2 Proverbial phrase of warning.

seeing as it waxed in age, so it increased in beauty. The shepherd every night at his coming home would sing and dance it on his knee and prattle, that in a short time it began to speak and call him "Dad" and her "Mam." At last when it grew to ripe years, that it was about seven years old, the shepherd left keeping of other men's sheep, and with the money he found in the purse, he bought him the lease of a pretty farm and got a small flock of sheep, which when Fawnia (for so they named the childe) came to the age of ten years, he set her to keep, and she with such diligence performed her charge as the sheep prospered marvelously under her hands. Fawnia thought Porrus had been her father and Mopsa her mother (for so was the shepherd and his wife called), honored and obeyed them with such reverence that all the neighbors praised the dutiful obedience of the child. Porrus grew in a short time to be a man of some wealth and credit, for Fortune so favored him in having no charge but Fawnia that he began to purchase land, intending after his death to give it to his daughter; so that diverse rich farmers' sons came as wooers to his house, for Fawnia was something cleanly attired, being of such singular beauty and excellent wit, that whoso saw her would have thought she had been some heavenly nymph and not a mortal creature— insomuch that, when she came to the age of sixteen years, she so increased with exquisite perfection both of body and mind as her natural disposition did bewray that she was born of some high parentage. But the people thinking she was daughter to the shepherd Porrus rested only, amazed at her beauty and wit; yea, she won such favor and commendations in every man's eye, as her beauty was not only praised in the country, but also spoken of in the court. Yet such was her submiss modesty, that although her praise daily increased, her mind was no whit puffed up with pride, but humbled herself as became a country maid and the daughter of a poor shepherd. Every day she went forth with her sheep to the field, keeping them with such care and diligence as all men thought she was very painful,[1] defending her face from the heat of the sun with no other veil but with a garland made of bows and flowers, which attire became her so gallantly as she seemed to be the goddess Flora herself for beauty. Fortune,[2] who all this while had showed a friendly face, began now to turn her back and

1 Diligent.

2 For information on the goddesses Flora and Fortune, see extended notes, pp. 138 and 123.

to show a louring countenance, intending as she had given Fawnia a slender check,[1] so she would give her a harder mate; to bring which to pass, she laid her train on this wise.[2] Egistus had but one only son called Dorastus, about the age of twenty years, a prince so decked and adorned with the gifts of nature, so fraught[3] with beauty and virtuous qualities, as not only his father joyed to have so good a son and all his commons rejoiced that god had sent them such a noble prince to succeed in the kingdom. Egistus, placing all his joy in the perfection of his son, seeing that he was now marriageable, sent ambassadors to the king of Denmark to entreat a marriage between him and his daughter, who willingly consenting, made answer, that the next spring if it please Egistus with his son to come into Denmark, he doubted not but they should agree upon reasonable conditions. Egistus, resting satisfied with this friendly answer, thought convenient in the meantime to break with his son; finding therefore on a day fit opportunity, he spake to him in these fatherly terms:

> Dorastus, thy youth warneth me to prevent the worst, and mine age to provide the best. Opportunities neglected are signs of folly. Actions measured by time are seldom bitten with repentance. Thou art young, and I old. Age hath taught me that which thy youth cannot yet conceive.
>
> I therefore will counsel thee as a father, hoping thou wilt obey as a child. Thou seest my white hairs are blossoms for the grave, and thy fresh color fruit for time and fortune, so that it behooveth me to think how to die and for thee to care how to live. My crown I must leave by death, and thou enjoy my kingdom by succession, wherein I hope thy virtue and prowess shall be such, as though my subjects want my person, yet they shall see in thee my perfection. That nothing either may fail to satisfy thy mind or increase thy dignities, the only care I have is to see thee well married before I die and thou become old.

1 Slight reproach.

2 I.e., Fortune now provides a harder one, as is about to be explained (setting Fawnia's gaze in Dorastus's direction).

3 Full of.

Dorastus, who from his infancy delighted rather to die with Mars in the field than to dally with Venus in the chamber, fearing to displease his father and yet not willing to be wed, made him this reverent answer:

> Sir, there is no greater bond than duty, nor no straiter law then nature. Disobedience in youth is often galled with despite in age. The command of the father ought to be a constraint to the child. So parents' wills are laws; so they pass not all laws. May it please your grace therefore to appoint whom I shall love, rather than by denial I should be appeached of disobedience. I rest content to love, though it be the only thing I hate.

Egistus, hearing his son to fly so far from the mark, began to be somewhat choleric, and therefore made him his hasty answer:

> What, Dorastus, canst thou not love? Cometh this cynical passion of prone desires or peevish forwardness? What, dost thou think thyself too good for all, or none good enough for thee? I tell thee, Dorastus, there is nothing sweeter than youth nor swifter decreasing while it is increasing. Time passed with folly may be repented, but not recalled. If thou marry in age, thy wife's fresh colors will breed in thee dead thoughts and suspicion, and thy white hairs her loathsomeness and sorrow. For Venus's affections are not fed with kingdoms or treasures, but with youthful conceits and sweet amours. Vulcan was allotted to shake the tree, but Mars allowed to reap the fruit.[1] Yield, Dorastus, to thy father's persuasions, which may prevent thy perils. I have chosen thee a wife, fair by nature, royal by birth, by virtues famous, learned by education, and rich by possessions, so that it is hard to judge whether her bounty or fortune, her beauty or virtue, be of greater force. I mean, Dorastus, Euphrania, daughter and heir to the King of Denmark.

Egistus, pausing here a while, looking when his son should make him answer, and seeing that he stood still as one in a trance, he shook him up thus sharply:

---

1 Egistus suggests that, while Vulcan had the power to stir Venus's affections, Mars had the youthfulness to take advantage of them.

> Well, Dorastus, take heed. The tree Alpya wasteth not with fire, but withereth with the dew. That which love nourisheth not, perisheth with hate. If thou like Euphrania, thou breedest my content, and in loving her thou shalt have my love; otherwise ...

and with that he flung from his son in a rage, leaving him a sorrowful man, in that he had by denial displeased his father, and half angry with himself that he could not yield to that passion whereto both reason and his father persuaded him.

But see how Fortune is plumed with time's feathers, and how she can minister strange causes to breed strange effects. It happened not long after this that there was a meeting of all the farmers' daughters in Sicilia, whither Fawnia was also bidden as the mistress of the feast, who, having attired herself in her best garments, went among the rest of her companions to the merry meeting, there spending the day in such homely pastimes as shepherds use.

As the evening grew on and their sports ceased, each taking their leave at other, Fawnia, desiring one of her companions to bear her company, went home by the flock to see if they were well folded,[1] and as they returned, it fortuned that Dorastus (who all that day had been hawking, and killed store of game) encountered by the way these two maids, and casting his eye suddenly on Fawnia, he was half afraid, fearing that with Acteon he had seen Diana,[2] for he thought such exquisite perfection could not be found in any mortal creature.

As thus he stood in a maze, one of his pages told him that the maid with the garland on her head was Fawnia, the fair shepherd, whose beauty was so much talked of in the court. Dorastus, desirous to see if nature had adorned her mind with any inward qualities as she had decked her body with outward shape, began to question with her whose daughter she was, of what age, and how she had been trained up; who answered him with such modest reverence and sharpness of wit that Dorastus thought her outward beauty was but a counterfeit to darken her inward qualities, wondering how so courtly behavior could be found

1 Properly penned up.

2 Reference to a tale from Ovid's *Metamorphoses* (see also Appendix A2, p. 263). The young huntsman Actaeon accidentally saw the goddess Diana naked, bathing with her nymphs. Diana transformed him into a stag who was overrun and torn apart by his own hounds.

in so simple a cottage, and cursing Fortune that had shadowed wit and beauty with such hard fortune.

As thus he held her a long while with chat, Beauty seeing him at discovert,[1] thought not to lose the vantage but stroke him so deeply with an envenomed shaft as he wholly lost his liberty and became a slave to love, which before contemned love, glad now to gaze on a poor shepherd who before refused the offer of a rich princess; for the perfection of Fawnia had so fired his fancy as he felt his mind greatly changed and his affections altered, cursing love that had wrought such a change and blaming the baseness of his mind that would make such a choice. But thinking these were but passionate toys that might be thrust out at pleasure to avoid the siren that enchanted him, he put spurs to his horse, and bade this fair shepherd farewell.

Fawnia (who all this while had marked the princely gesture of Dorastus), seeing his face so well featured, and each limb so perfectly framed, began greatly to praise his perfection, commending him so long, till she found herself faulty and perceived that if she waded but a little further, she might slip over the shoes.[2] She therefore seeking to quench that fire which never was put out went home, and feigning herself not well at ease, got her to bed, where casting a thousand thoughts in her head, she could take no rest; for if she waked, she began to call to mind his beauty, and thinking to beguile such thoughts with sleep, she then dreamed of his perfection; pestered thus with these unacquainted passions, she passed the night as she could in short slumbers.

Dorastus (who all this while rode with a flea in his ear[3]) could not by any means forget the sweet favor of Fawnia, but rested so bewitched with her wit and beauty as he could take no rest. He felt fancy to give the assault and his wounded mind ready to yield as vanquished, yet he began with divers considerations to suppress this frantic affection, calling to mind that Fawnia was a shepherd, one not worthy to be looked at of a prince, much less to be loved of such a potentate, thinking what a discredit it were to himself, and what a grief it would be to his father, blaming fortune and accusing his own folly that should be so fond[4] as but once to cast a glance at such a country slut.

---

1 Off his guard.

2 I.e., Fawnia is afraid of getting in over her head.

3 A nagging reminder.

4 Foolish.

As thus he was raging against himself, love, fearing if she dally long to lose her champion, stepped more nigh and gave him such a fresh wound as it pierced him at the heart, that he was fain to yield, maugre[1] his face, and to forsake the company and get him to his chamber, where being solemnly set, he burst into these passionate terms:

Ah, Dorastus, art thou alone? No, not alone while thou art tried with these unacquainted passions. Yield to fancy; thou canst not by thy father's counsel, but in a frenzy thou art by just destinies. Thy father were content if thou couldest love, and thou therefore discontent, because thou dost love. O divine Love, feared of men because honored of the gods, not to be suppressed by wisdom, because not to be comprehended by reason: without law, and therefore above all law.

How now, Dorastus, why dost thou blaze that with praises which thou hast cause to blaspheme with curses? Yet why should they curse love which are in love?

Blush, Dorastus, at thy fortune, thy choice, thy love. Thy thoughts cannot be uttered without shame, nor thy affections without discredit. Ah Fawnia, sweet Fawnia, thy beauty Fawnia. Shamest not thou Dorastus to name one unfit for thy birth, thy dignities, thy kingdoms? Die, Dorastus! Dorastus, die! Better hadst thou perish with high desires than live in base thoughts. Yea, but beauty must be obeyed, because it is beauty, yet framed of the gods to feed the eye, not to fetter the heart.

Ah, but he that striveth against Love shooteth with them of Scyrum against the wind, and with the Cockatrice pecketh against the steel. I will therefore obey, because I must obey. Fawnia, yea Fawnia shall be my fortune, in spite of fortune. The Gods above disdain not to love women beneath. Phoebus liked Sibilla, Jupiter Io, and why not I then Fawnia, one something inferior to these in birth, but far superior to them in beauty, born to be a shepherd, but worthy to be a goddess.

Ah Dorastus, wilt thou so forget thyself as to suffer affection to suppress wisdom, and love to violate thine honor? How sour will thy choice be to thy father, sorrowful to thy subjects, to thy friends a grief, most gladsome to thy foes? Subdue then thy affection, and cease to love her whom thou couldst not love, unless blinded with too much

1 In spite of.

> love. Tush, I talk to the wind, and in seeking to prevent the causes, I further the effects. I will yet praise Fawnia, honor, yea, and love Fawnia, and at this day follow content, not counsel. Do, Dorastus! Thou canst but repent.

And with that his Page came into the chamber, whereupon he ceased from complaints, hoping that time would wear out that which fortune had wrought. As thus he was pained, so poor Fawnia was diversely perplexed, for the next morning getting up very early, she went to her sheep, thinking with hard labors to pass away her new conceived amours, beginning very busily to drive them to the field, and then to shift the folds. At last (wearied with toil) she sate her down, where (poor soul) she was more tried with fond affections, for love began to assault her, insomuch that as she sate upon the side of a hill, she began to accuse her own folly in these terms:

> Infortunate Fawnia, and therefore infortunate because Fawnia. Thy shepherd's hook showeth thy poor state, thy proud desires an aspiring mind. The one declareth thy want, the other thy pride. No bastard hawk must soar so high as the Hobby.[1] No fowl gaze against the sun but the Eagle. Actions wrought against nature reap despite, and thoughts above Fortune disdain.
>
> Fawnia, thou art a shepherd, daughter to poor Porrus. If thou rest content with this, thou art like to stand; if thou climb thou art sure to fall. The herb Anita[2] growing higher than six inches becometh a weed. Nilus flowing more than twelve cubits procureth a dearth.[3] Daring affections that pass measure are cut short by time or fortune. Suppress then, Fawnia, those thoughts which thou mayest shame to express. But, ah Fawnia! Love is a Lord, who will command by power, and constrain by force.
>
> Dorastus, ah, Dorastus is the man I love. The worse is thy hap, and the less cause hast thou to hope. Will Eagles catch at flies? Will Cedars stoop to brambles, or mighty Princes look at such homely trulls?[4] No, no, think this: Dorastus's disdain is greater than thy desire. He is a

1 No inferior hawk unfit for hunting should fly as high as a bird of prey.
2 Probably anise: a warning not to aspire above her humble state.
3 The Nile reaching a height over 12 cubits (18 feet) creates drought.
4 Wenches.

> Prince respecting his honor, thou a beggar's brat forgetting thy calling. Cease then not only to say but to think to love Dorastus, and dissemble thy love, Fawnia, for better it were to die with grief than to live with shame. Yet in despite of love I will sigh, to see if I can sigh out love.

Fawnia, somewhat appeasing her griefs with these pithy persuasions, began after her wonted manner to walk about her sheep and to keep them from straying into the corn, suppressing her affection with the due consideration of her base estate, and with the impossibilities of her love, thinking it were frenzy, not fancy, to covet that which the very destinies did deny her to obtain.

But Dorastus was more impatient in his passions, for love so fiercely assailed him, that neither company nor music could mitigate his martyrdom, but did rather far the more increase his malady. Shame would not let him crave counsel in this case, nor fear of his father's displeasure reveal it to any secret friend; but he was fain to make a Secretary of himself and to participate his thoughts with his own troubled mind. Lingering thus awhile in doubtful suspense, at last stealing secretly from the court without either men or Page, he went to see if he could espy Fawnia walking abroad in the field, but as one having a great deal more skill to retrieve the partridge with his spaniels than to hunt after such a strange prey he sought, but was little the better; which cross luck drove him into a great choler, that he began both to accuse love and fortune. But as he was ready to retire, he saw Fawnia sitting all alone under the side of a hill, making a garland of such homely flowers as the fields did afford. This sight so revived his spirits that he drew nigh with more judgment to take a view of her singular perfection, which he found to be such as in that country attire she stained all the courtly Dames of Sicilia. While thus he stood gazing with piercing looks on her surpassing beauty, Fawnia cast her eye aside and spied Dorastus, which sudden sight made the poor girl to blush and to dye her crystal cheeks with a vermilion red, which gave her such a grace as she seemed far more beautiful. And with that she rose up, saluting the Prince with such modest courtesies, as he wondered how a country maid could afford such courtly behavior. Dorastus, repaying her courtesy with a smiling countenance, began to parley with her on this manner:

> Fair maid (quoth he) either your want is great, or a shepherd's life very sweet, that your delight is in such country labors. I cannot conceive what pleasure you should take, unless you mean to imitate the nymphs, being yourself so like a nymph. To put me out of this doubt, show me what is to be commended in a shepherd's life and what pleasures you to countervail these drudging labors.

Fawnia with blushing face made him this ready answer:

> Sir, what richer state than content or what sweeter life than quiet. We shepherds are not born to honor, nor beholding unto beauty, the less care we to fear fame or fortune. We count our attire brave enough if warm enough and our food dainty if to suffice nature. Our greatest enemy is the wolf; our only care in safe keeping our flock. Instead of courtly ditties we spend the days with country songs. Our amorous conceits are homely thoughts: delighting as much to talk of Pan and his country pranks, as ladies to tell of Venus and her wanton toys. Our toil is in shifting the folds and looking to the lambs' easy labors. Oft singing and telling tales, homely pleasures our greatest wealth not to covet, our honor not to climb, our quiet not to care. Envy looketh not so low as shepherds. Shepherds gaze not so high as ambition. We are rich in that we are poor with content, and proud only in this: that we have no cause to be proud.

This witty answer of Fawnia so inflamed Dorastus's fancy as he commended himself for making so good a choice, thinking, if her birth were answerable to her wit and beauty, that she were a fit mate for the most famous prince in the world. He therefore began to sift her more narrowly on this manner:

> Fawnia, I see thou art content with country labors because thou knowest not courtly pleasures. I commend thy wit, and pity thy want, but wilt thou leave thy father's cottage and serve a courtly mistress.
>
> Sir (quoth she) beggars ought not to strive against fortune nor to gaze after honor, lest either their fall be greater or they become blind. I am born to toil for the court, not in the court; my nature unfit for their nurture, better live then in mean degree than in high disdain.
>
> Well said Fawnia (quoth Dorastus) I guess at thy thoughts; thou art in love with some country shepherd.

No sir (quoth she). Shepherds cannot love that are so simple, and maids may not love that are so young.

Nay, therefore (quoth Dorastus) maids must love, because they are young, for Cupid is a child, and Venus, though old, is painted with fresh colors.

I grant (said she) age may be painted with new shadows, and youth may have imperfect affections; but what art concealeth in one, ignorance revealeth in the other.

Dorastus, seeing Fawnia held him so hard, thought it was vain so long to beat about the bush. Therefore he thought to have given her a fresh charge, but he was so prevented by certain of his men, who missing their master, came posting to seek him, seeing that he was gone forth all alone; yet before they drew so nigh that they might hear their talk, he used these speeches:

Why Fawnia, perhaps I love thee, and then thou must needs yield, for thou knowest I can command and constrain.

Truth sir (quoth she) but not to love, for constrained love is force, not love; and know this, sir, mine honesty is such, as I had rather die than be a concubine even unto a king, and my birth is so base as I am unfit to be a wife to a poor farmer.

Why then (quoth he) thou canst not love Dorastus?

"Yes," said Fawnia, "when Dorastus becomes a shepherd."

And with that, the presence of his men broke off their parley, so that he went with them to the palace, and left Fawnia sitting still on the hillside, who seeing that the night drew on, shifted her folds,[1] and busied herself about other work to drive away such fond fancies as began to trouble her brain. But all this could not prevail, for the beauty of Dorastus had made such a deep impression in her heart, as it could not be worn out without cracking, so that she was forced to blame her own folly in this wise:

Ah, Fawnia, why dost thou gaze against the sun, or catch at the wind? Stars are to be looked at with the eye, not reached at with the hand. Thoughts are to be measured by fortunes, not by desires. Falls come not

---

1 Sheep enclosures.

by sitting low, but by climbing too high. What then shall all fear to fall, because some hap to fall? No, luck cometh by lot, and fortune windeth those threads which the destinies spin. Thou art favored Fawnia of a prince, and yet thou art so fond to reject desired favors. Thou hast denial at thy tongue's end and desire at thy heart's bottom; a woman's fault to spurn at that with her foot which she greedily catcheth at with her hand. Thou lovest Dorastus, Fawnia, and yet seemest to lour. Take heed. If he retire, thou wilt repent, for unless he love, thou canst but die. Die then Fawnia! For Dorastus doth but jest. The lion never preyeth on the mouse, nor falcons stoop not to dead stales.[1] Sit down then in sorrow. Cease to love, and content thyself that Dorastus will vouchsafe to flatter Fawnia, though not to fancy Fawnia. Heigh ho! Ah fool! It were seemlier for thee to whistle as a shepherd than to sigh as a lover.

And with that she ceased from these perplexed passions, folding her sheep, and hieing[2] home to her poor cottage. But such was the inconstant sorrow of Dorastus to think on the wit and beauty of Fawnia, and to see how fond he was being a prince and how froward[3] she was being a beggar. Then he began to lose his wonted[4] appetite, to look pale and wan; instead of mirth, to feed on melancholy; for courtly dances to use cold dumps,[5] insomuch that not only his own men, but his father and all the Court began to marvel at his sudden change, thinking that some lingering sickness had brought him into this state; wherefore he caused Physicians to come, but Dorastus neither would let them minister nor so much as suffer them to see his urine, but remained still so oppressed with these passions, as he feared in himself a farther inconvenience. His honor wished him to cease from such folly, but love forced him to follow fancy. Yea, and in despite of honor, love won the conquest, so that his hot desires caused him to find new devices, for he presently made himself a shepherd's coat that he might go unknown and with the less suspicion to prattle with Fawnia, and conveyed it secretly into a thick grove hard joining to the palace, whither finding fit time and opportunity, he went all alone, and putting off his princely

1 Stuffed decoys.
2 Hurrying.
3 Ill-disposed.
4 Customary.
5 Distant melancholy.

apparel, got on those shepherd's robes and taking a great hook in his hand (which he had also gotten) he went very anciently to find out the mistress of his affection; but as he went by the way, seeing himself clad in such unseemly rags, he began to smile at his own folly and to reprove his fondness in these terms:

"Well," said Dorastus, "thou keepest a right decorum, base desires and homely attires. Thy thoughts are fit for none but a shepherd and thy apparel such as only become a shepherd, a strange change from a Prince to a peasant. What is it thy wretched fortune or thy willful folly? Is it thy cursed destinies or thy crooked desires that appointeth thee this penance? Ah, Dorastus, thou canst but love, and unless thou love, thou art like to perish for love[.] Yet, fond fool, choose flowers, not weeds; diamonds, not pebbles; ladies, which may honor thee, not shepherds which may disgrace the. Venus is painted in silks, not in rags; and Cupid treadeth on disdain when he reacheth at dignity. And yet, Dorastus, shame not at thy shepherd's weed. The heavenly Gods have sometime earthly thoughts: Neptune became a ram, Jupiter a bull, Apollo a shepherd.[1] They gods, and yet in love; and thou a man appointed to love."

Devising thus with himself, he drew nigh to the place where Fawnia was keeping her sheep, who casting her eye aside and seeing such a mannerly shepherd, perfectly limbed, and coming with so good a pace, she began half to forget Dorastus and to favor this pretty shepherd, whom she thought she might both love and obtain. But as she was in these thoughts, she perceived then it was the young prince Dorastus, wherefore she rose up and reverently saluted him. Dorastus, taking her by the hand, repaid her courtesy with a sweet kiss, and praying her to sit down by him, he began thus to lay the battery:[2]

If thou marvel, Fawnia, at my strange attire, thou wouldst more muse at my unaccustomed thoughts; the one disgraceth but my outward shape, the other disturbeth my inward senses. I love Fawnia, and therefore what love liketh I cannot mislike. Fawnia, thou hast

1 Examples from Ovid of gods metamorphosing into earthly forms.

2 Begin the siege.

promised to love, and I hope thou wilt perform no less. I fulfilled thy request, and now thou canst but grant my desire. Thou wert content to love Dorastus when he ceased to be a Prince and to become a shepherd, and see I have made the change, and therefore not to miss of my choice.

"Truth," quoth Fawnia, "but all that wear cowls are not Monks. Painted eagles are pictures, not eagles. Zeuxis's[1] grapes were like grapes, yet shadows. Rich clothing make not princes, nor homely attire beggars. Shepherds are not called shepherds because they wear hooks and bags, but that they are born poor and live to keep sheep, so this attire hath not made Dorastus a shepherd, but to seem like a shepherd."

"Well, Fawnia," answered Dorastus. "Were I a shepherd I could not but like thee, and being a prince, I am forced to love thee. Take heed, Fawnia. Be not proud of beauty's painting, for it is a flower that fadeth in the blossom. Those which disdain in youth are despised in age. Beauty's shadows are tricked up with time's colors, which being set to dry in the sun are stained with the sun, scarce pleasing the sight ere they begin not to be worth the sight, not much unlike the herb Ephemeron, which flourisheth in the morning and is withered before the sun setting. If my desire were against law, thou mightest justly deny me by reason, but I love thee, Fawnia, not to misuse thee as a concubine, but to use thee as my wife. I can promise no more, and mean to perform no less."

Fawnia, hearing this solemn protestation of Dorastus, could no longer withstand the assault, but yielded up the fort in these friendly terms:

Ah, Dorastus, I shame to express that thou forcest me with thy sugared speech to confess. My base birth caused the one, and thy high dignities the other. Beggars' thoughts ought not to reach so far as kings, and yet my desires reach as high as princes. I dare not say, Dorastus, I love thee, because I am a shepherd, but the gods know I have honored Dorastus (pardon if I say amiss) yea and loved Dorastus with such dutiful affection as Fawnia can perform, or Dorastus desire.

1 Reference to a celebrated Greek artist (fifth century BCE) known for his highly realistic paintings.

I yield, not overcome with prayers, but with love, resting Dorastus's handmaid ready to obey his will, if no prejudice at all to his honor, nor to my credit.

Dorastus hearing this friendly conclusion of Fawnia, embraced her in his arms, swearing that neither distance, time, nor adverse fortune should diminish his affection, but that in despite of the destinies he would remain loyal unto death. Having thus plight their troth[1] each to other, seeing they could not have the full fruition of their love in Sicilia, for that Egistus consent would never be granted to so mean a match, Dorastus determined as soon as time and opportunity would give them leave to provide a great mass of money and many rich and costly jewels for the easier carriage, and then to transport themselves and their treasure into Italy, where they should lead a contented life, until such time as either he could be reconciled to his father, or else by succession come to the kingdom. This device was greatly praised of Fawnia, for she feared if the King his father should but hear of the contract, that his fury would be such as no less than death would stand for payment. She therefore told him that delay bred danger; that many mishaps did fall out between the cup and the lip; and that to avoid anger, it were best with as much speed as might be to pass out of Sicilia lest Fortune might prevent their pretence with some new despite. Dorastus, whom love pricked forward with desire, promised to dispatch his affairs with as great haste, as either time or opportunity would give him leave. And so resting upon this point, after many embracing and sweet kisses, they departed.

Dorastus, having taken his leave of his best beloved Fawnia, went to the grove where he had his rich apparel, and there uncasing himself as secretly as might be, hiding up his shepherd's attire till occasion should serve again to use it, he went to the palace, shewing by his merry countenance that either the state of his body was amended or the case of his mind greatly redressed. Fawnia, poor soul, was no less joyful that being a shepherd, Fortune had favored her so, as to reward her with the love of a prince, hoping in time to be advanced from the daughter of a poor farmer to be the wife of a rich king, so that she thought every hour a year, till by their departure they might prevent danger, not ceasing still

1 Pledged to marry.

to go every day to her sheep, not so much for the care of her flock as for the desire she had to see her love and lord, Dorastus, who oftentimes when opportunity would serve repaired thither to feed his fancy with the sweet content of Fawnia's presence; and although he never went to visit her but in his shepherd's rags, yet his oft repair made him not only suspected but known to diverse of their neighbors, who for the good will they bare to old Porrus, told him secretly of the matter, wishing him to keep his daughter at home, least she went so oft to the field that she brought him home a young son, for they feared that Fawnia being so beautiful, the young prince would allure her to folly. Porrus was stricken into a dump at these news, so that thanking his neighbors for their good will, he hied him home to his wife, and calling her aside, wringing his hands, and shedding forth tears, he brake[1] the matter to her in these terms:

> I am afraid, wife, that my daughter Fawnia hath made herself so fine, that she will buy repentance too dear. I hear news, which if they be true, some will wish they had not proved true. It is told me by my neighbors that Dorastus, the king's son, begins to look at our daughter Fawnia, which if it be so, I will not give her a halfpenny for her honesty at the year's end. I tell thee, wife, nowadays beauty is a great stale[2] to trap young men, and fair words and sweet promises are two great enemies to maiden's honesty; and thou knowest where poor men entreat and cannot obtain, there princes may command and will obtain. Though kings' sons dance in nets, they may not be seen, but poor men's faults are spied at a little hole. Well, it is a hard case where King's lusts are laws, and that they should bend poor men to that which they themselves willfully break.
>
> Peace husband (quoth his wife) take heed what you say. Speak no more than you should, lest you hear what you would not. Great streams are to be stopped by sleight,[3] not by force; and princes to be persuaded by submission, not by rigor. Do what you can, but no more than you may, lest in saving Fawnia's maidenhead, you lose your own head. Take heed I say. It is ill jesting with edged tools and bad sporting

1 Broke.

2 Decoy.

3 Craft, trickery.

> with Kings. The Wolf had his skin pulled over his ears for but looking into the Lion's den.
>
> Tush, wife (quoth he) thou speakest like a fool. If the king should know that Dorastus had begotten our daughter with child (as I fear it will fall out little better) the king's fury would be such as no doubt we should both lose our goods and lives. Necessity therefore hath no law, and I will prevent this mischief with a new device that is come in my head, which shall neither offend the king nor displease Dorastus. I mean to take the chain and the jewels that I found with Fawnia and carry them to the King, letting him then to understand how she is none of my daughter, but that I found her beaten up with the water, alone in a little boat wrapped in a rich mantle, wherein was enclosed this treasure. By this means I hope the king will take Fawnia into his service, and we whatsoever chanceth shall be blameless.

This device pleased the good wife very well, so that they determined as soon as they might know the king at leisure to make him privy to this case. In the meantime Dorastus was not slack in his affairs but applied his matters with such diligence that he provided all things fit for their journey. Treasure and jewels he had gotten great store, thinking there was no better friend than money in a strange country. Rich attire he had provided for Fawnia, and, because he could not bring the matter to pass without the help and advice of someone, he made an old servant of his called Capnio, who had served him from his childhood, privy to his affairs, who, seeing no persuasions could prevail to divert him from his settled determination, gave his consent and dealt so secretly in the cause, that within short space he had gotten a ship ready for their passage. The mariners seeing a fit gale of wind for their purpose wished Capnio to make no delays, lest if they pretermitted[1] this good weather, they might stay long ere they had such a fair wind. Capnio, fearing that his negligence should hinder the journey, in the night time conveyed the trunks full of treasure into the ship, and by secret means let Fawnia understand that the next morning they meant to depart. She upon this news slept very little that night, but got her up very early and went to her sheep, looking every minute when she should see Dorastus, who tarried not long for fear delay might breed

1 Disregarded, allowed to pass.

danger, but came as fast as he could gallop, and without any great circumstance took Fawnia up behind him and rode to the haven where the ship lay, which was not three quarters of a mile distant from that place. He no sooner came there, but the mariners were ready with their cock-boat to set them aboard, where being couched together in a cabin, they passed away the time in recounting their old loves till their man Capnio could come.

Porrus, who had heard that this morning the king would go abroad to take the air, called in haste to his wife to bring him his holiday hose and his best jacket, that he might go like an honest substantial man to tell his tale. His wife, a good cleanly wench, brought him all things fit and sponged[1] him up very handsomely, giving him the chain and jewels in a little box, which Porrus for the more safety put in his bosom. Having thus all his trinkets in a readiness, taking his staff in his hand, he bad his wife kiss him for good luck, and so he went towards the palace. But as he was going, Fortune (who meant to show him a little false play) prevented his purpose in this wise.

He met by chance in his way Capnio, who trudging as fast as he could with a little coffer under his arm to the ship and spying Porrus, whom he knew to be Fawnia's father, going towards the palace, being a wily fellow, began to doubt the worst, and therefore crossed him the way and asked him whither he was going so early this morning.

Porrus (who knew by his face that he was one of the court) meaning simply, told him that the King's son Dorastus dealt hardly with him, for he had but one daughter who was a little beautiful, and that his neighbors told him the young prince had allured her to folly. He went therefore now to complain to the king how greatly he was abused.

Capnio (who straightway smelt the whole matter) began to soothe him in his talk, and said that Dorastus dealt not like a Prince to spoil any poor man's daughter in that sort. He therefore would do the best for him he could, because he knew he was an honest man:

> But (quoth Capnio) you lose your labor in going to the palace, for the king means this day to take the air of the sea and to go aboard of a ship that lies in the haven. I am going before, you see, to provide all things in a readiness, and if you will follow my counsel, turn back with me to

1 Cleaned.

> the haven, where I will set you in such a fit place as you may speak to the king at your pleasure.

Porrus, giving credit to Capnio's smooth tale, gave him a thousand thanks for his friendly advice and went with him to the haven, making all the way his complaints of Dorastus yet concealing secretly the chain and the jewels. As soon as they were come to the seaside, the mariners, seeing Capnio, came a land with their cock-boat, who, still dissembling the matter, demanded of Porrus if he would go see the ship, who unwilling and fearing the worst, because he was not well acquainted with Capnio made his excuse that he could not brook the Sea, therefore would not trouble him.

Capnio, seeing that by fair means he could not get him aboard, commanded the mariners that by violence they should carry him into the ship, who like sturdy knaves hoisted the poor shepherd on their backs, and bearing him to the boat, launched from the land.

Porrus, seeing himself so cunningly betrayed, durst not cry out, for he saw it would not prevail, but began to entreat Capnio and the mariners to be good to him and to pity his estate. He was but a poor man that lived by his labor. They, laughing to see the shepherd so afraid, made as much haste as they could and set him aboard. Porrus was no sooner in the ship, but he saw Dorastus walking with Fawnia, yet he scarce knew her, for she had attired herself in rich apparel, which so increased her beauty, that she resembled rather an angel than a creature.

Dorastus and Fawnia were half astonished to see the old shepherd, marveling greatly what wind had brought him thither, till Capnio told them all the whole discourse: how Porrus was going to make his complaint to the king, if by policy he had not prevented him, and therefore now sith he was aboard for the avoiding of further danger, it were best to carry him into Italy.

Dorastus praised greatly his man's device, and allowed of his counsel, but Fawnia, (who still feared Porrus, as her father) began to blush for shame, that by her means he should either incur danger or displeasure.

The old shepherd hearing this hard sentence—that he should on such a sudden be carried from his wife, his country, and kinsfolk, into a foreign land amongst strangers—began with bitter tears to make his complaint and on his knees to entreat Dorastus that pardoning his unadvised folly he would give him leave to go home, swearing that he would keep all things as secret as they could wish. But these protestations could not prevail, although Fawnia entreated Dorastus very earnestly, but the mariners hoisting their main sails weighed anchors and hailed into the deep, where we leave them to the favor of the wind and seas, and return to Egistus.

Who having appointed this day to hunt in one of his forests called for his son Dorastus to go sport himself, because he saw that of late he began to lour, but his men made answer that he was gone abroad none knew whither, except he were gone to the grove to walk all alone as his custom was to do every day.

The king, willing to waken him out of his dumps, sent one of his men to go seek him, but in vain, for at last he returned, but find him he could not, so that the king went himself to go see the sport; where passing away the day, returning at night from hunting, he asked for his son, but he could not be heard of, which drove the king into a great choler, whereupon most of his noblemen and other courtiers, posted abroad to seek him, but they could not hear of him through all Sicilia, only they missed Capnio his man, which again made the king suspect that he was not gone far.

Two or three days being passed and no news heard of Dorastus, Egistus began to fear that he was devoured with some wild beasts, and upon that made out a great troop of men to go seek him, who coasted through all the country and searched in every dangerous and secret place, until at last they met with a fisherman that was sitting in a little covert hard by the seaside mending his net, when Dorastus and Fawnia took shipping, who being examined if he either knew or heard where the king's son was, without any secrecy at all revealed the whole matter, how he was sailed two days past and had in his company his man Capnio, Porrus and his fair daughter Fawnia. This heavy news was presently carried to the king, who half dead for sorrow commanded Porrus's wife to be sent for, she being come to the palace after due examination, confessed that her neighbors had oft told her that the king's son was too familiar with Fawnia her daughter; whereupon her husband fearing the worst, about two days past (hearing the king should go an hunting) rose early in the morning and went to make his complaint, but since she neither heard of him nor saw him, Egistus, perceiving the woman's unfeigned simplicity, let her depart without incurring further displeasure, conceiving such secret grief for his Son's reckless folly that he had so forgotten his honor and parentage by so base a choice to dishonor his father, and discredit himself, that with very care and thought he fell into a quartan fever,[1] which was so unfit for his aged years and complexion, that he became so weak as the physicians would grant him no life.

But his son Dorastus little regarded either father, country, or kingdom in respect of his lady Fawnia, for Fortune, smiling on his young novice, lent him so lucky a gale of wind, for the space of a day and a night, that the mariners lay and slept upon the hatches; but on the next morning about the break of the day, the air began to be overcast, the winds to rise, the seas to swell. Yea, presently there arose such a fearful tempest, as the ship was in danger to be swallowed up with every sea. The main mast with the violence of the wind was thrown overboard, the sails were torn, the tackling went in sunder, the storm raging still so furiously that poor Fawnia was almost dead for fear, but that she was greatly comforted with the presence of Dorastus. The tempest continued three days, all which time the Mariners every minute looked for death, and the air was so darkened with clouds that the Master could not tell by his compass in what coast they were. But upon the fourth day about ten of the clock, the wind began to cease, the sea to wax calm, and the sky to be clear, and the Mariners descried the coast of Bohemia, shooting of their ordnance for joy that they had escaped such a fearful tempest.

Dorastus, hearing that they were arrived at some harbor, sweetly kissed Fawnia, and bad her be of good cheer. When they told him that the port belonged unto the chief city of Bohemia where Pandosto kept his court, Dorastus began to be sad, knowing that his Father hated no man so much as Pandosto, and that the king himself had sought secretly to betray Egistus. This considered, he was half afraid to go on land but that Capnio counseled him to change his name and his country, until such time as they could get some other bark to transport them into Italy. Dorastus, liking this device, made his case privy to the mariners, rewarding them bountifully for their pains and charging them to say that he was a gentleman of Trapalonia called Meleagrus. The shipmen, willing to show what friendship they could to Dorastus, promised to be as secret as they could or he might wish, and upon this they landed in a little village a mile distant from the city, whereafter they had rested a day, thinking to make provision for their marriage, the fame of Fawnia's

1 A fever that recurs every four days.

beauty was spread throughout all the city, so that came to the ears of Pandosto, who then being about the age of fifty had notwithstanding young and fresh affections, so that he desired greatly to see Fawnia and to bring this matter the better to pass, hearing they had but one man and how they rested at a very homely house. He caused them to be apprehended as spies and sent a dozen of his guard to take them, who being come to their lodging told them the king's message. Dorastus, no whit dismayed, accompanied with Fawnia and Capnio, went to the court (for they left Porrus to keep the stuff)[1] who being admitted to the king's presence, Dorastus and Fawnia with humble obeisance saluted his majesty.

Pandosto, amazed at the singular perfection of Fawnia, stood half astonished, viewing her beauty, so that he had almost forgot himself what he had to do. At last with stern countenance, he demanded their names and of what country they were and what caused them to land in Bohemia:

> Sir (quoth Dorastus) know that my name Meleagrus is a knight born and brought up in Trapalonia, and this gentlewoman, whom I mean to take to my wife, is an Italian born in Padua, from whence I have now brought her. The cause I so small a train with me is for that her friends unwilling to consent, I intended secretly to convey her into Trapalonia, whither as I was sailing, by distress of weather I was driven into these coasts. Thus have you heard my name, my country, and the cause of my voyage.

Pandosto, starting from his seat as one in choler, made this rough reply:

> Meleagrus, I fear this smooth tale hath but small truth, and that thou coverest a foul skin with fair paintings. No doubt this lady by her grace and beauty is of her degree more meet for a mighty prince than for a simple knight, and thou like a perjured traitor hath bereft her of her parents to their present grief and her ensuing sorrow. Till therefore I hear more of her parentage and of thy calling, I will stay you both here in Bohemia.

1 I.e., the box with jewels and chain that the infant Fawnia wore when he found her.

Dorastus, in whom rested nothing but kingly valor, was not able to suffer the reproaches of Pandosto, but that he made him this answer:

> It is not meet for a king, without due proof to appeach any man of ill behavior nor upon suspicion to infer belief. Strangers ought to be entertained with courtesy, not to be entreated[1] with cruelty, least being forced by want to put up injuries, the gods revenge their cause with rigor.

Pandosto, hearing Dorastus utter these words, commanded that he should straight be committed to prison, until such time as they heard further of his pleasure, but as for Fawnia, he charged that she should be entertained in the court, with such courtesy as belonged to a stranger and her calling. The rest of the shipmen he put into the dungeon.

Having thus hardly handled the supposed Trapalonians, Pandosto, contrary to his aged years, began to be somewhat tickled with the beauty of Fawnia, insomuch that he could take no rest but cast in his old head a thousand new devises. At last he fell into these thoughts:

> How art thou pestered, Pandosto, with fresh affections and unfit fancies, wishing to possess with an unwilling mind, and a hot desire troubled with a cold disdain? Shall thy mind yield in age to that thou hast resisted in youth? Peace, Pandosto, blab not out that which thou mayest be ashamed to reveal to thyself. Ah, Fawnia is beautiful, and it is not for thine honor (fond fool) to name her that is thy captive and another man's concubine. Alas, I reach at that with my hand which my heart would fain refuse: playing like the bird ibis in Egypt, which hateth serpents, yet feedeth on her eggs.
>
> Tush, hot desires turn oftentimes to cold disdain. Love is brittle where appetite not reason bears the sway. Kings' thoughts ought not to climb so high as the heavens, but to look no lower than honor. Better it is to peck at the stars with the young eagles than to prey on dead carcasses with the vulture. Tis more honorable for Pandosto to die by concealing love than to enjoy such unfit love. Doth Pandosto then love? Yea. Whom? A maid unknown, yea, and perhaps immodest,

---

1 Treated.

> straggled[1] out of her own country, beautiful but not therefore chaste; comely in body but perhaps crooked in mind. Cease then, Pandosto, to look at Fawnia, much less to love her. Be not overtaken with a woman's beauty, whose eyes are framed by art to enamor, whose heart is framed by nature to enchant, whose false tears know their true times, and whose sweet words pierce deeper than sharp swords.

Here Pandosto ceased from his talk, but not from his Love. For although he sought by reason and wisdom to suppress this frantic affection, yet he could take no rest; the beauty of Fawnia had made such a deep impression in his heart. But on a day walking abroad into a Park, which was hard adjoining to his house, he sent by one of his servants for Fawnia, unto whom he uttered these words:

> Fawnia, I commend thy beauty and wit, and now pity thy distress and want, but if thou wilt forsake Sir Meliagrus, whose poverty, though a knight, is not able to maintain an estate answerable to thy beauty and yield thy consent to Pandosto, I will both increase thee with dignities and riches.
>
> No sir, answered Fawnia. Meliagrus is a knight that hath won me by love, and none but he shall wear me. His sinister mischance shall not diminish my affection but rather increase my good will. Think not though your grace hath imprisoned him without cause, that fear shall make me yield my consent. I had rather be Meliagrus's wife, and a beggar, than live in plenty and be Pandosto's concubine.

Pandosto, hearing the assured answer of Fawnia, would, notwithstanding, prosecute his suit to the uttermost, seeking with fair words and great promises to scale the fort of her chastity, swearing that if she would grant to his desire, Meleagrus should not only be set at liberty, but honored in his court amongst his nobles; but these alluring baits could not entice her mind from the love of her new betrothed mate Meleagrus, which Pandosto seeing, he left her alone for that time to consider more of the demand. Fawnia, being alone by herself, began to enter into these solitary meditations:

1 Strayed.

> Ah, infortunate Fawnia, thou seest to desire above fortune is to strive against the gods and fortune. Who gazeth at the sun weakeneth his sight. They which stare at the sky fall oft into deep pits. Haddest thou rested content to have been a shepherd, thou needst not to have feared mischance. Better had it been for thee, by sitting low, to have had quiet than by climbing high to have fallen into misery. But, alas, I fear not mine own danger but Dorastus's displeasure. Ah, sweet Dorastus, thou art a prince but now a prisoner, by too much love procuring thine own loss. Haddest thou not loved Fawnia, thou haddest been fortunate. Shall I then be false to him that hath forsaken kingdoms for my cause? No. Would my death might deliver him, so mine honor might be preserved.

With that, fetching a deep sigh, she ceased from her complaints and went again to the palace, enjoining a liberty without content, and proffered pleasure with small joy. But poor Dorastus lay all this while in close prison, being pinched with a hard restraint and pained with the burden of cold and heavy irons, sorrowing sometimes that his fond affection had procured him this mishap; that by the disobedience of his parents, he had wrought his own despite; another, while cursing the gods and fortune, that they should cross him with such sinister chance, uttering at last his passions in these words:

> Ah unfortunate wretch, born to mishap. Now thy folly hath his desert. Art thou not worthy for thy base mind to have bad fortune? Could the destinies favor thee, which hast forgot thine honor and dignities? Will not the gods plague him with despite that paineth his father with disobedience? Oh gods, if any favor or justice be left, plague me, but favor poor Fawnia, and shroud her from the tyrannies of wretched Pandosto, but let my death free her from mishap, and then welcome death.

Dorastus, pained with these heavy passions, sorrowed and sighed, but in vain, for which he used the more patience.

But again to Pandosto, who broiling at the heat of unlawful lust could take no rest but still felt his mind disquieted with his new love, so that his nobles and subjects marveled greatly at this sudden alteration, not being able to conjecture the cause of this his continued care. Pandosto, thinking every hour a year till he had talked once again with Fawnia, sent for her secretly into his chamber; whither though Fawnia unwillingly coming, Pandosto entertained her very courteously using these familiar speeches, which Fawnia answered as shortly in this wise:

PANDOSTO. Fawnia, are you become less willful and more wise, to prefer the love of a king before the liking of a poor knight. I think ere this you think it is better to be favored of a king than of a subject.

FAWNIA. Pandosto, the body is subject to victories, but the mind not to be subdued by conquest. Honesty is to be preferred before honor, and a dram of faith weigheth down a ton of gold. I promised Meleagrus to love, and will perform no less.

PANDOSTO. Fawnia, I know thou art not so unwise in thy choice as to refuse the offer of a king, nor so ungrateful as to despise a good turn. Thou art now in that place where I may command, and yet thou seest I entreat. My power is such as I may compel by force, and yet I sue by prayers. Yield, Fawnia, thy love to him which burneth in thy love. Meleagrus shall be set free, thy countrymen discharged, and thou both loved and honored.

FAWNIA. I see, Pandosto, where lust ruleth it is a miserable thing to be a virgin, but know this, that I will always prefer fame before life, and rather choose death then dishonor.

Pandosto, seeing that there was in Fawnia a determinate courage to love Meleagrus and a resolution without fear to hate him, fleeing away from her in a rage, swearing if in short time she would not be won by reason: he would forget all courtesy and compel her to grant by rigor. But these threatening words no whit dismayed Fawnia, but that she still both despited and despised Pandosto. While thus these two Lovers strove, the one to win love, the other to live in hate, Egistus heard certain news by merchants of Bohemia that his son Dorastus was imprisoned by Pandosto, which made him fear greatly that his son should be but hardly entreated, yet considering that Bellaria and he were cleared by the oracle of Apollo from that crime wherewith Pandosto had unjustly charged them, he thought best to send with all speed to Pandosto, that he should set free his son Dorastus and put to death Fawnia and her father Porrus. Finding this by the advice of counsel the speediest remedy to release his son, he caused presently two of his ships to be rigged and thoroughly furnished with provision of men and victuals and sent divers of his nobles, ambassadors, into Bohemia, who, willing to obey their king and receive their young prince, made no delays for fear of danger, but with as much speed as might be, sailed towards Bohemia. The wind and seas favored them greatly, which made them hope of some good hap, for within three days they were landed, which Pandosto no sooner heard of their arrival, but he in person went to meet them, entreating them with such sumptuous and familiar courtesy that they might well perceive how sorry he was for the former injuries he had offered to their king, and how willing (if it might be) to make amends. As Pandosto made report to them how one Meleagrus, a knight of Trapolonia, was lately arrived with a lady called Fawnia in his land, coming very suspiciously, accompanied only with one servant, and an old shepherd. The ambassadors perceived by the half what the whole tale meant and began to conjecture that it was Dorastus, who, for fear to be known, had changed his name; but dissembling the matter, they shortly arrived at the court, where after they had been very solemnly and sumptuously feasted, the noblemen of Sicilia being gathered together, they made report of their embassage, where they certified Pandosto that Meleagrus was son and heir to the king Egistus, and that his name was Dorastus. How contrary to the king's mind he had privily conveyed away that Fawnia, intending to marry her, being but daughter to that poor shepherd Porrus, whereupon the King's request was that Capnio, Fawnia, and Porrus might be murthered and put to death and that his son Dorastus might be sent home in safety.

Pandosto having attentively and with great marvel heard their embassage, willing to reconcile himself to Egistus and to show him how greatly he esteemed his favor, although love and fancy forbade him to hurt Fawnia, yet in despite of love he determined to execute Egistus's will without mercy, and therefore he presently sent for Dorastus out of prison, who marveling at his unlooked-for courtesy, found at his coming to the king's presence, that which he least doubted of, his father's ambassadors, who no sooner saw him but with great reverence they honored him; and Pandosto, embracing Dorastus, set him by him very lovingly in a chair of estate. Dorastus, ashamed that his folly was bewrayed, sate a long time as one in a muse, till Pandosto told him the sum of his father's embassage, which he had no sooner heard but he was touched at the quick for the cruel sentence that was pronounced against Fawnia. But neither could his sorrow nor persuasions prevail, for Pandosto commanded that Fawnia, Porrus, and Capnio should be brought to his presence, who were no sooner come, but Pandosto having his former Love turned to a disdainful hate, began to rage against Fawnia in these terms:

> Thou disdainful vassal, thou currish kite, assigned by the destinies to base fortune, and yet with an aspiring mind gazing after honor! How durst thou presume, being a beggar, to match with a prince, by thy alluring looks to enchant the son of a king to leave his own country to fulfill thy disordinate lusts. O despiteful mind! A proud heart in a beggar is not unlike to a great fire in a small cottage, which warmeth not the house but burneth it. Assure thyself thou shalt die, and thou old doting fool, whose folly hath been such, as to suffer thy daughter to reach above thy fortune, look for no other meed but the like punishment. But Capnio, thou which hast betrayed the king and has consented to the unlawful lust of thy lord and master, I know not how justly I may plague thee. Death is too easy a punishment for thy falsehood, and to live (if not in extreme misery) were not to show the equity. I therefore award that thou shalt thine eyes put out, and continually, while thou dyest, grind in a mill like a brute beast.

The fear of death brought a sorrowful silence upon Fawnia and Capnio, but Porrus seeing no hope of life, burst forth into these speeches:

> Pandosto, and ye noble ambassadors of Sicilia, seeing without cause I am condemned to die, I am yet glad I have opportunity to disburden my conscience before my death. I will tell you as much as I know, and yet no more than is true; whereas I am accused that I have been a supporter of Fawnia's pride, and she disdained as a vile beggar, so it is that I am neither father unto her, nor she daughter unto me.
>
> For so it happened that I being a poor shepherd in Sicilia, living by keeping other men's flocks, one of my sheep straying down to the seaside as I went to seek her, I saw a little boat driven upon the shore, wherein I found a babe of six days old, wrapped in a mantle of scarlet, having about the neck this chain. I, pitying the child and desirous of the treasure, carried it home to my wife, who with great care nursed it up and set it to keep sheep. Here is the chain and the jewels, and this

> Fawnia is the child whom I found in the boat. What she is or of what parentage, I know not, but this I am assured of, that she is none of mine.

Pandosto would scarce suffer him to tell out his tale, but that he required the time of the year, the manner of the boat, and other circumstances, which when he found agreeing to his count, he suddenly leapt from his seat and kissed Fawnia, wetting her tender cheeks with his tears, and crying, "My daughter Fawnia, ah sweet Fawnia, I am thy father, Fawnia." This sudden passion of the king drove them all into a maze, especially Fawnia and Dorastus. But when the king had breathed himself a while in this new joy, he rehearsed before the ambassadors the whole matter, how he had entreated his wife Bellaria for jealousy, and that this was the child whom he sent to float in the seas.

Fawnia was not more joyful that she had found such a father than Dorastus was glad he should get such a wife. The ambassadors rejoiced that their young Prince had made such a choice, that those kingdoms which through enmity had long time been dissevered, should now through perpetual amity be united and reconciled. The citizens and subjects of Bohemia (hearing that the king had found again his daughter, which was supposed dead, joyful that there was an heir apparent to their kingdom) made bonfires and shows throughout the city. The courtiers and knights appointed jousts and tourneys to signify their willing minds in gratifying the king's hap.[1]

Eighteen days being past in these princely sports, Pandosto, willing to recompense old Porrus of a shepherd made him a knight, which done, providing a sufficient navy to receive him and his retinue, accompanied with Dorastus, Fawnia, and the Sicilian ambassadors. He sailed towards Sicilia, where he was most princely entertained by Egistus, who, hearing this comical event, rejoiced greatly at his son's good hap, and without delay (to the perpetual joy of the two young lovers) celebrated the marriage, which was no sooner ended, but Pandosto (calling to mind how first he betrayed his friend Egistus, how his jealousy was the cause of Bellaria's death, that contrary to the law of nature he had lusted after his own daughter) moved with these desperate thoughts, he fell into a melancholy fit, and to close up the comedy with a tragical

---

1 Good fortune.

stratagem, he slew himself, whose death being many days bewailed of Fawnia, Dorastus, and his dear friend Egistus, Dorastus taking his leave of his father, went with his wife and the dead corpse into Bohemia, where after they were sumptuously entombed, Dorastus ended his days in contented quiet.

FINIS.

2. FROM OVID, *METAMORPHOSES*

[Ovid's *Metamorphoses* was a seminal text for the grammar school curriculum that Shakespeare most likely studied in Stratford. This collection of myths records the often violent intervention of the gods into the lives of mortals, a collision of immortal and mortal that typically resulted in the metamorphosis or transformation of humans as they fled from their godly pursuers. Arthur Golding published an English translation of all fifteen books in 1567, a popular edition reprinted numerous times in the late sixteenth and early seventeenth centuries that proved influential for Shakespeare and his fellow writers. Francis Meres is perhaps the earliest critic of Shakespeare's devotion to Ovid. Writing in his 1598 *Palladis Tamia, Wits Treasury*, Meres comments that "the sweet wittie soule of Ovid lives in mellifluous and hony-tongued Shakespeare, witness his *Venus and Adonis*, his *Lucrece*, his sugred *Sonts among his private friends*."[1] As Jonathan Bate observes, "The soul that has been metamorphosed into Shakespeare is that of Ovid, the poet of metamorphosis" (3). Indeed, the myths presented below are Ovidian instances of metamorphosis that inform Shakespeare's own poetic modulations of myth into dramatic form and allow its readers to experience the human dimension of metamorphosis that is as much psychological and emotional as it is corporeal. Source: *Shakespeare's Ovid: Being Arthur Golding's Translation of the Metamorphoses*. Ed. W.H. Rouse. London: De la More Press, 1904. <http://archive.org/stream/shakespearesovid00oviduoft/shakespearesovid00oviduoft_djvu.txt>.]

1 internetshakespeare.uvic.ca/Library/SLT/life/early%20maturity/meres.html.

a. Pygmalion

[Book 10 of Ovid's *Metamorphoses* contains the tale of Pygmalion, a sculptor who falls in love with the ivory statue he fashions to compensate for his disgust over female libertines. The goddess Venus takes pity on Pygmalion and his devotion to his statue and animates it to provide a resolution that fulfills Pygmalion's desire for a perfect love. While Shakespeare clearly draws on the Pygmalion myth for this play, Hermione's own restoration is more nuanced: Hermione's "statue" is not the creation of a masculine wish-fulfillment but rather a product of Hermione and Paulina's feminine collusion. Shakespeare uses this myth to demonstrate the enforced artifice of Hermione's privation and later restoration to a Leontes responsible for her isolation and purposeful deprivation.]

And the time shall come ere many years be spent,
That in thy flower a valiant prince shall join himself with thee,
And leave his name upon the leaves for men to read and see.
While Phoebus[1] thus did prophesy, behold the blood of him
Which dyed the grass, ceased blood to be, and up there sprang
a trim
And goodly flower, more orient than the purple cloth ingrain,
In shape a lily, were it not that lillies do remain
Of silver color, whereas these of purple hue are seen.
Although that Phoebus had the cause of this great honor been,
Yet thought he not the same enough. And therefore did he write
His sighs upon the leaves thereof: and so in color bright
The flower hath a writ thereon, which letters are of grief.
So small the Spartans thought the birth of Hyacinth reproof
Unto them, that they worship him from that day unto this.
And as their fathers did before, so they do never miss
With solemn pomp to celebrate his feast from year to year.
But if perchance that Amathus the rich in metals, were
Demanded if it would have bred the prophets it would swear,
Yea even as gladly as the folk whose brews sometime did bear
A pair of welked[2] horns: whereof they Cerastes named are.

1 Apollo.
2 Ridged.

Before their door an Altar stood of Jove that takes the care
Of alyents[1] and of travelers, which loathsome was to see,
For lewdness wrought thereon. If one that had a stranger be
Had looked thereon, he would have thought there had on it been killed
Some sucking calves or lambs. The blood of strangers there was spilled.
Dame Venus sore offended at this wicked sacrifice,
To leave her cities and the land of Cyprus did devise
But then bethinking her, she said: What hath my pleasant ground,
What have my cities trespassed? what fault in them is found?
Nay rather let this wicked race by exile punished been,
Or death, or by some other thing that is a mean between
Both death and exile. What is that? save only for to change
Their shape. In musing with herself what figure were most strange,
She cast her eye upon a horn. And there withal she thought
The same to be a shape right meet upon them to be brought:
And so she from their mighty limbs their native figure took,
And turned them into boisterous bulls with grim and cruel look.
Yet durst the filthy prophets stand in stiff opinion that
Dame Venus was no goddess till she being wroth thereat,
To make their bodies common first compelled them everychone[2]
And after changed their former kind. For when that shame was gone,
And that they waxed brazen fast, she turned them to stone,
In which between their former shape was difference small or none.
Whom for because Pygmalion saw to lead their life in sin
Offended with the vice whereof great store is packed within
The nature of the womankind, he led a single life.
And long it was ere he could find in heart to take a wife.

1 Aliens.
2 Everyone.

Now in the while by wondrous art an image he did grave
Of such proportion, shape, and grace as nature never gave
Nor can to any woman give. In this his work he took
A certain love. The look of it was right a maiden's look,
And such a one as that ye would believe had life, and that
Would moved be, if womanhood and reverence letted[1] not.
So artificial was the work. He wondreth at his art
And of his counterfeited corse[2] conceiveth love in heart.
He often touched it, feeling if the work that he had made
Were very flesh or ivory still. Yet could he not persuade
Himself to think it ivory, for he oftentimes it kissed
And thought it kissed him again. He held it by the fist,
And talked to it. He believed his fingers made a dint
Upon her flesh, and feared lest some black or bruised print
Should come by touching over hard. Sometime with pleasant bourds[3]
And wanton toys he dallyingly doth cast forth amorous words.
Sometime (the gifts wherein young maids are wonted to delight)
He brought her ouches,[4] fine round stones, and lilies fair and white,
And pretty singing birds, and flower of thousand sorts and hue,
In gorgeous garments furthermore he did her also deck,
And painted balls, and amber from the tree distilled new.
And on her fingers put me rings, and chains about her neck.
Rich pearls were hanging at her ears, and tablets at her breast.
All kind of things became her well. And when she was undressed,
She seemed not less beautiful. He laid her in a bed
The which with scarlet dyed in tyre[5] was richly overspread,
And terming her his bedfellow, he couched down her head
Upon a pillow soft, as though she could have felt the same.
The feast of Venus hallowed through the isle of Cyprus, came

1 Prevented.
2 Corpse, body.
3 Jokes.
4 Brooches.
5 Rich purple.

And bullocks white with gilden horns were slain for sacrifice,
And up to heaven of frankincense the smoky fume did rise.
When as Pygmalion having done his duty that same day,
Before the altar standing, thus with fearful heart did say:
"If that you goddess can all things give, then let my wife (I pray)
(He durst not say be yon same wench of ivory, but) be like
My wench of ivory." Venus (who was nought at all to seek
What such a wish as that did mean) then present at her feast,
For handsel[1] of her friendly help did cause three times, at least
The fire to kindle and to spire thrice upward in the air.
As soon as he came home, straightway Pygmalion did repair
Unto the image of his wench, and leaning on the bed,
Did kiss her. In her body straight a warmness seemed to spread.
He put his mouth again to hers, and on her breast did lay
His hand. The ivory waxed soft: and putting quite away
All hardness, yielded underneath his fingers, as we see
A piece of wax made soft against the sun, or drawn to be
In divers shapes by chafing it between one's hands, and so
To serve to uses. He amazed stood wavering to and fro
Tween joy, and fear to be beguiled, again he burnt in love,
Again with feeling he began his wished hope to prove.
He felt it very flesh in deed. By laying on his thumb,
He felt her pulses beating. Then he stood no longer dumb
But thanked Venus with his heart, and at the length he laid
His mouth to hers who was as then become a perfect maid.
She felt the kiss, and blushed thereat: and lifting fearfully
Her eyelids up, her lover and the light at once did spy.
The marriage that herself had made the goddess blessed so,
That when the moon with fulsome light nine times her course
    had go,
This lady was delivered of a son that Paphos hight,[2]
Of whom the island takes that name.

1 Omen.
2 Was named.

b. Ceres and Proserpina

[The myth of a mother and daughter forcefully separated and reunited forms a major source for Shakespeare's account of Hermione and Perdita's 16-year separation. In Ovid, Proserpina's abduction by the god of the underworld, Dis, compels Ceres to search above and below the waters to find her daughter. She is assisted in her search by a number of nymphs who themselves are metamorphosed figures, including the fountains Cyan and Arethusa. Though the god Jove exercises his power to restore Ceres and Proserpina, the reunion is limited to a six-month period, spring-time, when Ceres's fertility holds sway over the earth; Dis claims her for the remainder of the year, winter, when Ceres is dormant and estranged from her daughter.]

While in this garden Proserpine was taking her pastime,
In gathering either violets blue, or lilies white as lime,
And while of maidenly desire she filled her maundy[1] and lap,
Endeavoring to outgather her companions there, by hap
Dis spied her: loved her: caught her up: and all at once well
    near,
So hasty, hot, and swift a thing is love as may appear.
The lady with a wailing voice affright did often call
Her mother and her waiting maids, but mother most of all.
And as she from the upper part her garment would have rent,
By chance she let her lap slip down, and out her flowers went.
And such a silly simpleness her childish age yet bears,
That even the very loss of them did move her more to tears.
The catcher drives his chariot forth, and calling every horse
By name, to make away apace he doth them still enforce:
And shakes about their necks and manes their rusty bridle reins
And through the deepest of the lake perforce he them
    constrains.
And through the Palic[2] pools, the which from broken ground
    do boil
And smell of brimstone very rank: and also by the soil
Where as the Bacchies, folk of Corinth with the double seas,

1 Wicker basket.
2 Slavic river.

Between unequal havens twain did rear a town for ease.
Between the fountains of Cyan and Arethuse of Pise
An arm of sea that meets enclosed with narrow horns there lies.
Of this the pool called Cyan which beareth greatest fame
Among the nymphs of Sicily did algates[1] take the name.
Who vauncing[2] her unto the waste amid her pool did know
Dame Proserpine, and said to Dis: Ye shall no further go:
You cannot Ceres' son-in-law be, will she so or no.
You should have sought her courteously and not enforst her so.
And if I may with great estates my simple things compare,
Anapus was in love with me: but yet he did not fare
As you do now with Proserpine. He was content to woo
And I unforst and unconstrained consented him unto.
This said, she spreaded forth her arms and stopt him of his way.
His hastier wrath Saturnus's son[3] no longer then could stay.
But cheering up his dreadful steeds did smite his royal mace
With violence in the bottom of the pool in that same place.
The ground straight yielded to his stroke and made him way to Hell,
And down the open gap both horse and chariot headlong fell.
Dame Cyan taking sore to heart as well the ravishment
Of Proserpine against her will, as also the contempt ...
Against her fountain's privilege, did shroud in secret heart
An inward corsie[4] comfortless, which never did depart
Until she melting into tears consumed away with smart.
The selfsame waters of the which she was but late ago
The mighty goddess, now she pines and wastes herself into.
Ye might have seen her limbs wax lithe, ye might have bent her bones.
Her nails waxed soft: and first of all did melt the smallest ones:
As hair and fingers, legs and feet: for these same slender parts
Do quickly into water turn, and afterward converts
To water, shoulder, back, breast, side: and finally in stead
Of lively blood, within her veins corrupted there was spread

1 Always.
2 Advancing.
3 Dis.
4 Grievance.

Thin water: so that nothing now remained whereupon
Ye might take hold, to water all consumed was anon.
The careful mother in the while did seek her daughter dear
Through all the world both sea and land, and yet was near the near.
The morning with her dewy hair her slugging never found,
Nor yet the evening star that brings the night upon the ground.
Two seasoned pine trees at the mount of Aetna[1] did she light
And bare[2] them restless in her hands through all the dankest night.
Again as soon as cheerful day did dim the stars, she sought
Her daughter still from east to west. And being overwrought
She caught a thirst: no liquor yet had come within her throat.
By chance she spied near at hand a thatched cote[3]
With peevish doors: she knocked thereat, and out there comes a trot.
The goddess asked her some drink and she denied it not:
But out she brought her by and by a draught of merry go down[4]
And therewithal a hotchpotch[5] made of steeped barley brown
And flax and coriander seed and other simples more
The which she in an earthen pot together sod[6] before.
While Ceres was a eating this, before her gazing stood ...
A hard fast boy, a shrewd pert wag, that could no manners good:
He laughed at her and in scorn did call her greedy gut.
The goddess being wroth therewith did on the hotchpotch put
The liquor ere that all was eat, and in his face it threw.
Immediately the skin thereof became of speckled hew,[7]
And into legs his arms did turn: and in his altered hide
A wriggling tail straight to his limbs was added more beside.

1 Volcanic mountain on east coast of Sicily.
2 Bore.
3 Roofed hut.
4 A strong wine.
5 Thick stew.
6 Baked.
7 Hue.

And to th' intent he should not have much power to worken scathe,
His body in a little room together knit she hath.
For as with pretty lizard he in fashion doth agree:
So than the lizard somewhat less in every point is he.
The poor old woman was amazed: and bitterly she wept:
She durst not touch the uncouth worm, which into corners crept.
And of the flecked spots like stars that on his hide are set
A name agreeing thereunto in Latin doth he get.
It is our swift whose skin with gray and yellow specks is fret.
What lands and seas the goddess sought it were too long to sayen.
The world did want. And so she went to Sicill back again.
And is in going every where she searched busily,
She also came to Cyane:[1] who would assuredly
Have told her all things, had she not transformed been before.
But mouth and tongue for utterance now would serve her turn no more.
Howbeit a token manifest she gave her for to know
What was become of Proserpine. Her girdle she did show
Still hovering on her holy pool, which slightly from her fell
As she that way did pass: and that her mother knew too well.
For when she saw it, by and by as though she had but then
Been new advertised of her chance, she piteously began
To rend her ruffled hair, and beat her hands against her breast.
As yet she knew not where she was. But yet with rage opprest,
She curst all lands, and said they were unthankful everychone,[2]
Yea and unworthy of the fruits bestowed them upon.
But bitterly above the rest she banned Sicilie,
In which the mention of her loss she plainly did espy.
And therefore there with cruel hand the earing ploughs[3] she brake,
And man and beast that tilde[4] the ground to death in anger strake.

1 A river goddess.
2 Everyone.
3 Plows for tilling.
4 Tilled.

She marred the seed, and eke[1] forbade the fields to yield their fruit.
The plenteousness of that same Ile[2] of which there went such bruit[3]
Through all the world, lay dead: the corn was killed in the blade:
Now too much drought, now too much wet did make it for to fade.
The stars and blasting winds did hurt, the hungry fowls did eat
The corn to ground: the tines[4] and briars did overgrow the wheat.
And other wicked weeds the corn continually annoy,
Which neither tilth[5] nor toil of man was able to destroy.
Then Arethuse, flood Alphey's love,[6] lifts from her Elean waves
Her head, and shedding to her ears her dewy hair that waves
About her forehead said: O thou that art the mother dear
Both of the maiden sought through all the world both far and near,
And eke of all the earthly fruits, forbear thine endless toil,
And be not wroth without a cause with this thy faithful soil:
The land deserves no punishment. Unwillingly, God wot,[7]
She opened to the ravisher that violently her smote.
It is not sure my native soil for which I thus entreat.
I am but here a sojourner, my native soil and seat
In Pisa and from Ely town I fetch my first descent.
I dwell but as a stranger here: but sure to my intent
This country likes me better far than any other land.
Here now I Arethusa dwell: here am I settled: and
I humbly you beseech extend your favor to the same.
A time will one day come when you to mirth may better frame, ...
And have your heart more free from care, which better serve me may

1 Also.
2 I.e., Sicily.
3 Report, rumor.
4 Thorns.
5 Tillage.
6 In Greek mythology, Arethusa was a water nymph pursued by the river god Alpheus; "Elean" refers to Elis, a region in southern Greece.
7 Knows.

To tell you why I from my place so great a space do stray,
And unto Ortygy[1] am brought through so great seas and waves.
The ground doth give me passage free, and by the lowest caves
Of all the earth I make my way, and here I raise my head,
And look upon the stars again neared out of knowledge fled.
Now while I underneath the earth the lake of Styx did pass,
I saw your daughter Proserpine with these same eyes. She was
Not merry, neither rid of fear as seemed by her cheer.
But yet a queen, but yet of great god Dis the stately fere;[2]
But yet of that same droopy realm the chief and sovereign peer.
Her mother stood as stark as stone, when she these news did hear,
And long she was like one that in another world had been.
But when her great amazedness by greatness of her teen[3]
Was put aside, she gets her to her chariot by and by
And up to heaven in all post haste immediately doth sty.[4]
And there beslubbered all her face: her hair about her ears,
To royal Jove in way of plaint this spiteful tale she bears:
As well for thy blood as for mine a suitor unto thee
I hither come. If no regard may of the mother be ...
Yet let the childe her father move, and have not lesser care
Of her (I pray) because that I her in my body bare.
Behold our daughter whom I sought so long is found at last:
If finding you it term, when of recovery means is past.
Or if you finding do it call to have a knowledge where
She is become. Her ravishment we might consent to bear,
So restitution might be made. And though there were to me
No interest in her at all, yet forasmuch as she
Is yours, it is unmeet she be bestowed upon a thief.
Jove answered thus: "My daughter is a jewel dear and life,
A collop[5] of mine own flesh cut as well as out of thine.
But if we in our hearts can find things rightly to define,
This is not spite but love. And yet madam in faith I see
No cause of such a son in law ashamed for to be,

1 Ortigya, an island that is the historical center of Syracuse, Sicily.
2 Spouse.
3 Anger.
4 Climb.
5 Slice of meat; see also p. 76, note 5.

So you contented were therewith. For put the case that he
Were destitute of all things else, how great a matter is't
Jove's brother for to be? but sure in him is nothing mist.
Nor he inferior is to me save only that by lot
The Heavens to me, the Hells to him the destinies did allot.
But if you have so sore desire your daughter to divorce,
Though she again to Heaven repair I do not greatly force.
But yet conditionally that she have tasted there no food:
For so the destinies have decreed." He ceased: and Ceres stood
Full bent to fetch her daughter out: but destinies her withstood,
Because the maid had broke her fast. For as she happed one day
In Pluto's orchard recklessly from place to place to stray,
She gathering from a bowing tree a ripe powngarnet,[1] took
Seven kernels out and sucked them. None chanced hereon to look,
Save only one Ascalaphus[2] whom Orphne, erst[3] a dame
Among the other elves of Hell not of the basest fame,
Bare to her husband Acheron within her dusky den.
He saw it, and by blabbing it ungraciously as then,
Did let[4] her from returning thence. A grievous sigh the queen
Of Hell did fetch, and of that wight[5] that had a witness been
Against her made a cursed bird.[6] Upon his head she shed
The water of the Phlegeton:[7] and by and by his head
Was nothing else but beak and down, and mighty glaring eyes.
Quite altered from himself between two yellow wings he flies.
He groweth chiefly into head and hooked talons long
And much ado he hath to flask[8] his lazy wings among.
The messenger of morning was he made, a filthy fowl,
A sign of mischief unto men, the sluggish screeching owl.
This person for his lavish tongue and telling tales might seem
To have deserved punishment. But what should men esteem

1 Pomegranate.

2 Ascalaphus was the son of Orphne and Acheron.

3 Formerly.

4 Prevent.

5 Person.

6 Ascalaphus was transformed into an owl for revealing that Proserpina had eaten a pomegranate from Pluto's (Dis's) orchard.

7 Fiery river in Hades.

8 Flap.

To be the very cause why you, Acheloy's daughters,[1] wear
Both feet and feathers like to birds, considering that you bear
The upper parts of maidens still? And comes it so to pass
Because when Lady Proserpine a gathering flowers was,
Ye mermaids kept her company? Whom after you had sought
Through all the earth in vain, anon of purpose that your thought
Might also to the seas be known, ye wished that ye might
Upon the waves with hovering wings at pleasure rule your flight.
And had the gods to your request so pliant, that ye found
With yellow feathers out of hand your bodies clothed round:
Yet lest that pleasant tune of yours ordained to delight
The hearing, and so high a gift of music perish might
For want of utterance, human voice to utter things at will
And countenance of virginity remained to you still.
But mean between his brother and his heavy sister go'th
God Jove, and parteth equally the years between them both.
And now the goddess Proserpine indifferently doth reign
Above and underneath the earth, and so doth she remain
One half year with her mother and the residue with her fere.
Immediately she altered is as well in outward cheer
As inward mined. For where her look might late before appear
Sad even to Dis, her countenance now is full of mirth and grace
Even like as Phoebus having put the watery clouds to chase,
Doth show himself a conqueror with bright and shining face.
Then fruitful Ceres void of care in that she did recover
Her daughter, prayed thee, Arethuse, the story to discover....
What caused thee to fleet so far and wherefore[2] thou became
A sacred spring? The waters whist.[3]

1 I.e., the Sirens, mythological sisters whose beautiful voices lured sailors to their death.

2 Why.

3 Were hushed.

c. Callisto

[Callisto was a nymph of chastity—a devotee of the huntress Diana—who, after being forcibly taken by Jove and impregnated by the god in his disguise as Diana, is further victimized by both Diana and Juno, the former in banishing Callisto when the pregnancy is discovered and the latter in transforming Callisto into a bear in the heat of her wrath caused by her husband's infidelity. Callisto's son, Arcas, later confronts his mother while he is hunting, and despite Callisto's desire to embrace her son, Arcas fearfully seeks to slay this approaching beast of the forest. Jove, in the throes of pity, transforms Callisto into the Ursa Major constellation and her son into the Ursa Minor constellation in order that mother and son may be reunited. Within this myth, Shakespeare may have found two ideas for *The Winter's Tale*: mother and child reunited after a prolonged separation, and the bear as a victimized object of a hunt more deserving of pity than vengeance.]

There is no cause of further stay. To spite her heart withal,
Her husband's leman[1] bare a boy that Arcas men did call.
On whom she casting louring look with fell and cruel mind
Said: was there, arrant strumpet thou, none other shift to find
But that thou needs must be with bairn? that all the world must see
My husband's open shame and thine in doing wrong to me?
But neither unto heaven nor hell this trespass shalt thou bear.
I will bereave thee of thy shape through pride whereof thou were
So hardy to entice my fere. Immediately with that
She raught her by the foretop fast[2] and fiercely threw her flat
Against the ground. The wretched wench her arms up meekly cast,
Her arms began with grisly hair to wax all rugged fast.
Her hands gan warp and into paws ylfavoredly[3] to grow,
And for to serve instead of feet. The lips that late ago
Did like the mighty Jove so well, with side and flaring flaps
Became a wide deformed mouth. And further lest perhaps

1 Lover.

2 Seized her firmly by the hair.

3 Ill-favoredly, ugly.

Her prayers and her humble words might cause her to relent:
She did bereave her of her speech. Instead whereof there went
An ireful, hoarse, and dreadful voice out from a threatening throat:
But yet the selfsame mind that was before she turned her coat
Was in her still in shape of bear. The grief whereof she shows
By thrusting forth continual sighs, and up she ghastly throws
Such kind of hands as then remained unto the starry sky.
And for because she could not speak she thought Jove inwardly
To be unthankful. Oh how oft she daring not abide
Alone among the desert[1] woods, full many a time and tide
Would stalk before her house in grounds that were her own erewhile?[2]
How oft oh did she in the hills the barking hounds beguile[3]
And in the lands where she herself had chased erst[4] her game,
Now fly herself to save her life when hunters sought the same?
Full oft at sight of other beasts she hid her head for fear,
Forgetting what she was herself. For though she were a bear,
Yet when she spied other bear she quooked[5] for very pain:
And feared wolves although her sire among them did remain.

1 Remote.
2 Lately.
3 Deceive.
4 Formerly.
5 Quaked.

APPENDIX B: ANALOGS

1. FROM JAMES VI OF SCOTLAND, *BASILIKON DORON* (1599)

[The *Basilikon Doron* (a Greek phrase meaning "royal gift") is a richly important document for the role it plays in defining the Jacobean court and its use of domestic metaphor for describing regal power and responsibility. In addition, this treatise is a useful reminder of how the future James I of England viewed his relationship with his family and his subjects, all of whom are directed to view him as their royal father. Written in 1599 and intended as an informative and instructive handbook for James's son, Prince Henry (1594–1612), *Basilikon Doron* is a political reinforcement of the dramatic issues that Leontes raises in the *The Winter's Tale*: the legitimacy of his fatherhood and the replication of his image in his son Mamillius. The same sense of political and iconic replication is on display in James's initial private document to his son. In addition, James I's pedantic qualities are prominent in this text as he attempts to shape his son in his own royal image, intending the Jacobean image of kingship to extend generationally to embrace his progeny.

The treatise is divided into three sets of guidelines: the king's responsibility as a good Christian to emulate God and his goodness; the king's responsibility to avoid becoming tyrannical by governing his subjects both judiciously and wisely, taking the time to study both his subjects and their needs, and the best way to provide prudent government; the king's responsibility to behave moderately in "things indifferent," those behaviors that are daily displays of monarchical prerogative.

The excerpts below present the opening sonnet and preamble to James's son, followed by paternal advice in book two on how to conduct oneself in the office, especially in its fulfillment through the matrimonial state. Both sections are useful touchstones for *The Winter's Tale* in providing the discursive context for issues that Shakespeare dramatizes in Leontes's immoderate conduct towards his family and his fear of domestic illegitimacy caused by the presumed adultery of Hermione. Source: <http://www.stoics.com/basilikon_doron.html>.]

Book I. Of a King's Christian Duty Towards God

GOD gives not kings the style of gods in vain,
For on his throne his scepter do they sway,
And as their subjects ought them to obey,
So kings should fear and serve their god again
If then ye would enjoy a happy reign.
Observe the statutes of your heavenly king,
And from his law, make all your laws to spring.
Since his lieutenant here ye should remain,
Reward the just, be steadfast, true, and plain,
Repress the proud, maintaining aye[1] the right,
Walk always so, as ever in his sight,
Who guards the godly, plaguing the profane.
And so ye shall in princely virtues shine,
Resembling right your mighty king divine.

TO HENRY MY DEAREST SON, AND NATURAL SUCCESSOR.

WHOM-to can so rightly appertain this book of instructions to a prince in all the points of his calling, as well general, as a Christian towards God; as particular, as a king towards his people? Whom-to, I say, can it so justly appertain, as unto you my dearest son? Since I the author thereof, as your natural father, must be careful for your godly and virtuous education, as my eldest son, and the first fruits of God's blessing towards me in thy posterity; and as a king must timously[2] provide for your training up in all the points of a king's office since ye are my natural and lawful successor therein, that being rightly informed hereby of the weight of your burthen, ye may in time begin to consider, that being born to be a king, ye are rather born to *onus*, than *honos*,[3] not excelling all your people so far in rank and honor, as in daily care and hazardous painstaking, for the dutiful administration of that great office, that God hath laid upon your shoulders. Laying so a just symmetry and proportion betwixt the height of your honorable place and the heavy weight of your great charge, and consequently, in case of failing, which God forbid, of the sadness of your

1 Ever.

2 Promptly.

3 I.e., born to a burden rather than an honor (Latin).

fall, according to the proportion of that height. I have therefore for the greater ease to your memory, and that ye may, at the first cast up any part that ye have to do with, divided this treatise in three parts: the first teacheth you your duty towards God as a Christian; the next, your duty in your office as a king; and the third informeth you how to behave yourself in indifferent things, which of themselves are neither right nor wrong, but according as they are rightly or wrong used, and yet will serve according to your behavior therein, to augment or impair your fame and authority at the hands of your people. Receive and welcome this book then as a faithful preceptor and counselor unto you, which, because my affairs will not permit me ever to be present with you, I ordain to be a resident faithful admonisher of you. And because the hour of death is uncertain to me, as unto all flesh, I leave it as my testament and latter will unto you. Charging you in the presence of GOD, and by the fatherly authority I have over you, that ye keep it ever with you, as carefully, as Alexander did the *Iliads* [*sic*] of Homer. Ye will find it a just and impartial counselor, neither flattering you in any vice, not importuning you at unmeet times. It will not come uncalled, neither speak unspeered at;[1] and yet conferring with it when ye are at quiet, ye shall say with Scipio that ye are *nunquam minus solus, quam cum solus*.[2] To conclude then, I charge you, as ever ye thinks to deserve my fatherly blessing, to follow and put in practice, as far as lyeth in you, the precepts hereafter following. And if ye follow the contrary course, I take the Great God to record that this book shall one day be a witness betwixt me and you; and shall procure to be ratified in Heaven, the curse that in that case here I give unto you. For I protest before that Great God, I had rather not be a father and childless, than be a father of wicked children. But hoping, yea, even promising unto myself, that God, who in his great blessing sent you unto me, shall in the same blessing, as he hath given me a son, so make him a good and a godly son; not repenting him of his mercy showed unto me, I end, with my earnest prayer to God, to work effectually unto you, the fruits of that blessing, which here from my heart I bestow upon you.

Your loving Father
I. R. [Jacobus Rex]

---

1 Unasked.
2 Never less alone than when you are alone (Latin).

IV. *Book II. Of the King's Duty in His Office*

But the principal blessing that ye can get of good company will stand in your marrying of a godly and virtuous wife, for she must be nearer unto you than any other company, being flesh of your flesh, and bone of your bone, as Adam said of Hevah.[1] And because I know not but God may call me, before ye be ready for marriage, I will shortly set down to you here my advice therein.

First of all consider, that marriage is the greatest earthly felicity or misery that can come to a man, according as it pleaseth God to bless or curse the same. Since then without the blessing of God, ye cannot look for a happy success in marriage, ye must be careful both in your preparation for it and in the choice and usage of your wife, to procure the same. By your preparation, I mean, that ye must keep your body clean and unpolluted, till ye give it to your wife, whom-to only it belongeth. For how can ye justly crave to be joined with a pure virgin, if your body be polluted? Why should the one half be clean, and the other defiled? And although I know fornication is thought but a light and venial sin by the most part of the world, yet remember well what I said to you in my first book anent[2] conscience, and count every sin and breach of God's law, not according as the vain world esteemeth of it, but as God the judge and maker of the law accounteth of the same. Here God commanding by the mouth of Paul to abstain from fornication, declaring that the fornicator shall not inherit the kingdom of heaven; and by the mouth of John, reckoning our fornication amongst other grievous sins, that debar the committers amongst dogs and swine from entry in that spiritual and heavenly Jerusalem. And consider, if a man shall once take upon him, to count that light which God calleth heavy, and venial that which God calleth grievous; beginning first to measure any one sin by the rule of his lust and appetites and not of his conscience; what shall let him to do so with the next, that his affections shall stir him to, the like reason serving for all, and so to go forward till he place his whole corrupted affections in God's room? And then what shall come of him, but as a man given over to his own filthy affections, shall perish into them? And because we are all of that nature, that sibbest[3] examples touch us nearest, consider the difference of success that God granted

1 Eve (Hebrew).
2 Regarding.
3 Familial.

in the marriages of the king my grandfather, and me your own father: the reward of his incontinency (proceeding from his evil education) being the sudden death at one time of two pleasant young princes; and a daughter only born to succeed to him, whom he had never the hap, so much as once to see or bless before his death; leaving a double curse behind him to the land, both a woman of sex, and a new born babe of age to reign over them. And as for the blessing God hath bestowed on me in granting me both a greater continence and the fruits following thereupon, yourself and sib folks to you are (praise be to God) sufficient witnesses; which I hope the same God of his infinite mercy shall continue and increase, without repentance to me and my posterity. Be not ashamed then, to keep clean your body, which is the temple of the Holy Spirit, notwithstanding all vain allurements to the contrary, discerning truly and wisely of every virtue and vice, according to the true qualities thereof, and not according to the vain conceits of men.

As for your choice in marriage, respect chiefly the three causes wherefore marriage was first ordained by God; and then join three accessories, so far as they may be obtained, not derogating to the principles.

The three causes it was ordained for are for staying of lust, for procreation of children, and that man should by his wife get a helper like himself. Defer not then to marry till your age, for it is ordained for quenching the lust of your youth. Especially a king must tymouslie[1] marry for the weal[2] of his people. Neither marry ye, for any accessory cause or worldly respects, a woman unable, either through age, nature, or accident, for procreation of children, for in a king that were a double fault, as well against his own weal, as against the weal of his people. Neither also marry one of known evil conditions or vicious education; for the woman is ordained to be a helper and not a hinderer to man.

The three accessories, which as I have said ought also to be respected, without derogating to the principal causes, are beauty, riches, and friendship by alliance, which are all blessings of God. For beauty increaseth your love to your wife, contenting you the better with her, without caring for others; and riches and great alliance do both make her the abler to be a helper unto you. But if over great respect being had to these accessories, the principal causes be overseen (which is over

1 Timely.

2 Welfare, benefit.

oft practiced in the world) as of themselves they are a blessing being well used; so the abuse of them will turn them in a curse. For what can all these worldly respects avail when a man shall find himself coupled with a devil, to be one flesh with him, and the half marrow[1] in his bed? Then (though too late) shall he find that beauty without bounty, wealth without wisdom, and great friendship without grace and honesty are but fair shows and the deceitful masques of infinite miseries.

But have ye respect, my Son, to these three special causes in your marriage, which flow from the first institution thereof, & *coetera omnia adjicientur vobis*.[2] And therefore I would rathest[3] have you to marry one that were fully of your own religion; her rank and other qualities being agreeable to your estate. For although that to my great regret, the number of any princes of power and account, professing our religion be but very small; and that therefore this advice seems to be the more strait and difficile;[4] yet ye have deeply to weigh and consider upon these doubts, how ye and your wife can be of one flesh and keep unity betwixt you, being members of two opposite churches. Disagreement in religion bringeth ever with it disagreement in manners; and the dissention betwixt your preachers and hers will breed and foster a dissension among your subjects, taking their example from your family; besides the peril of the evil education of your children. Neither pride you that ye will be able to frame and make her as ye please; that deceived Solomon the wisest king that ever was, the grace of perseverance not being a flower that groweth in our garden.

Remember also that marriage is one of the greatest actions that a man doth in all his time, especially in taking of his first wife; and if he marry first basely beneath his rank, he will ever be the less accounted of thereafter. And lastly, remember to choose your wife as I advised you to choose your servants: that she be of a whole and clean race, not subject to the hereditary sicknesses, either of the soul or the body. For if a man will be careful to breed horses and dogs of good kinds, how much more careful should he be, for the breed of his own loins? So shall ye in your marriage have respect to your conscience, honor, and natural weal in your successors.

---

1 Spouse, partner.

2 All things will be added unto you (Latin).

3 Rather.

4 Strict and difficult.

When ye are married, keep inviolably your promise made to God in your marriage, which standeth all in doing of one thing, and abstaining from another: to treat her in all things as your wife, and the half of yourself; and to make your body (which then is no more yours, but properly hers) common with none other. I trust I need not to insist here to dissuade you from the filthy vice of adultery; remember only what solemn promise ye make to God at your marriage, and since it is only by the force of that promise that your children succeed to you, which otherwayes[1] they could not do, equitie and reason would, ye should keep your part thereof. God is ever a severe avenger of all perjuries; and it is no oath made in jest that giveth power to children to succeed to great kingdoms. Have the king my grandfather's example before your eyes, who by his adultery bred the wrack of his lawful daughter and heir in begetting that bastard Moray,[2] who unnaturally rebelled and procured the ruin of his own sovereign and sister. And what good her posterity hath gotten sensyne[3] of some of that unlawful generation, Bothwell[4] his treacherous attempts can bear witness. Keep precisely then your promise made at marriage, as ye would wish to be partaker of the blessing therein.

And for your behavior to your wife, the Scripture can best give you counsel therein: Treat her as your own flesh, command her as her lord, cherish her as your helper, rule her as your pupil, and please her in all things reasonable; but teach her not to be curious in things that belong her not. Ye are the head, she is your body. It is your office to command, and hers to obey, but yet with such a sweet harmony as she should be as ready to obey, as ye to command; as willing to follow, as ye to go before; your love being wholly knit unto her, and her affections lovingly bent to follow your will.

And to conclude, keep specially three rules with your wife: first, suffer her never to meddle with the politick government of the commonweal, but hold her at the oeconomicke[5] rule of the house; and yet all to be

1 Otherwise.

2 James Stewart, 1st Earl of Moray, Queen Mary's illegitimate half-brother and Protestant rival to the Catholic queen's Scottish throne.

3 Since then.

4 James Hepburn, 4th Earl of Bothwell; third husband of Mary, Queen of Scots. Bothwell was tried and acquitted of the assassination of Queen Mary's consort, Henry Stuart, Lord Darnley, who was James I's father.

5 Economic.

subject to your direction; keep carefully good and chaste company about her, for women are the frailest sex; and be never both angry at once but when ye see her in passion, ye should with reason danton[1] yours. For both when ye are settled, ye are meetest[2] to judge of her errors; and when she is come to herself, she may be best made to apprehend her offence and reverence your rebuke.

2. FROM ROBERT GREENE, *THE SECOND AND LAST PART OF CONEY-CATCHING AND THE THIRD AND LAST PART OF CONEY-CATCHING* (1592)

[Autolycus is a successful coney-catcher in Shakespeare's play. The art of swindling is a chief topic for Robert Greene, whose 1588 novel *Pandosto* formed the primary source for Shakespeare's play (see Appendix A1, p. 201). Within a few years of this novel, Greene began to publish a series of pamphlets dealing with "cony-catching," the art of cutting purses or robbing unsuspected gulls. In the second and third of his pamphlets, published in 1592, Greene depicts the kinds of roguish thievery demonstrated by Autolycus: his robbing of the young clown by feigning his own victimizing at the hands of thieves. The young clown's naiveté invites Autolycus's success, and Greene's text supplies us with a historical correlative to Shakespeare's dramatization.

In the second excerpt, Greene demonstrates how the act of ballad-singing allows for an audience ripe for swindling. Like Autolycus with the Bohemian rustics, Greene's cutpurse uses his skill as a singer to generate his own ill-gotten gains. Both these examples testify to Shakespeare's historical veracity in describing the vocation of robbing that is emblematic of Autolycus's prodigious skill. Source: <http://www.luminarium.org/renascence-editions/greene4.html>.]

Book 2

While I was writing this discovery of foisting,[3] & was desirous of any intelligence that might be given me, a gentleman, a friend of mine, reported unto me this pleasant tale of a foist, and as I well remember it grew to this effect. There walked in the middle walk a plain country

1 Subdue.

2 Most fit.

3 Picking purses.

farmer, a man of good wealth, who had a well-lined purse, only barely thrust up in a round slop,[1] which a crew of foists having perceived, their hearts were set on fire to have it, & every one had a fling at him, but all in vain, for he kept his hand close in his pocket, and his purse fast in his fist like a subtle churl, that either had been forewarned of Paul's,[2] or else had aforetime smoked some of that faculty. Well, howsoever it was impossible to do any good with him he was so wary. The foists spying this, strained their wits to the highest string how to compass this boung,[3] yet could not all their politick conceits fetch the farmer over; for jostle him, chat with him, offer to shake him by the hand, all would not serve to get his hand out of his pocket. At last one of the crew that for his skill might have been doctorat in his mystery, amongst them all, choose out a good foist, one of a nimble hand and great agility, and said to the rest thus: "Masters, it shall not be said such a base peasant shall slip away from such a crew of gentlemen foists as we are and not have his purse drawn, and therefore this time I'll play the stall myself, and if I hit him not home, count me for a bungler for ever, and so left them and went to the farmer and walked directly before him and next him three or four turns, at last standing still," he cried "Alas, honest man, help me! I am not well", & with that sunk down suddenly in a sown,[4] the poor farmer seeing a proper young gentleman (as he thought) fall dead afore him, stepped to him, held him in his arms, rubbed him & chafed[5] him. At this there gathered a great multitude of people about him, and the whilst the foist drew the farmer's purse and away; by that the other thought the feat was done, he began to come something to himself again, and so half staggering, stumbled out of Paul's, and went after the crew where they had appointed to meet, and there boasted of his wit and experience. The farmer, little suspecting this villainy, thrust his hand into his pocket and missed his purse, searched for it, but lining and shells & all was gone, which made the country man in a great maze[6] that he stood still in a dump so long, that a gentleman perceiving it asked what

1 Breeches pocket.
2 St. Paul's Cathedral, presumably a place frequented by pickpockets.
3 Purse.
4 Swoon.
5 Warmed.
6 In a daze, amazement.

he ailed: "What ail I, sir?" quoth he. "Truly, I am thinking how men may long as well as women." "Why dost thou conjecture that, honest man?" quoth he. "Marry, sir," answers the farmer. "The gentleman even now that sound[1] here, I warrant him breeds his wife's child, for the cause of his sudden qualm that he fell down dead grew of longing." The gentleman demanded how he knew that. "Well enough, sir," quoth he. "And he hath his longing too, for the poor man longed for my purse, and thanks be to God he hath it with him." At this all the hearers laughed, but not so merrily as the foist and his fellows, that then were sharing his money.

Book 3

Another tale of a cozening companion, who would needs try his cunning in this new invented art, and how by his knavery (at one instant) he beguiled half a dozen and more.

Of late time there hath a certain base kind of trade been used, who though divers poor men, & doubtless honest apply themselves to, only to relieve their need, yet are there some notorious varlets do the same, being compacted with such kind of people as this present treatise manifesteth to the world, and what with outward simplicity on the one side, and cunning close treachery on the other, divers honest citizens and day-laboring men, that resort to such places as I am to speak of, only for recreation as opportunity serveth, have been of late sundry times deceived of their purses. This trade, or rather unsufferable loitering quality, in singing of ballets,[2] and songs at the doors of such houses where plays are used, as also in open markets and other places of this city, where is most resort; which is nothing else but a sly fetch to draw many together, who listening unto an harmless ditty, afterward walk home to their houses with heavy hearts. From such as are hereof true witnesses to their cost, do I deliver this example. A subtle fellow, belike emboldened by acquaintance with the former deceit, or else being but a beginner to practice the same, calling certain of his companions together, would try whether he could attain to be master of his art or no, by taking a great many of fools with one train. But let his intent and what else besides, remain to abide the censure after the matter is heard,

1 Swooned, fainted.

2 Ballads.

& come to Gracious street, where this villainous prank was performed. A roguing mate, & such another with him, were there got upo[n] a stall singing of ballets which belike was some pretty toy, for very many gathered about to hear it, & divers buying, as their affections served, drew to their purses & paid the singers for the[m]. The sly mate and his fellows, who were dispersed among them that stood to hear the songs: well noted where every man that bought, put up his purse again, and to such as would not buy, counterfeit warning was sundry times given by the rogue and his associate, to beware of the cut purse, and look to their purses, which made them often feel where their purses were, either in sleeve, hose, or at girdle, to know whether they were safe or no. Thus the crafty copesmates[1] were acquainted with what they most desired, and as they were scattered, by shouldering, thrusting, feigning to let fall something, and other wily tricks fit for their purpose. Here one lost his purse, there another had his pocket picked, and to say all in brief, at one instant, upon the complaint of one or two that saw their purses were gone, eight more in the same company found themselves in like predicament. Some angry, others sorrowful, and all greatly discontented looking about them, knew not who to suspect or challenge, in that the villains themselves that had thus beguiled them made show that they had sustained like loss. But one angry fellow, more impatient then all the rest, he falls upon the ballad singer and beating him with his fists well favoredly, says, if he had not listened his singing, he had not lost his purse, and therefore would not be other wise persuaded, but that they two and the cutpurses were compacted together. The rest that had lost their purses likewise, and saw that so ma[n]y complain together, they jump in opinion with the other fellow, & begin to tug & hale the ballad singers, when one after one, the false knaves began to shrink away with the purses. By means of some officer then being there prese[n]t, the two rogues were had before a Justice, and upon his discrete examination made, it was found that they and the cut-purses were compacted together, and that by this unsuspected villainy, they had deceived many. The fine fool-taker himself, with one or two more of that company, was not long after apprehended, when I doubt not but they had their reward answerable to their deserving, for I hear of

1 Associates.

their journey westward, but not of their return.[1] Let this forewarned those that listen singing in the streets.

3. FROM *GOD'S HANDI-WORK IN WONDERS* (1615)

[Autolycus's skill in generating gulls for his thievery is predicated on his ability to sing and to sell broadsheet ballads that are Shakespeare's equivalent of a tabloid: lurid titles and promises of spectacular tales. "Littered under Mercury," Autolycus shares in the eloquence that he uses to promote his own mischievous enterprise, the selling of stolen "sheets," ribbons, linens, and other merchandise acquired through robbery and chicanery. The kind of tales that Autolycus offers incorporates the act of childbirth, in this instance the birthing of monstrous deformities. In his dialogue with Mopsa and Dorcas, Autolycus offers a "doleful" ballad of how a "usurer's wife was brought to bed of twenty money-bags at a burden, and how she longed to eat adder's heads and toads carbonadoed" (4.4.250–52, TLN 2085–87). Autolycus's claims of a truthful origin for the ballad echoes Leontes's own concern about bastardized origins for his own offspring.

The genre of "monstrous-birth" ballads is typified in the excerpt provided below from the 1615 *God's Handi-Work in Wonders, Miraculously Shown upon Two Women, Lately Delivered of Two Monsters*. The provocative titles that Autolycus sells have their historical correlative in the tales that tell of the deformities that God bestows on nature's "chek" to instill modesty and "check our vicious condition," ironic qualities in the hands of Autolycus, who uses these very lurid tales to promote his own moral deformity. Source: *Gods Handi-Work in wonders*. London, 1615. London. STC 1067, <http://estc.bl.uk/S105736>.]

Another strange wonder at Arnheim, a towne in Gelderland the 23. Of Januarie. 1615.

This ugly and feareful monster was born the 23 of January in the yeare of our Saviour Jesus Christ, a Thousand Six Hundred and Fifteen, an ensample to us of the great wrath of GOD, because of our manifold and great sins, which nowadays in every place doth bear sway, as cursing, swearing, blaspheming of GOD, whoredom, drunkenness, and

---

1 I.e., their execution.

the like, the which is truly to be lamented. And every man may let this feareful monster or token of God be unto him a looking glass, whereby to amend his life, and repent; for this birth was very wonderful and scene of many credible persons that do witness hereunto, and hath been openly declared and published throughout the whole town of Arnheim, and chanced as hereafter followeth.

A citizen's wife in the said town, a comely woman (whose name for certain causes I let pass) being great with child, and looked every day, her husband (being one that had almost spent all his goods amongst whores and thieves) did not leave the same, but without any regard of his wife or her time so near, followed his naughty accustomed use. For he was rather amongst other naughty company than in his house or by his wife, which did not a little grieve his wife, who often rebuked him, both with good and bad words. All would not help, it made him to be more earnest against her and to use her so much the worse, the which grieved her very sore. She being now great with child (as aforesaid), upon a time her husband accompanied himself again with his companions and whores, yea in an open house, he both drunk, danced and leapt, both night and day, and thus used all manner of filthy concupiscence with them.

This came to his wife's ear, whereupon the having intelligence thereof, was in great chase, ran thither in a fury, told him his own, and rebuked him for it, and said he should something regard her great belly and tarry at home, and leave the company of those wicked women, for she had but small goodness at his hands, and hath scarce to eat or drink at home. Her husband, little regarding her words, was in a raging anger, and would have beat his wife. The company which were in the said house would not suffer him, and said, he should bethink himself better, be more wiser, and not deal in such sort with his wife, seeing she was great with child, and looked every day to be brought a bed. Her husband in his great anger and unadvisedly made answer: she may bear the devil of hell. His wife on the other side being sore vexed, answered therefore, "I would I might bear a devil, so should I once be rid of this woe & misery, wherewithal thou dost so vex me, for thou wilt by no means leave the whore-hunting but be always in their company, both drunken and half mad, the which I woeful woman must both hear and see."

Thus in her anger she returned him again, and shortly the time came, as soon as the neighbor's midwife were come, she began for very great pains to cry out fearfully, and not long after was brought abed of this wonderful monster, with so fearful proportioned limbs, the which as soon as the woman was delivered thereof, it ran underneath the bed. The proportion of his body and limbs was as hereafter followeth, and was seen of many persons, both men and women, which witness the same openly:

First, this child being a monster was over his whole body very rough with hair, and all black, except his belly which was like a swan.

Secondly, the two feet upon the which it did stand were like to a peacock's feet.

Thirdly, his eyes were to behold, fearful, for they shined like fire, and were very great.

Fourthly, he had a mouth like unto a stork or crane, altogether black and very fearful to behold.

Fifthly, it had a tail like unto an deer.

Sixthly, it had two horns upon his head, which hung over him.

Seventhly, it had instead of hands and fingers, claws like unto a fowl.

In sum it was not found in any point like to a Christian body, but was very fearful and horrible to behold.

After that it had now (with great trembling and fear) been seen of many men in the town, and every man astonished thereat, in the end they smothered it betwixt two beds and so killed it.

My brother in Christ, and reader hereof, let not this which is here declared seem a fable unto thee, for this and the like wonders, many have been heard of here and there, as monsters by sea, signs in the air, both of men and cattle.

By this we do perceive and mark that the Lord's coming is at hand, and that shortly hereupon will follow the judgment day, whereas we must not only give account of our sins but also of all vain works, words, and deeds. For nowadays the common sort of people are holy bent to wicked company, whereas is cursing, swearing, eating, drinking, breaking of wedlock, and whoredom, like as was this aforesaid man of Arnheim. Good people amend your sinful lives, and call to God for grace.

Also this may be a looking glass unto every wedded woman, whereby to refrain casting out of such unadvised words, like as did this aforesaid wife her time of delivery being so near, but rather to have patience, by pacifying her wrath, and commit all matters to almighty God that he may amend all that, which in her husband is amiss, also to pray for him, that it will please God to turn his heart, that he may acknowledge his sins and so amend his sinful life. The almighty God, wonderful in his creations, grant us all his grace, that we may amend our wicked lives, confess his power, and have everlasting life in Jesus Christ our Lord. Amen.

WORKS CITED AND BIBLIOGRAPHY

PRIMARY TEXTS

DiGangi, Mario, ed. *The Winter's Tale: Texts and Contexts*. New York: Bedford, 2008.

Dolan, Frances, ed. *The Winter's Tale* (The Pelican Shakespeare). New York: Penguin Putnam, 1999.

Fergusson, Francis, ed. *The Winter's Tale*. The Laurel Shakespeare. New York: Dell, 1959.

Greene, Robert. *Pandosto the triumph of time*. London, 1588. STC (2nd ed.) 12285. Early English Books Online.

Johnson, Samuel, ed. *The Plays of William Shakespeare*. Vol. 2. London: Printed for J. and R. Tonson ..., 1765. 8 vols.

Kittredge, George. *The Complete Works of Shakespeare*. Boston: Ginn and Company, 1936.

Mowat, Barbara, and Paul Werstine, eds. *The Winter's Tale*. New York: Washington Square P, 1998.

Orgel, Stephen, ed. *The Winter's Tale*. New York: Oxford UP, 1996.

Pafford, J.H.P., ed. *The Winter's Tale*. Arden Shakespeare. London: Routledge, 1996.

Pitcher, John A., ed. *The Winter's Tale*. Third Series (Arden Shakespeare). London: Methuen, 2010.

Quiller-Couch, Arthur, and John Dover Wilson, eds. *The Winter's Tale*. New Cambridge Shakespeare. New York: Macmillan, 1931.

Schanzer, Ernest, ed. *The Winter's Tale*. Harmondsworth, Middlesex: Penguin, 1969.

Snyder, Susan. ed. *The Winter's Tale*. Cambridge: Cambridge UP, 2007.

Turner, Robert, and Virginia Haas, eds. *A New Variorum Edition of Shakespeare, The Winter's Tale*. New York: Modern Language Association, 2005.

SECONDARY WORKS

Adelman, Janet. *The Common Liar: An Essay on Antony and Cleopatra*. Yale Studies in English 181. New Haven, CT: Yale UP, 1973.

———. "Masculine Authority and the Maternal Body: The Return to Origins in the Romances." *Suffocating Mothers: Fantasies of Maternal Origin in Shakespeare's Plays, Hamlet to The Tempest*. New York: Routledge, 1992. 193–238.

Barber, C.L. "'Thou That Begetst Him That Did Thee Beget': Transformation in *Pericles* and *The Winter's Tale*." *Shakespeare Survey* 22 (1969): 59–65.

———, and Richard P. Wheeler. *The Whole Journey: Shakespeare's Power of Development*. Berkeley: U of California P, 1986.

Barkan, Leonard. "'Living Sculptures': Ovid, Michelangelo, and *The Winter's Tale*." *English Literary History* 48 (1981): 639–67.

Bartholomeusz, Dennis. *The Winter's Tale in Performance in England and America, 1611–1976*. Cambridge: Cambridge UP, 1982.

Barton, Anne. "Leontes and the Spider: Language and Speaker in Shakespeare's Last Plays." *Shakespeare: The Last Plays*. Ed. Kiernan Ryan. London: Longman, 1999. 22–42.

Bate, Jonathan. *Shakespeare and Ovid*. Oxford: Oxford UP, 1993.

Belsey, Catherine. *Shakespeare and the Loss of Eden: The Construction of Family Values in Early Modern Culture*. Basingstoke: Palgrave, 2001.

Bergeron, David. "The Apollo Mission in *The Winter's Tale*." Hunt, ed. 361–79.

———. "The Restoration of Hermione in *The Winter's Tale*." Kay and Jacobs. 125–33.

———. *Shakespeare's Romances and the Royal Family*. Lawrence: UP of Kansas, 1985.

Bethell, S.L. *The Winter's Tale: A Study*. London: Staples, 1947.

Bishop, T.G. *Shakespeare and the Theatre of Wonder*. Cambridge: Cambridge UP, 1996.

Bliss, Lee. "Tragicomic Romance for the King's Men, 1609–1611: Shakespeare, Beaumont, and Fletcher." *Comedy from Shakespeare to Sheridan: Change and Continuity in the English and European Dramatic Tradition*. Ed. A.R. Braunmuller and J.C. Bulman. Newark: U of Delaware P, 1986. 148–64.

Blount, Thomas. *Glossographia, or a Dictionary*. (1656) Ed. Ian Lancashire. Toronto: U of Toronto Library and U of Toronto P, 2014. Date consulted: [5 October 2011]. URL: <leme.library.utoronto.ca> (LEME).

Bristol, Michael D. "In Search of the Bear: Spatiotemporal Form and the Heterogeneity of Economies in *The Winter's Tale*." *Shakespeare Quarterly* 42 (1991): 145–67.

Bullokar, William. *An English Expositor*. (1616) *Lexicons of Early Modern English*. Ed. Ian Lancashire. Toronto, ON: U of Toronto Library and U of Toronto P, 2014. Date consulted: [5 October 2011]. URL: <leme.library.utoronto.ca> (LEME).

Cavell, Stanley. "Recounting Gains, Showing Losses: Reading *The Winter's Tale*." *Disowning Knowledge in Seven Plays of Shakespeare*. Cambridge UP, 1987.

Clubb, Louise. "The Tragicomic Bear." *Comparative Literature Studies* 9 (1972): 17–30.

Coghill, Nevill. "Six Points of Stage-Craft in *The Winter's Tale*." *Shakespeare Survey* 11 (1958): 31–42.

Colie, Rosalie L. *Shakespeare's Living Art*. Princeton, NJ: Princeton UP, 1974.

Dessen, Alan. "Massed Entries and Theatrical Options in *WT*." *Medieval and Renaissance Drama in England* 8 (1996): 119–27.

Diehl, Huston. *Staging Reform, Reforming the Stage*. Ithaca, NY: Cornell UP, 1997.

Edwards, Philip. "Shakespeare's Romances: 1900–1957." *Shakespeare Survey* 11 (1958): 1–18.

Enterline, Lynn. "'You Speak a Language that I Understand Not': The Rhetoric of Animation in *The Winter's Tale*." *Shakespeare Quarterly* 48 (1997): 17–44.

Erickson, Peter. "Patriarchal Structures in *The Winter's Tale*." *PMLA* 97.5 (1982): 819–29.

Ewbank, Inga-Stina. "The Triumph of Time in *The Winter's Tale*." *The Winter's Tale: Critical Essays*. Ed. Maurice Hunt. New York: Garland, 1995. 139–55.

Felperin, Howard. *Shakespearean Romance*. Princeton, NJ: Princeton UP, 1972.

———. "'Tongue-tied Our Queen': The Deconstruction of Presence in *The Winter's Tale*." *Shakespeare and the Question of Theory*. Ed. Patricia Parker and Geoffrey Hartman. London: Routledge, Chapman & Hall, 1985. 3–18.

French, Marilyn. *Shakespeare's Division of Experience*. New York: Ballantine, 1983.

Frey, Charles. *Shakespeare's Vast Romance: A Study of The Winter's Tale*. Columbia: U of Missouri P, 1980.

Frye, Northrop. *The Anatomy of Criticism*. Princeton, NJ: Princeton UP, 1957.

———. *The Myth of Deliverance: Reflections on Shakespeare's Problem Comedies*. Toronto: U of Toronto P, 1983.

———. *A Natural Perspective: The Development of Shakespearean Comedy and Romance*. New York: Columbia UP, 1965.

———. "Recognition in *The Winter's Tale*." *Fables of Identity: Studies in Poetic Mythology*. New York: Harcourt Brace Jovanovich, 1963. 107–18.

———. "Romance as Masque." *Shakespeare's Romances Reconsidered*. Ed. Carol McGinnis Kay and Henry E. Jacobs. Lincoln: U of Nebraska P, 1978. 11–39.

Garber, Marjorie. *Shakespeare after All*. New York: Pantheon Books, 2004.

———. *Shakespeare's Ghost Writers: Literature as Uncanny Causality*. London: Methuen, 1987.

Goldberg, Jonathan. "Fatherly Authority: The Politics of Stuart Family Images." *Rewriting the Renaissance*. Ed. Margaret W. Ferguson, Maureen Quillian, and Nancy J. Vickers. Chicago: U of Chicago P, 1986.

———. *James I and the Politics of Literature*. Baltimore: Johns Hopkins UP, 1983.

Granville-Barker, Harley. "Preface to *The Winter's Tale*." *Prefaces to Shakespeare*. Hunt, ed. 76–81.

Greenblatt, Stephen. *Hamlet in Purgatory*. Princeton, NJ: Princeton UP, 2002.

Greg, W.W. *The Shakespeare First Folio: Its Bibliographical and Textual History*. Oxford: Oxford UP, 1955.

Gurr, Andrew. "The Bear, the Statue, and Hysteria in *The Winter's Tale*." *Shakespeare Quarterly* 34 (1983): 420–25.

Hall, Joan Lord. *The Winter's Tale: A Guide to the Play*. Westport, CT: Greenwood P, 2005.

Hinman, Charlton. *The Printing and Proof-Reading of the First Folio of Shakespeare*. 2 vols. Oxford: Clarendon, 1963.

Howard-Hill, T.H. *Ralph Crane and Some Shakespeare First Folio Comedies*. Bibliographical Society of the U of Virginia: U of Virginia P, 1972.

Hunt, Maurice. "'Bearing Hence': Shakespeare's *The Winter's Tale*." *Studies in English Literature* 44.2 (2004): 333–43.

———, ed. *The Winter's Tale: Critical Essays*. New York: Garland, 1995.

James I of England. *The Political Works of James I*. Ed. Charles H. McIlwain. Cambridge, MA: Harvard UP, 1918.

Jensen, Phebe. "Singing Psalms to Horn-Pipes: Festivity, Iconoclasm, and Catholicism in *The Winter's Tale*." *Shakespeare Quarterly* 55 (2004): 279–306.

Kay, Carol McGinnis, and Henry E. Jacobs, eds. *Shakespeare's Romances Reconsidered*. Lincoln: U of Nebraska P, 1978.

Knapp, James A. "Visual and Ethical Truth in *The Winter's Tale*." *Shakespeare Quarterly* 55 (2004): 253–78.

Knight, G. Wilson. "'Great Creating Nature': An Essay on *The Winter's Tale*." *The Crown of Life*. London: Methuen, 1948. 76–128.

Kurland, Stuart. "'We Need No More of Your Advice': Political Realism in *The Winter's Tale*." *Studies in English Literature* 31.2 (1991): 365–86.

Lamb, Mary Ellen. "Engendering the Narrative Act: Old Wives' Tales in *The Winter's Tale*, *Macbeth*, and *The Tempest*." *Criticism* 40 (Fall 1998): 529–53.

Lupton, Julia Reinhard. *Afterlives of the Saints: Hagiography, Typology, and Renaissance Literature*. Stanford, CA: Stanford UP, 1996.

Lyne, Raphael. *Shakespeare's Late Work* (Oxford: Oxford UP, 2007).

McDonald, Russ. "Poetry and Plot in *The Winter's Tale*." *Shakespeare Quarterly* 36 (1985): 315–29.

Miko, Stephen J. "Winter's Tale." *Studies in English Literature* 29 (1989): 259–75.

Morse, William R. "Metacriticism and Materiality: The Case of Shakespeare's *The Winter's Tale*." *English Literary History* 58 (1991): 283–94.

Mowat, Barbara A. "Rogues, Shepherds, and the Counterfeit Distressed: Texts and Infracontexts of *The Winter's Tale* 4.3." *Shakespeare Studies* 22 (1994): 58–76.

———. "'What's In a Name?': Tragicomedy, Romance, or Late Comedy." *A Companion to Shakespeare's Works*. Ed. Richard Dutton and Jean E. Howard. 4 vols. Maldon, MA: Blackwell, 2003.

Muir, Kenneth. *The Sources of Shakespeare's Plays*. 1977; rpt. Oxford: Routledge, 2005.

———, ed. *Shakespeare: The Winter's Tale, A Casebook*. London: Macmillan, 1969.

Neely, Carol Thomas. *Broken Nuptials in Shakespeare's Plays*. New Haven, CT: Yale UP, 1985.

Orgel, Stephen. *Illusion of Power*. Berkeley: U of California P, 1975.

———. "The Poetics of Incomprehensibility." *Shakespeare Quarterly* 42 (1991): 431–37.

———. "*The Winter's Tale*: A Modern Perspective." Mowat and Werstine 257–72.

Overton, Bill. *The Winter's Tale: The Critics Debate*. Atlantic Highlands, NJ: Humanities P International, 1989.

Palfrey, Simon. *Late Shakespeare: A New World of Words* (Oxford: Oxford UP, 1997).

Panofsky, Erwin. *Studies in Iconology*. Oxford: Oxford UP, 1939.

Proudfoot, Richard. "Verbal Reminiscence and the Two-Part Structure of *The Winter's Tale*." *Shakespeare Survey* 29 (1976): 67–78.

Rabkin, Norman. *Shakespeare and the Problem of Meaning*. Chicago: U of Chicago P, 1981.

Randall, Dale B.J. "'This Is the Chase': or, The Further Pursuit of Shakespeare's Bear." *Shakespeare Jahrbuch* 121 (1985): 89–95.

Ravelhofer, Barbara. "'Beasts of Recreation': Henslowe's White Bears." *English Literary Renaissance* 323 (2002): 287–323.

Reid, Stephen. "*The Winter's Tale*." *American Imago* 2 (1980): 263–78.

Rutter, Carol Chillington. "Shakespeare Performances in England 2009." *Shakespeare Survey* 63 (2010): 338–75.

Ryan, Kiernan, ed. *Shakespeare: The Last Plays*. New York: Longman, 1999.

Schwalkwyk, David. "'A Lady's "Verily" Is as Potent as a Lord's': Women, Word, and Witchcraft in *The Winter's Tale*." *English Literary Renaissance* 22 (1992): 242–72.

Schwartz, Murray M. "Leontes' Jealousy in *The Winter's Tale*." *American Imago* 30 (1973): 250–73.

———. "*The Winter's Tale*: Loss and Transformation." *American Imago* 32 (1975): 145–99.

Shaheen, Naseeb. *Biblical References in Shakespeare's Plays*. Newark: U of Delaware P, 1989.

Smith, Bruce. "Sermons in Stone: Shakespeare and Renaissance Sculpture." *Shakespeare Studies* 17 (1985): 1–23.

Snyder, Susan. "Mamillius and Gender Polarization in *The Winter's Tale*." *Shakespeare: A Wayward Journey*. Newark: U of Delaware P, 2002.

———. "Memorial Art in *The Winter's Tale* and Elsewhere: 'I will kill thee / And love thee after.'" *Shakespeare: A Wayward Journey*. Newark: U of Delaware P, 2002.

———. "*The Winter's Tale* Before and After." *Shakespeare: A Wayward Journey*. Newark: U of Delaware P, 2002.

Stewart, J.I.M. *Character and Motive in Shakespeare: Some Recent Appraisals Examined*. London: Longmans, 1949.

Tatspaugh, Patricia E. *Shakespeare at Stratford: The Winter's Tale*. London: Thomson Learning, 2002.

Tennenhouse, Leonard. *Power on Display: The Politics of Shakespeare's Genres*. London: Methuen, 1986.

Tilley, M.P. *A Dictionary of the Proverbs in England in the Sixteenth and Seventeenth Centuries: A Collection of the Proverbs Found in English Literature and the Dictionaries of the Period*. Ann Arbor: U of Michigan P, 1950.

Tillyard, E.M.W. *Shakespeare's Last Plays*. London: Chatto and Windus, 1938.

Traversi, Derek. *Shakespeare: The Last Phase*. Stanford, CA: Stanford UP, 1955.

Vanita, Ruth. "Mariological Memory in *The Winter's Tale* and *Henry VIII*." *Studies in English Literature* 40.2 (2000): 311–37.

Venezky, Alice. "Current Shakespearian Productions in England and France." *Shakespeare Quarterly* 2 (1951): 335–42.

Ward, David. "Affection, Intention, and Dreams in *The Winter's Tale*." *Modern Language Review* 82.3 (1987): 545–54.

Warren, Roger. "Shakespeare Late Plays at Stratford, Ontario." *Shakespeare Survey* 40 (1988): 155–68.

———. *Staging Shakespeare's Late Plays*. Oxford: Clarendon, 1990.

Wells, Stanley, ed. *Perymedes the Blacksmith* and *Pandosto* by Robert Greene. New York: Garland, 1988.

———, and Gary Taylor. *William Shakespeare: A Textual Companion*. New York: W.W. Norton, 1997.

Williamson, Hugh R. *The Day Shakespeare Died*. London: Michael Joseph, 1962.

Young, David. *The Heart's Forest: A Study of Shakespeare's Pastoral Plays*. New Haven, CT: Yale UP, 1972.

Ziegler, Georgiana. "Parents, Daughters, and 'That Rare Italian Master': A New Source for *The Winter's Tale*." *Shakespeare Quarterly* 36 (1985): 204–12.

from the publisher

A name never says it all, but the word "broadview" expresses a good deal of the philosophy behind our company. We are open to a broad range of academic approaches and political viewpoints. We pay attention to the broad impact book publishing and book printing has in the wider world; we began using recycled stock more than a decade ago, and for some years now we have used 100% recycled paper for most titles. As a Canadian-based company we naturally publish a number of titles with a Canadian emphasis, but our publishing program overall is internationally oriented and broad-ranging. Our individual titles often appeal to a broad readership too; many are of interest as much to general readers as to academics and students.

Founded in 1985, Broadview remains a fully independent company owned by its shareholders—not an imprint or subsidiary of a larger multinational.

The interior of this book is printed on 100% recycled paper.